A Century Of Jazz

A Century Of

Roy Carr

hamlyn

Executive Editor: **Mike Evans**
Editor: **Humaira Husain**
Production Controller: **Mark Walker**
Picture Research: **Roy Carr, Maria Gibbs**
Art Director: **Keith Martin**
Art Editor: **Leigh Jones**
Design: **Paul Aarons**

First published in 1997 by
Hamlyn, an imprint of
Octopus Publishing Group Limited
2-4 Heron Quays
London E14 4JP

First published in paperback 1999

This edition first printed 2004

Reprinted 2005, 2006

Copyright © 1997 Octopus Publishing Group Limited

A Catalogue record for this book is available from the British Library
ISBN 0-600-61609-6

Printed and bound in China

Contents

A SHOW FOR THE ENTIRE FAMILY
Mr. Dynamite
JAMES BROWN
N.Y. APOLLO Theatre
THUR. JULY 28 8:00 P.M.
GET ... OUT...COME EARLY!

RED HOT ON IMPULSE
STARRING:
ALICE COLTRANE
PHAROAH SANDERS
JOHN COLTRANE
OLIVER NELSON
MAX ROACH
CHARLES MINGUS
ARCHIE SHEPP

impulse!

Contents

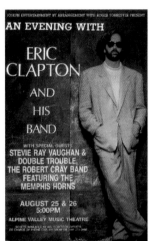

1897-1920

Way Dow

Jazz had its roots in the fertile soil of the American South in the latter part of the last century, where newly-emancipated slaves with a rhythmic tradition that harked back to their forefathers' Africa were part of a musical melting pot that also involved military brass band music, English Victorian hymns, French and Spanish influences and even the popular 'minstrel' songs of the day.

Yonder in New Orleans

THE LEVEE AT NEW ORLEANS.

JAZZ HISTORIANS have as much trouble forcing their theories onto the available historical facts as anthropologists do when they try to explain how and why the human race had apes for ancestors. Neither can identify the moment when either took recognisable shape. Did jazz evolve because of the instruments available or because of the musicians who played them? The answer involves elements of both, most likely, and a lot more besides.

Like the Three Witches in *Macbeth*, everyone tends to throw their ingredients into the pot in varying proportions and call the resulting stew 'jazz'. Slavery, a European musical notation, the American Civil War, the 'call and response' techniques in African music, 'lining out' in Christian church practises, all played their part in the development of what we have come to call 'jazz'.

When the Civil War ended in 1865, one curious outcome was the glut of brass band instruments no longer required to stiffen the sinews of the fool-hardy and the timorous. Although hostilities had ended, martial music was still in vogue, for parades, at dances and, conveniently so for the present narrative, at funerals.

New Orleans has claimed or been accorded the honour of creating the marching band tradition at funerals, as much for the presence of a large black population as for its polyglot mixture of English, French, Spanish and Caribbean communities. Playing music on the way to and from the

Left and top right: Late 19th Century New Orleans, around the time jazz was born Right: The only picture of Buddy Bolden, standing second left

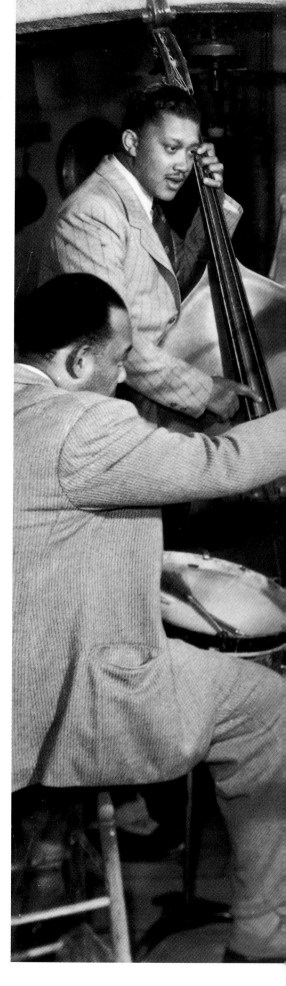

cemetery was a continuation of the African tradition of honouring the dead. It's quite likely that black citizens in other parts of the newly United States did much the same thing. It's also probable that they did it best in the Crescent City.

For all its high-profile vices, New Orleans also supported more wholesome forms of entertainment such as a number of opera companies, symphony orchestras including the Negro Philharmonic Society plus an insatiable lust for dancing enjoyed across all social classes.

Another musical strand in the DNA of jazz was 'ragtime' (ragged time), a technique again developed from the formal structures of marching music. It was largely played by black pianists whose main employment was in the brothels of America's principal cities. Its leading light was Scott Joplin, an itinerant Texas pianist who worked his way up through the logging camps of Mississippi and Arkansas to arrive in Missouri in 1894. His famous 'Maple Leaf Rag' was published five years later, although the first to be printed had been 'Harlem Rag' by Tom Turpin.

But these men and others like Louis Chauvin, Scott Hayden and Arthur Marshall were straight, formally trained musicians with no particular interest in, or aptitude for, improvisation.

Other musicians were drawn to ragtime, and back in the Crescent City, a fabled cornet player, Charles 'Buddy' Bolden, adapted its rhythms for his band which comprised of himself, a trombonist, two clarinetists, guitar and bass.

Bolden wasn't the only one, of course, to start to explore the rigours of collective improvisation.

Contemporaries like the cornet maestro King Oliver, clarinet stylists Johnny Dodds and Jimmie Noone, plus Creoles – the soprano saxophonist Sidney Bechet, cornetists Freddie Keppard and Buddie Petit, tailgate trombonist Kid Ory, and pianist Jelly Roll Morton (who characteristically claimed he'd invented jazz in 1902), all played their part in creating the vocabulary of the new music.

As far as the flamboyant Jelly Roll was concerned, it was about tapping out four-to-the-bar with a two-beat 'rag' draped over the top. One theory suggests that it was due to the tendency of the Creole musicians to 'jazz up' rags and blues that the new music first gained its popularity.

Right: A scene from the 1947 movie *New Orleans*, with a band that included Louis Armstrong, Barney Bigard on clarinet and Kid Ory on trombone Below: King Oliver's band with Louis Armstrong (centre) and pianist Lil Hardin

PRYTANIA
BREWING CO.
9 PRYTANIA ST. &
MA 0125

JULY
1917
SUN MON TUE WED THU FRI SAT
1 2 3 4 5 6 7
8 9 10 11 12 13 14
15 16 17 18 19 20 21
22 23 24 25 26 27 28
29 30 31

But every era needs its icon and Buddy Bolden has been elected. Unfortunately, he went mad in 1907 and spent the last 24 years of his life in an asylum.

Then there was the blues, another nebulous concoction drawn from the field hollers of plantation workers and adaptations of the hymns they heard in church on Sunday.

Instrumentalists emulated the melismatic convolutions of the blues singer, whose style involved the flattening of the third and the seventh notes of the diatonic scale.

And another curious echo of the martial theme could be heard in the fife and drum bands found in Mississippi and Tennessee, blending African polyrhythms with the earliest American traditions of such play.

The reality is that most of the musicians performed a haphazard selection of material, ranging from a quadrille or a mazurka through to 'Slow Drags' (likened to vertical copulation), 'Barrel House', 'Plantation Music' and 'Bumpy' tunes such as 'St.Louis Blues' in rough-house honky tonks and ballrooms like the legendary Funky Butt Hall (Union Son's Hall), the Odd Fellows Hall, Kid Brown's, Matranga's, Ponce's, Joe Segretta's and Spano's.

Significantly at the same time half a dozen top-dollar 'sporting houses' offered live music as an added inducement.

History likes simple solutions and the spread of this new music to other parts of America has been attributed to the (illegal) closing down by the US Navy Department, of the segregated 'red light' district of New

Orleans, Storyville, on 12 November, 1917. Prior to such drastic action, New Orleans' rampant sex industry had proved to be the main attraction for tens of thousands of tourists, itinerants and free-spending sailors.

By 1899, prostitution had become so widespread, that the local politician Joseph Story sponsored legislation confining all paid-for carnal pursuits to one area of the city – which was then named in his honour.

The closing of Storyville accelerated a migration already in progress, since many of the city's bands, like that led by Kentucky-born pianist Fate Marable, also played on the huge Mississippi riverboats that carried passengers, cargo and even the odd exotic floating brothel between New Orleans, Memphis and St. Louis.

Although these towns all had significant black sections, it was further north to Chicago that many of the best musicians like King Oliver and Louis Armstrong travelled.

Ironically, the first 'jazz' (or 'jass') band to actually maka a gramophone record, on 26 February 1917, was the Original Dixieland Jass Band, a quintet of white musicians from New Orleans led by the cornet player and self-publicist Nick LaRocca.

Their debut release 'Livery Stable Blues', recorded in New York City and coupled with 'Dixie Jass Band One-Step', proved an instant smash, and their subsequent hits like 'Tiger Rag' further established jazz in the public mind, initially at least, as just a fashionable craze, novelty 'good-time' music.

One rather cynical view holds that the Original Dixieland Jass Band – who were once dubbed 'Untuneful Harmonists Playing Peppery Melodies' – were in fact exploiting the musical resources of America's largest group of second-class citizens, being just the latest in a long line of crowd-pleasing 'minstrel' bands, only this time without the black pancake make-up. In retrospect, though, the prospect of LaRocca and his chums making a conscious decision to 'exploit' anyone seems highly unlikely.

Whatever, the ODJB were very soon superceded by the real thing, and although for many years it remained the daring thing for white socialites to 'slum it' at Chicago clubs and dives, or uptown Manhatten joints like New York's Cotton Club, jazz was to eventually establish itself as America's first and only indigenous music.

The Cornet

Bottom Left: A quaint saxophone quartet of the period with (l-r) baritone, tenor, alto and soprano
Below: Jelly Roll Morton's Red Hot Peppers
Bottom: The Superior Orchestra marching band, 1910, with Bunk Johnson second left, back row

Kings

The marching band tradition of New Orleans helped establish the cornet as the leading voice in early jazz, a status it retained into the Twenties.

WHEN JAZZ GAVE OUT its first squawk, it sounded like a cornet. In turn-of-the-century New Orleans he who played cornet was undoubtedly king. Most bands comprised seven pieces, with the cornet player taking the melody line. Originally, there were no less than six contenders, of which only half have been able to justify their status.

The undisputed original was Buddy Bolden (1877-1931). Not that his CV stands up to examination. No records, a legendary wax cylinder that has never been traced, the well-known solitary photograph and the memories of now-dead contemporaries who agreed that Bolden played as much ragtime as he played blues. Then there's the legend – the one about the sound of his cornet being heard 10 miles away, across the bayou, on the still night air. But less romantic is the truth that he eventually blew himself into terminal madness.

Freddie Keppard (1890-1933) is generally regarded as Bolden's successor. Quitting New Orleans in 1911, he passed up the opportunity to become the first jazzman to actually record, reasoning that other musicians might misappropriate his style. By the time Keppard eventually placed his sound on disc, in 1923, ill-health had already blighted his talent.

Bunk Johnson (1889-1949) is another with a vague reputation. Bunk didn't record until 1942, when he was hailed as something of a 'missing link' between Bolden and King Oliver, the first proven cornet king. Also figuring in the original equation was Manuel Perez (1871-1946) an apparent teen genius with Robichaux's Orchestra before moving on to head the acclaimed Imperial Band. Again, his actual ability is now merely the subject of faded memories.

Joe 'King' Oliver (1885-1938) who admitted Johnson's influence, swung to glory with his infectious 'Dippermouth Blues', was said to have dispensed with both Perez and Keppard on the same night by blasting outside the rivals' venues and then disappearing down the street in best Pied Piper mode, with their audiences following him in a mass appreciative manner.

An innovative musician, Oliver played in a clipped melodic style, and was to provide positive proof of his importance by taking a band first to California and then to Chicago, where, leading his Creole Jazz Band, he proved to be a sensation, both live and

on a series of classic recordings, some featuring the then 22-year old Louis Armstrong on second cornet. But Louis Armstrong (1901-1971) was too hot for Oliver to hold on to.

Not only the most remarkable cornet and trumpet player ever to emerge from New Orleans, 'Satchmo' (short for 'Satchlemouth') also sang, mugged, danced and soon became an all-round entertainer. But more importantly, within months he was changing the face of jazz forever.

FREDDIE KEPPARD

EARLY JAZZ GREATS

Right: Freddie Keppard, from a card series by cartoonist Robert Crumb

Below: The Hot Five (l-r) Louis Armstrong, Johnny St Cyr, Johnny Dodds, KidOry, and Lil Hardin

OKeh
ELECTRIC
FOR BEST RESULTS:
USE OKEH NEEDLES
8566
Fox Trot
STRUTTIN' WITH SOME BARBECUE
(Hardin)
LOUIS ARMSTRONG AND HIS
HOT FIVE
(82037)

The blues was one of the building-blocks of jazz, with chord structures and phrasing sharing a common lineage in the musical culture of Afro-America, but it has a rich history in its own right.

Woke Up This Morning

BLUES AND JAZZ are branches of the same tree, it's said. The music grew out of the clash of cultures when African ritual collided with European ceremonial and instinct encountered intellect. While jazz co-opted the disciplines of the marching band and the brash tones of brass and horn, the blues grew out of folk songs and ballads and was usually accompanied by violin and banjo.

Musicians who catered to the rural black communities called themselves songsters and their repertoire reflected the broad range of European songs and hymns first heard by their slave ancestors. As the century turned, the guitar, now readily available from mail-order catalogues, took on a more prominent role. What became identified as blues, utilising 8, 12 and 16-bar metric schemes, emerged in the first decades of this century. While the travelling Medicine Shows ensured its recognition throughout the South and regional styles flourished in several states, black popular songwriters marked the trend with ballads, by turns lachrymose and boasting, with the word 'blues' appended to them. Mamie Smith's 'Crazy Blues', recorded in August 1920, set the formula, and other 'classic blues' singers like Lucille Hegamin ('Jazz Me Blues'), Ida Cox ('Any Woman's Blues'), Alberta Hunter ('Jazzin' Baby Blues') and Viola McCoy ('Dying Crapshooter Blues') and the 'Empress', Bessie Smith, ('Give Me A Pig Foot And A Bottle Beer', 'Empty Bed Blues' and 'St. Louis Blues') soon followed.

Such was the demand, record companies like Paramount, Okeh and RCA Victor belatedly recognised the sales potential in the black community and cast their nets wider for talent. Less

Cordially Yours [signed] Jefferson

Left: A signed picture of Blind Lemon Jefferson
Right: Mississippi bluesman Charley Patton
Below: The 'Empress of the Blues' Bessie Smith

Columbia
The St. Louis Blues
(W. C. Handy)
BESSIE SMITH - Organ and Cornet Accomp.
14064-D
(140241)
MADE AND PAT'D IN U.S.A. JAN. 21,'13 AND MAY 22,'23 A
COLUMBIA PHONOGRAPH COMPANY, INC., NEW YORK, U.S.A.

Columbia
Viva-tonal Recording
ELECTRICAL PROCESS
Hard Driving Papa
(Brooks)
Vocal - Fletcher Henderson, piano
Joe Smith, cornet
BESSIE SMITH
14137-D
(142148)
MADE AND PAT'D IN ... 21,'13 AND MAY 22,'23 A
COLUMBIA PHONO ... NEW YORK, U.S.A.

Columbia
Viva-tonal Recording
ELECTRICAL PROCESS
Vocal
ONE AND TWO BLUES
(Brooks)
BESSIE SMITH and Her Blue Boys
14172-D
(142876)
MADE AND PAT'D IN U.S.A. JAN. 21,'13 AND MAY 22,'23 A
COLUMBIA PHONOGRAPH COMPANY, INC., NEW YORK, U.S.A.

formally trained musicians like Sylvester Weaver ('Guitar Rag'), Papa Charlie Jackson ('Salty Dog'), Blind Blake ('Diddie-Wa-Diddy') and Blind Lemon Jefferson ('Matchbox Blues') were among the big stars, accompanied as the 20s closed by Big Bill Broonzy ('House Rent Stomp'), Tampa Red ('It's Tight Like That') and Leroy Carr ('How Long, How Long').

The latter trio, along with Walter Davis ('M & O Blues'), Lonnie Johnson ('Falling Rain Blues'), Sonny Boy Williamson ('Good Morning Little Schoolgirl') and Memphis Minnie ('Me And My Chauffeur'), dominated blues in the 30s. But the decade saw much of the individuality disappear from the music, with the trend which saw regional variations vanishing in favour of a standardisation of style largely emanating from Chicago and New York. The market was dominated by RCA Victor and Columbia, and their subsidiaries, companies that held sway until World War II put an end to all recording.

In a move that impacted on post-war blues, some Mississippi musicians were to buck the main trend. The influence of Tommy Johnson ('Big Road Blues'), Son House ('My Black Mama') and the more prolific Charley Patton ('Pony Blues') on Muddy Waters and Howlin' Wolf dictated the direction of 50s Chicago blues. While Patton was the more accomplished, House was the more direct influence on Waters and Robert Johnson.

Largely unknown during his lifetime, Johnson's status has grown since his records were first anthologised in the 60s. By his adaptation of songs by men like House, Leroy Carr and Kokomo Arnold, and the use of rhythm patterns transposed from piano techniques, Johnson reinvented the blues as performance art. His small repertoire fed the mainstream: 'I Believe I'll Dust My Broom' gave a whole career to Elmore James and his followers, 'Sweet Home Chicago' has become an anthem for artists as diverse as Buddy Guy through to The Blues Brothers, and the Rolling Stones couldn't totally destroy the fragile beauty of 'Love In Vain'.

The Windy City

The history of jazz can be traced – through the first half of the century at least – in terms of the geography of jazz. Styles were named after the places where they evolved, and New Orleans was followed by Chicago and New York.

1

F NEW ORLEANS was the birthplace of jazz, Chicago was where it began to really grow and develop. In the Teens and Twenties, Chicago was the most exciting and almost certainly the most dangerous city in America. It was packed with dance halls, speakeasies, juke joints, cabarets and various houses of ill repute – the kind of places that needed something like jazz for a soundtrack. The city's entertainments were usually overseen by the racketeers and mobsters that came to symbolise the city in the era of 1920s prohibition, and the hot music fitted in perfectly with their needs. For a few years, Chicago reigned as the real centre of jazz in America.

Just as it was to be in New York and elsewhere, the tone of the city's music was set by the arrival of blacks from the South, part of the great migration which followed the end of the First World War and the closing down of the Storyville tenderloin district in New Orleans. Chicago's South Side was colonised by an army of bluesmen and instrumentalists, and among the names to make their way to the city and find work there were many of the most illustrious pioneers of New Orleans: trumpet players Freddie Keppard and Joe 'King' Oliver, and pianist Jelly Roll Morton. It was Oliver's Creole Jazz Band in particular which captivated audiences at the Lincoln Gardens.

Oliver was the third King of New Orleans brassmen, after Buddy Bolden and Keppard, and the Creole Jazz Band synthesised all that New Orleans jazz had created up to that point. A dense, crowded ensemble music that always felt exciting because of its swinging rhythms, this was exhilarating stuff to an audience eager for something potent. When Oliver finally recorded his repertoire, in 1923, he featured an extraordinary band: besides himself,

Left: Saxist Frankie Trumbauer who was also an ace aviator   Opposite: The legendary Bix

there were Johnny Dodds (clarinet), Kid Ory (trombone) and the young second cornetist, Louis Armstrong.

Armstrong exemplified the group of young innovators who were emerging from the ranks of black players in the city. Although his small-group recordings tended to be made with bands that didn't exist outside the record studios, he was still working in public at the Savoy Ballroom and the Sunset Cafe. Towards the end of the decade, one of the hottest groups in the city, the band led by clarinetist Jimmie Noone, worked at the Apex Club, and there the patrons had a chance to hear the miraculous new piano stylings of the young Earl Hines, a cigar-chomping virtuoso who was Louis Armstrong's match in terms of both style and imagination.

Jelly Roll Morton didn't record his band music at length until 1926-27 (there are a stack of piano solos from a few years earlier), but the results number among the truly classic sessions in jazz history. Morton put together an ensemble music so perfect in its detail that the records might as well have been written out – yet they are full of fine improvisations, touched with a natural swing that makes them infectiously exciting. But this was still really a

refinement of the classic New Orleans style, rather than a conscious development away from it. Even when Louis Armstrong recorded his immortal series of Hot Five and Hot Seven discs in the city around the same time, he was still performing in the polyphonic setting of his New Orleans background.

This was the oddity of Chicago in the 20s. The 'toddlin' town' fostered jazz without really encouraging it to evolve very much. Armstrong's unique virtuosity forced the music into a new mode of single-handed expression, but otherwise Chicago jazz still relied heavily on a vocabulary that was already threatened with decline.

When Morton went to New York at the end of the decade, he found it impossible to adapt to the new orchestral methods of Duke Ellington and Fletcher Henderson. The more blues-directed groups, whether in the slightly sophisticated manner of Lovie Austin or the rough-and-ready barrelhouse music of Jimmy Blythe, were similarly one-paced.

There was, though, at this time another strain of jazz that was starting to grow out of the city, one that would eventually personify what came to be known and understood as 'Chicago Jazz'.

Black audiences weren't the only ones spellbound by the new music. Many white teenagers began listening, and then began copying what they heard. Some of them came from the city's Austin High School. Inspired to emulate some of the music they had been hearing, they formed a clique that would later be recalled as the Austin High School Gang.

Among the line-up was the fiery cornetist, Jimmy McPartland (and his lesser-known brother Dick, who played banjo); the ferocious drummer, Dave Tough; Frank Teschemacher, who started on violin but would later become the most adventurous clarinetist of the era; and the suave, engaging saxman, Bud Freeman. McPartland and Freeman, who lived on into the 1990s, quickly became fully-developed personalities on their instruments, and it was only Teschemacher's death in a car wreck in 1932 that prevented him from holding a revered place in jazz.

They weren't only listening to the best black players. A white group called the New Orleans Rhythm Kings, seminal among early jazz bands yet one largely forgotten today, were a special influence. The NORK were fronted by three friends from the city that gave the group its name: cornetist Paul Mares,

Left : The Jean Goldkette Orchestra, with Beiderbecke fourth left and Trumbauer second right
Right: The Original Dixieland Jazz Band; clockwise from top left Eddie Edwards, Larry Shields, Tony Spargo, Nick LaRocca and Russell Robinson

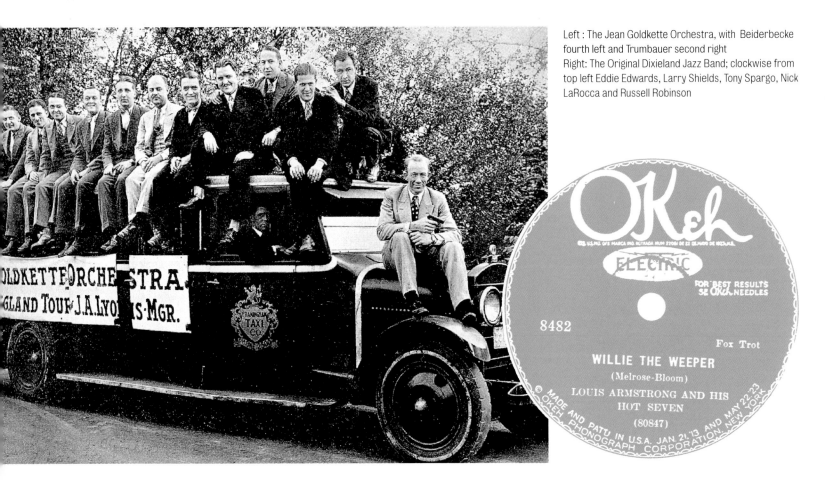

ORIGINAL DIXIELAND JAZZ BAND

Best Wishes To Our Pal Billie Jones
The Original Dixieland Jazz Band.

OKeh
LICENSED
FOR RADIO
BROADCAST
ELECTRIC
81   Fox Trot
                     Talk by
               Clarence Babcock
THE KING OF THE ZULU'S
(At A Chit'lin' Rag)
(Hardin)
LOUIS ARMSTRONG and
his HOT FIVE
(17344)
MADE AND PAT'D. IN U.S.A. RE. 16588 AND 1702563
COLUMBIA PHONOGRAPH COMPANY, INC.; NEW YORK

OKeh
ELECTRIC
FOR BEST RESULTS
USE OKEH NEEDLES
8519
WEARY BLUES
(Matthews)
LOUIS ARMSTRONG AND HIS
HOT FIVE
(80863)
MADE AND PAT'D IN U.S.A. JAN. 21, '13 AND RE. 16588
OKEH PHONOGRAPH CORPORATION NEW YORK

trombonist Georg Brunis (he changed the spelling from George Brunies on the advice of a numerologist) and the clarinet player Leon Roppolo. In a brilliant mixture of Oliver's band and the Original Dixieland Jazz Band, the group managed to purvey seamless, hot music that sounded smooth without sacrificing the intensity of the best jazz of the day. Mares and Roppolo in particular were outstanding players, who left a mark on a whole generation of young Chicagoans; their records for the local label Gennett, which had also recorded the crucial sides by the King Oliver band, remain a precious legacy.

Bix Beiderbecke

Name: Leon 'Bix' Beiderbecke
Checked In: 10 March 1903, Davenport, Indiana
Checked Out: 6 August 1931, New York City
Instruments: cornet, piano
All About Bix:
Made initial reputation in Chicago with The Wolverines (1924). In the same year struck up his life-long friendship with alto saxist Frankie Trumbauer and briefly joined Jean Goldkette Orchestra. Following short spell with Trumbauer-fronted group (1925-26), both joined Goldkette until band broke up late '27. Bix and 'Tram' then accepted invitation from self-styled King of Jazz, Paul Whiteman to join his popular Orchestra as featured soloists. However, by 1929, acute alcoholism and accompanying ill health caused Bix to quit Whiteman, erratically freelancing around New York, until his death, aged 28.
Style:
Not only the first white jazz legend and an alternative to Armstrong, but with his crisp, bell-like clarity, Bix can also be seen to have anticipated cool and the coming of Miles and Chet Baker.
Notable Disciples:
Jimmy McPartland, Bobby Hackett and Rex Stewart.
Image:
The original blueprint for the live fast, die young burn out. A fictionalized account of Bix's short life was the basis for Dorothy Baker's popular romantic novel, *Young Man With A Horn* (1938). In 1950, an overwrought movie adaptation cast Hollywood hero Kirk Douglas (Rick Martin) in the title role.
Further Reading:
Bix: Man & Legend (Sudhalter, Evans & Myatt).
Best heard:
'Singing The Blues', 'I'm Coming Virginia' and the Debussey-esque 'In A Mist', an exceptional piano solo.
The Legend Lives On:
In 1985, the plot of a popular British TV detective series, *The Beiderbecke Tapes*, involved the search for a rare set of the great cornetist's recordings.
Best Thing Said Of Bix:
'Four notes could change your life' (Hoagy Carmichael).

But there were plenty of others jockeying for position in this scene. Muggsy Spanier, another native of the city, learned his craft as a brassman by listening to Oliver; pianist Joe Sullivan worked the local vaudeville circuit; and a young clarinetist Benny Goodman was so precocious that he received his Musicians Union card at the age of thirteen. Outsiders drifted in: Pee Wee Russell (clarinet) from Texas, Bix Beiderbecke (cornet) and Frankie Trumbauer (saxophone) from the Mid-West.

The man who came to epitomise the whole Chicago school was actually from Indiana: Eddie Condon, the pugnacious rhythm guitar specialist. With his friend, vocalist Red McKenzie, he organised one of the great record sessions of the era; the 1928 tracks by the McKenzie-Condon Chicagoans. It was almost his swan-song to the city, since Condon left for New York the next year and made that his base from then on; eventually he opened his own club there in 1945.

Yet forever after, this wise-cracking Runyonesque figure was seen as the prime mover behind 'Chicagoan Jazz'.

In Condon's vernacular, that meant a clear, unfussy kind of dixieland, based around the patterns established in New Orleans but flavoured with a big-city tone and swaggering delivery that characterised the best of this music. They favoured a small repertoire of familiar tunes; absorbed the slightly looser rhythms of the swing era; and shifted the axis from ensemble playing to strings of carefully-crafted solos which were unpretentiously effective. Otherwise, the music of these bands was as close to timeless as anything jazz has ever produced.

Condon's groups involved dozens of other players over the years: Max Kaminsky, Billy Butterfield, Bobby Hackett, Wild Bill Davison (trumpet) Floyd O'Brien (trombone), Pee Wee Russell, Edmond Hall, Joe Marsala (clarinet), Bud Freeman (tenor sax), Jess Stacy (piano), Big Sid Catlett, Gene Krupa, George Wettling, (drums) and plenty more. It endured through decades of swing and bebop, and the so-called revivalism of the 40s and 50s owed much to Condon's championing of a style that was more resilient than most expected.

More durable, certainly, than the city which spawned it. When Condon left Chicago in 1929 it was dying as a centre of jazz. Those city fathers who weren't on the take initiated a crackdown on gangland vice in 1928, and although the culture of the town didn't exactly change overnight, the best days of Chicago nightlife were past. The Depression did the rest. By 1930, most of the action had moved to New York.

BLUEBIRD

B-10434

I THOUGHT I HEARD BUDDY BOLDEN SAY—Fox T
(Traditional—arr. by Jelly-Roll Morton)
Jelly-Roll Morton's New Orleans Jazzme
Sidney Bechet, sop. sax—Happy Cauldwell, tenor sax—
Albert Nicholas, clarinet—Sydney DeParis, trumpet—
Claude Jones, trombone—Wellman Braud, bass—
Zutty Singleton, drums—Lawrence Lucie,
guitar—Jelly-Roll Morton, piano & singing

VICTOR

Orthophonic
Recording

20415—

DOCTOR JAZZ—STOMP
(Joe Oliver)
Jelly-Roll Morton's Red Hot Peppers
Vocal refrain by Jelly-Roll Morton

"JELLY ROLL" MORTON
e originator of Jazz & stomps
AND HIS
RED HOT PEPPERS

Above and left: Louis Armstrong in familiar publicity shots, and below in England 1932 with members of the Jack Hylton Orchestra
Opposite: Native Chicagoan Mugsy Spanier

Chicago has never quite reasserted its importance as a jazz town ever since. It wasn't until the 1960s, when the black avant garde that was centred around the Association For The Advancement Of Creative Musicians established itself, notably in the Art Ensemble of Chicago, that the city once again seemed to propose its jazz eminence.

The blues, of course, has always been a big part of the city's musical culture, the electric blues of Muddy Waters, Buddy Guy and such in particular, and that has never changed; but for the most part, jazz moved on.

CD CHECKLIST
KING OLIVER
King Oliver: Volume One 1923-1929 (CBS)
NEW ORLEANS RHYTHM KINGS
NORK & Jelly Roll Morton (Milestone)
EDDIE CONDON
Dixieland All Stars (MCA)
MUGSY SPANIER
Muggsy Spanier: 1931-1939 (CDS)
PEE WEE RUSSELL
Jack Teagarden & Pee Wee Russell (Riverside/OJC)

Fact File

Eddie Condon, Bix Beiderbecke and Bing Crosby were all invited to a party while playing in Chicago.
Condon recalls driving home afterwards. 'I said to Bix: "Remember the guy you kept telling to shut up?." "Sure", Bix said, "Why didn't I knock him down? I'm too good natured." "I thought you'd like to know his name," I said. "The hell with his name," Bix said. "His name is Capone", I informed him, "Bottles Capone."'
On another occasion, clarinettist Mezz Mezzrow (right) was hauled from his bed and taken to a large garden tent where he was given a brace-and-bit and told to drain off barrels of beer, which had to be spiked because the Feds wouldn't let Capone's Blackhawk Brewery brew anything strong.
So Al would cart the innocuous brew to another part of town, where musicians would help dump most of the near-beer and revitalise it by pumping in a headier concoction, more likely to encourage instant appreciation of Mezzrow's nightly gigs. 'We sopped up a lot of learning at Capone's University of Gutbucket Arts,' Mezzrow later admitted.

New York, New York
. . . the very name
evokes the Twentieth
Century Big City, and
jazz, the quintessential
music of the big city,
soon found its natural
habitat in the honky
tonks of Harlem
before moving south
with the 'A' Train to
midtown Manhatten
and 52nd Street.

...and the Big Apple

HE 1990s: New York is the world capital of jazz, the place where literally thousands of aspiring players attempt to live and work. Yet in the early days of the music, it made room for jazz only as a kind of novelty music, the next big thing after ragtime but perhaps nothing more than that.

When the Original Dixieland Jazz Band made their New York debut at Reisenweber's Restaurant in 1917, they caused a sensation, though it was more for the sheer impact of their cacophony than anything else. While jazz continued to develop in New Orleans and Chicago, the prime cosmopolitan centre of America continued to consider jazz as little more than the ragged end of the otherwise polite dance music that was played in clubs, diners and dance halls.

There was an occasional initiative: small groups like The Georgians, led by the Italian-born trumpeter Frank Guarente, and The Original Memphis Five – both New York-based, despite their names! – split the difference between sweet and hot dance music, and their many early recordings show how popular their style was, well beyond the confines of the city. For the most part, though, the bigger dance bands were performing stiff arrangements of fox-trots that were only sometimes briefly enlivened by a breakaway horn solo here and there.

That was true, anyway, for the white dance orchestras. But something entirely different was happening elsewhere in the city, and it was coming out of what had become New York's premier black community.

By 1920, there were 200,000 blacks living in Harlem, a district composed of once-grand, but by then run-down, buildings.

Jazz was taking root here as a neighbourhood music at many of the fund-raising 'rent parties' which were enjoyed on every block, every weekend. At whatever beat-up piano would be in the room, the best local players would joust for attention. They were players of some stature, too, even if their names were hardly known

PAUL WHITEMAN'S RHYTHM BOYS
AL RINKER—HARRY BARRIS—"BING" CROSBY

Right: Paul Whiteman's Rhythm Boys, the vocal trio that included Bing Crosby, which worked as a novelty addition to the full Whiteman orchestra, pictured below

Opposite: A printed personnel sheet of the Whiteman band

beyond these few square miles at the time: James P. Johnson, Fats Waller, Willie `The Lion' Smith. Duke Ellington came in from Washington in 1922. William Basie played there long before getting stranded in Kansas City in 1927.

Harlem Piano became a tradition in itself, a fascinating mixture of ragtime, blues and show music, and a flamboyant exercise in showmanship and invention. That new expressiveness inevitably found its way into the small groups and then into the larger bands which began to work in and, soon enough, out of Harlem.

In the early 20s, there were perhaps no particularly outstanding bands, but there were many players who were feeling their way towards the virtuoso music of the latter part of the decade: old-school types such as Johnny Dunn (trumpet) and Fess Williams (clarinet) alongside budding masters like

Sidney Bechet (soprano sax) and Johnny Hodges (alto sax). But with talent starting to move into the city from the south – from New Orleans and Chicago – it was only a matter of time before New York could boast jazz bands of real substance.

One of the first was led by Fletcher Henderson, a talented if diffident pianist/arranger, who led a big group that played for white dancers at the Roseland Ballroom at 1658 Broadway.

Henderson began recording in 1921, and though his early discs demonstrate that the band wasn't all that different in approach to that of Sam Lanin, the youthful personnel were struggling towards a rough kind of improvising. By the time players such as Coleman Hawkins (tenor sax) came on board in 1923, the fuse was ready to be lit, and it happened with the arrival (from Chicago) of Louis Armstrong in 1924. Armstrong's solos,

Personnel of Paul Whiteman's Band.

Paul Whiteman	– Leader.
Charles Strickfadden) Frank Trumbauer) Chester Hazlett)	– Saxophones.
"Red Maier	– Saxophone and Flute.
"Izzy" Friedman	– Tenor Saxophone, and clarinet.
"Milford Liebrook	– Bass saxophone and other
Bill Rank) Boyce Cullen) Jack Fulton.	– Trombone. Trombone and Vocal. Trombone and comedian.
Wilbur Hall) "Bix" Beiderbecke) "Harry (Goldie) Goldfield) Charlie Margulis	Trumpet.
Mike Traffacante	– Bass.
Kurt Deiterle) Mischa Russell) Matt Malneck) Herman Vian) Joe Venuti) John Bonam	– Violin.
Ed. Lang.)	– Guitar.
Roy Barge) Len Hayton)	– Piano.
George Marsh.	– Drums.
Bernard Daly	– Flute, piccolo etc.)
Mike Pingatore.	– Banjo.
Rhythm Boys	– Vocalists.

bubbling out of Henderson's still relatively quiescent scores, remain amazing listening experiences over sixty years later. From that point, with the added participation of arranger Don Redman and a band roster that would eventually include many of the smartest and most formidable black players in New York, the Henderson band became the primary force in orchestrating the new music.

Then there was Ellington, who was also inspired by a brassman – the growl specialist Bubber Miley, who made Duke 'forget about all the sweet music' – and went on to piece together the nucleus of a band that would stay together for fifty years.

Ellington went into the Cotton Club in 1926, and began attracting a white audience curious to see what all the excitement was that was spreading through the music venues of the district. Soon, they were coming in such numbers that the Club – and other places such as Connie's Inn and Small's Paradise – eventually closed their doors to

Eddie Condon

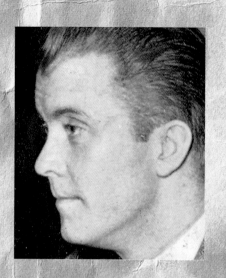

Name: Albert Edwin Condon
Checked In: 16 November 1905, Goodland, Indiana
Checked out: 4 August 1973, New York City
Instrument: Rhythm guitar
Other attributes:
Raconteur, television celebrity, club owner, bon vivant and author. Of the three books Condon penned, *We Called It Music* (1947) is the most illuminating.

His role in the cosmic scheme of things:
Even Damon Runyan would have been hard-pressed to create a wise-cracking character as colourful as Condon. Though early in his career, he moved from Chicago to New York (1929), Condon was forever regarded as the embodiment of Prohibition era Chicago Jazz.

Roots:
Integral part of the Austin High School Gang and (Red) McKenzie-Condon Chicagoans 1927.

Notable firsts:
Presented one of the first jazz programmes on TV in 1942. Between 1942-46, successfully organised a regular series of all-star concerts at both New York's Town Hall and Carnegie Hall. Opened his own New York jazz club in 1945.

Some famous sidemen:
Bobby Hackett (cornet), Max Kaminsky, Billy Butterfield, Wild Bill Davison (trumpet), Jack Teagarden, George Brunis (trombone), Pee Wee Russell (clarinet), Bud Freeman (tenor sax), Fats Waller, Joe Sullivan (piano), Gene Krupa, Big Sid Catlett, George Wettling (drums).

Health Care Advice:
While the Herculean drinking habits of both Condon and his band elevated them as the most likely candidates to sponsor bourbon or scotch, it was the laxative qualities of Kelloggs All-Bran that Condon felt an overwhelming desire to put his name to.

Cutting one-liners:
Condon's expertise at having the last word is revealed in his retort against bebop 'We don't flatten our fifths, we drink 'em', while on hearing the news that controversial French critic Hughes Panassie was to produce jazz dates in the US: 'Do I tell him how to jump on a grape?'

black patrons. But that audience took their business elsewhere, to hear King Oliver and Chick Webb at the Savoy Ballroom, or Luis Russell at the Saratoga Club.

These bandleaders and their sidemen came to set the tone for much of the most exciting music that New York could brag about. It's something of an irony, therefore, that 'New York jazz' of the 20s later came to suggest a different scene altogether, that of the white musicians who dominated much of the session and studio work in the period. New York recording studios were frantically busy throughout the decade, and even after the Depression set in there was still a terrific amount of recording being done. But although leaders such as Henderson and Ellington were always busy making records, their output paled in comparison to such counterparts as Ben Selvin, Paul Whiteman, Nat Shilkret or Fred Rich.

Whiteman, who almost slyly adopted the title 'The King Of Jazz', ran a big and unwieldy dance orchestra, but hired some of the best white players of the era – including Bix Beiderbecke (cornet) and Frankie Trumbauer (alto sax) – to give it a frisson of jazz excitement. The society playboy Roger Wolfe Kahn was able to run a band more or less to amuse himself, but he stuffed it with so many good players that the surviving records number among the best examples of the hotter dance music from that scene.

The roll-call of such musicians includes many now more or less forgotten by all but scholars of the era: Leo McConville (trumpet), Fud Livingston (clarinet/tenor sax), Adrian

Rollini (bass sax), Don Murray (clarinet), Bobby Davis (alto sax), Tommy Gott (trumpet) and many more. Yet the 'leaders' of the scene did more than merely turn up in sessionman settings. They also led small-group recording dates that became among the most revered and listened-to records of their day, at least by the early jazz fans.

Today, these sessions have fallen into some disrepute, with the rootsier records of Louis Armstrong's Hot Five or Jelly Roll Morton's Red Hot Peppers commanding much more respect. In their day, though, the white New Yorkers carried enormous respect.

The records featuring Bix Beiderbecke are somewhat atypical. Bix, a young veteran from the college jazz scene around Richmond, Indiana, played thoughtful and sometimes painfully beautiful solos on his cornet in musical settings that ranged from the gentle pre-dixieland of the Frankie Trumbauer and Bix And His Gang titles to the often puffing arrangements of the Whiteman orchestra.

Dead of alcoholism and pneumonia at 28, Beiderbecke became a melancholy doomed

Previous spread: Left, the Don Redman sax section, and right, the great Art Tatum
Left: The Hawk, Coleman Hawkins, in full flight
Right: Duke Ellington checks out an English music mag

youth symbol of Scott Fitzgerald's Jazz Age. But his serene methods were rather different to the meticulous virtuosity favoured by such men as trumpeter Red Nichols and trombonist Miff Mole, two names that dominated the New York school. They played on literally hundreds of dates right through the decade. The most famous sessions – by Nichols and his Five Pennies (though they were sometimes up to thirteen in number!) and Mole and his Molers – remain trim, poised examples of the kind of jazz that these players bequeathed to the history of jazz.

Nichols, who was still only 25 at the end of the decade, and Mole, whose wit and agility reinvented the trombone the way Coleman Hawkins restyled the saxophone, formed a frequent partnership that lent a certain wry distinction to much of the music. Among their confederates were the Dorsey brothers, Tommy (trombone) and Jimmy (alto sax), who would go on to become major figures in the big band Swing era of a decade later; the trombone player Glenn Miller, likewise; Jack Teagarden, whose mastery would eventually eclipse that of Mole himself; the violin and guitar duo of Joe Venuti and Eddie Lang; and Adrian Rollini, whose rotund yet flexible bass saxophone lines were a signature element in many of the records.

They may sound somewhat timelocked today, but records such as 'Feelin' No Pain', 'Hurricane' or 'Stringing The Blues' are an integral part of the New York music of the era. They also went all around the world and were

Brunswick
MADE IN UNITED STATES OF AMERICA
Not Licensed for Radio Broadcast
(B 18737)   Fox Trot
ECHOES OF HARLEM
-Duke Ellington-
DUKE ELLINGTON and his ORCHESTRA
7650
BRUNSWICK RECORD CORPORATION
US PAT 1637544 M REE MARCA INDUSTRIAL REGISTRATA

DECCA
TRADE MARK REGISTERED
NOT LICENSED FOR RADIO BROADCAST
(GB 6039)   FOX TROT
HARLEM SPEAKS
(Ellington-Mills)
DUKE ELLINGTON and his FAMOUS ORCHESTRA
800 A

VICTOR
Orthophonic Recording
"HIS MASTER'S VOICE"
For best results use Victor Needles   22587-A
MOOD INDIGO—Fox Trot
(Estoy muy Triste)
(Ellington-Bigard-Mills)
Duke Ellington and His Cotton Club Orchestra
RCA Victor Company, Inc.
Camden, N.J.
VE

JOHN KIRBY'S ORCHESTRA

Boogie

'A left hand like God' is how someone once described the great Boogie Woogie players, but the awesome power of the walking bass was used to support often subtle reworkings of simple blues figures, and was a direct influence on Kansas City big bands, post-War Rhythm and Blues and, into the 1950s, classic Rock'n'Roll.

BRUNSWICK RECORD CORPORATION NEW YORK
MADE IN U.S.A.
FULL-RANGE RECORDING
Vocalion
5186
(25026)
CAFE SOCIETY RAG
Fox Trot - Vocal Chorus by Joe Turner
-Ammons-Lewis-Johnson-
ALBERT, MEADE, PETE and THEIR THREE PIANOS

received as enthusiastically as the new music of Armstrong and Morton.

As the Depression made its mark and the era of speakeasies and flappers came to an end, New York's jazz moved on too. Besides Duke Ellington and Fletcher Henderson, other bands grew up throughout the early 1930s, including those of Cab Calloway, Jimmie Lunceford, Don Redman, Benny Carter, Teddy Hill, Lucky Millinder and many more. Count Basie – he originally hailed from just across the Hudson in Red Bank, New Jersey – returned, from Kansas City, in 1936. Benny Goodman and Tommy Dorsey and Artie Shaw and Woody Herman – when they weren't touring on strings of one-nighters – annexed the vast new audience for big-band swing.

Another new era was upon the music – and this time, it was centred around the Big Apple, New York City.

Woogie

Left: 'Greetings, Cats!!' – an advertisement for the touring boogie trio of Ammons, Johnson and Lewis, plus of course blues shouter Joe Turner

Below: Playing the part of a house decorator, Meade Lux Lewis rides the boogie gravy train in the 1947 movie *New Orleans*

'If you wanna hear some boogie, then I know the place, it's just an old piano and a knocked-out bass.' (Freddie Slack)

The often-underrated Chicago pianist Jimmy Yancey claimed he invented boogie-woogie. He didn't, of course. But nobody ever got around to filing a claim at the patent office, so the honour's still up for grabs.

A keyboard styling, whose rhythms often echoed locomotives, with the keyboardists attempting to musically depict the over-the-points clatter, the full-head-of-steam whistle, allied to the excitement of onrushing expresses and the almost 'Runaway Train' humour of happy-go-lucky locos, the genre grew up in booze-fumed backrooms and bars somewhere in America's great South.

If there was a birth-certificate, it had no name on it. That is until Clarence 'Pinetop' Smith opted to provide a christening, cutting 'Pinetop's Boogie Woogie' at a Chicago studio in 1928, the first time that anyone had recorded anything using the term 'boogie', though Clay Custer's

'The Rocks' had prodded the same idiom five years earlier. Pinetop hardly stayed around to pick up congratulations. Within months of the recording session, he was dead, accidentally shot in the crossfire at some Chicago club fracas. Out went the innovator.

But there were others. Fine exponents of eight-to-the-bar piano artistry, pianists like Jimmy Yancey, 'Cripple' Clarence Lofton, Cow Cow Davenport, Romeo Nelson, Charles Avery, Hersal Thomas, Montana Taylor and Meade 'Lux' Lewis, who claimed to have constructed his classic 'Honky Tonk Train Blues' at a house party in 1923. Not that it mattered. Boogie hardly teetered above life-support machine level until 1938.

It was then that the entrepreneur John Hammond sought Lewis and the portly powerhouse that was Albert Ammons, both of whom were driving taxis in Chicago when their Warholsworth of fame came up. They were thrust into the limelight, alongside fellow boogie man Pete Johnson at Carnegie Hall's 'Spirituals To Swing' concert in December 1938. The three pianists proved a sensation. The Carnegie date brought the Boogie Woogie Trio (as the three now billed themselves) both a flood of bookings on the New York Club circuit plus visits from record company hirelings bearing contracts.

When the big bands latched on, boogie mania got underway. Every main name swing outfit in the States headed for the nearest studio in order to log their contribution to the revival. Tommy Dorsey notched a million seller with his version of Pinetop's original 'Boogie Woogie', Earl Hines went Top 20 via 'Boogie Woogie On The St Louis Blues', while Harry James, Glenn Miller, Bob Crosby, Will Bradley, Gene Krupa and Woody Herman could be counted among the others who gained huge paychecks from releasing boogie recordings. However, Count Basie ('Basie Boogie') and Lionel Hampton ('Hamp's Boogie') required no additional help in this department.

Commercialism soon ran rife. Opportunistic songwriters weighed in. The Andrews Sisters were heard on every jukebox and radio station, harmonizing on such massive hits as 'Beat Me

Daddy, Eight To The Bar', 'Scrub Me, Mama, With A Boogie Beat', 'Rhumboogie' and 'Boogie Woogie Bugle Boy' (revived by Bette Midler in 1972). But when commercialism stepped in, jazz went out the highest window.

Overkill coincided with Over There. During World War II, American Forces entertainers sold boogie to a world that really needed something more than songs about booglie wooglie piggies. The fad took a time to fade. But fade it did, remnants surviving in various forms of Rhythm and Blues (Louis Jordan) and rock 'n' roll (Bill Haley's 'Rock-A-Beatin' Boogie'). Even so, boogie on its own terms still exists. In 1976, Keith Emerson, the flamboyant keyboard player with pomp-rock power trio ELP, dusted off Meade Lux's 'Honky Tonk Train Blues' and took it high into the UK pop charts.

Elsewhere, during the 70s and 80s, black music thrived on a series of 'boogie' songs that, though more often than not owing little or even nothing to the genre's history, at least kept the memory of this unique musical category alive.

And as recently as 1993, the blues veteran John Lee Hooker dented the British charts with 'Boogie At Russian Hill', a rhythmic reminder that some guitarists had also played a part in the music's history.

But boogie woogie remains mainly part of the pianist's prerogative and, as long as the (bass-providing) left hand knows exactly what the right hand is doing, then Pinetop Smith's legacy will always be stomping stuff.

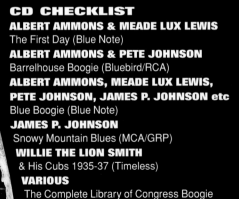

CD CHECKLIST
ALBERT AMMONS & MEADE LUX LEWIS
The First Day (Blue Note)
ALBERT AMMONS & PETE JOHNSON
Barrelhouse Boogie (Bluebird/RCA)
ALBERT AMMONS, MEADE LUX LEWIS, PETE JOHNSON, JAMES P. JOHNSON etc
Blue Boogie (Blue Note)
JAMES P. JOHNSON
Snowy Mountain Blues (MCA/GRP)
WILLIE THE LION SMITH
& His Cubs 1935-37 (Timeless)
VARIOUS
The Complete Library of Congress Boogie Woogie Recordings (Folkways)

Above: Stride and boogie albums featuring Willie 'The Lion' Smith and Meade Lux Lewis

Left: Albert Ammons

You had to have a great left hand to even attempt to participate in the stride school of pianists.

The style owed something to East Coast ragtime, and was a feature of 20s Harlem gin mills and rent parties, where a strong bass-line and an even stronger constitution was needed in order for the pianists to survive.

Top of the heap were James P. Johnson and the splendidly named William Bonaparte Bertholoff Smith, better known as Willie 'The Lion' Smith. Claimed Willie, 'Jimmie (James P) gave me the title because of my spunk and enterprise. I named him "The Brute". Later, we gave Fats Waller the name "Filthy" and the three of us, plus a guy called "Lippy" (Raymonde Boyette), used to run all over town playing piano.'

Naturally, Jelly Roll Morton, who claimed to have invented most things connected with jazz, including jazz itself, staked a claim as originator, and could, in truth, stay with the best of them. But it was 'The Lion' who nailed stride as church shouts played keyboard-style.

'When James P, Fats and I would get a romp-down about going, that was playing rocky, like the Baptist people sing. You don't play a chord to that – you got to move it and the piano.'

A lot of piano was moved in Harlem during the 20s, great two-handed stuff, with both hands contributing equally. And, as things lurched on, there were students ready to learn, get involved and then add their own individual traits to whatever they had fashioned.

Art Tatum took the genre into a fantasy-land, providing the kind of technique that even concert pianists would not be able to match. Count Basie opted for a far simpler approach,

Truly a super-star of his day, Fats Waller's tunes like 'Ain't Misbehavin'' were huge hits and remain in the annals of the greatest popular songs

by using the notes sparingly, while it was Duke Ellington who added the sophistication.

Thelonious Monk and later, Cecil Taylor, were two of the final links in the chain, bringing pure eccentricity to a style that had, incredibly, linked ragtime to bebop and beyond.

But maybe it was New York-born Willie Smith who really epitomised everything that stride had going for it, Duke Ellington once observing: 'When you came into the Capitol Palace, in 1923, you were either in step with the Lion, literally, or you had to stop and get out.'

JAZZ 100 Fact File

The boogie woogie idiom was responsible for providing many of the worst titles ever to clutter the jazz catalogue. Boogie, at least in the late Thirties and Forties, was a hip thing. Or so Tin Pan Alley songwriters imagined. Accordingly, they dug deep for titles that, or so they imagined, would make teenagers flip. Billy Maxted, for instance, who eventually replaced Freddy Slack in the boogie seat of the Will Bradley band, recorded a ditty that answered to the name 'Fry Me A Cookie With A Can Of Lard', one of Bradley's own biggest hits being 'Scrub Me Mama With A Boogie Beat', sung with true deserving passion by drummer Ray McKinley.
Bradley was forever hooked by boogie and even as late as 1959 was to be found recording an album of a dozen boogie tracks for the RCA label in the company of Johnny Guarnieri.
Not that everyone was an admirer. One club habitee, not entertained by Pete Johnson's attempt to play some eight-to-the-bar on an out-of-tune piano, requested the pianist to play 'The Silent Rag'.
'How does it go?' asked Johnson, unfamiliar with the title. 'Well, first you take your foot of the pedal,' instructed the customer, 'Then you take your hands off the keys. After which you take your ass off the seat and get outta here.'

Call Me MR BIG

–The Rise Of The Swing Bands

The era of big band Swing represented the first real instance of jazz music, or very close derivatives of jazz, becoming part of the mainstream of popular music. The tunes became standards that people whistled on their way to work, the musicians became superstars mobbed by fans, and top names like Artie Shaw, Glenn Miller and Harry James sold records by the million. Swing was the pop of its day.

Swing on the Silver Screen:
Opposite, the Count Basie band in a scene from *Hit Parade 1943*, this page, the 'King of Swing' Benny Goodman in *The Girl He Left Behind* and, top right, in a still from the movie *Orchestra Wives*, the pioneer of the 'Sweet' big band sound, Glenn Miller

SWING THRIVED on a riff. Or rather a succession of riffs, the repeated phrase that acted like a mindworm. Think Glenn Miller and you think 'In The Mood', the twelve-bar instrumental that practically won the Second World War. There's a guy somewhere trying to locate a war movie of that era that doesn't contain a few bars of that very flag-waver. And he's encountering problems.

The riff, the big band, the excitement as entire trombone sections waved their horns to the heavens in unison, as gum-chewing drummers embarked on percussive sorties that found them frantically hitting everything in sight, and as trumpet players perpetually sought notes that were beyond the range of Gabriel. Where did it all begin ?

As always there's no easy answer. Rarely does a genre simply develop overnight.

TOMMY DORSEY

AT 30 YEARS OF AGE, TOMMY DORSEY IS A VETERAN OF JAZZ, HAVING PLAYED WITH THEM ALL FROM GOLDKETTE DOWN TO WHITEMAN, NOT TO MENTION THE FAMOUS DORSEY BROTHERS ORCHESTRA. HE INVENTED THE STYLE OF SWINGING THE CLASSICS AND STILL DOES THAT BETTER THAN HIS MANY IMITATORS. RELAXED SWING, PLAYED WITH BEAUTIFUL TONE, IS HIS SWING STOCK-IN-TRADE.

CHICK CHICK CHICK CHICK CHICK

HE LIVES ON A BIG FARM IN THE COUNTRY AND INTENDS TO SETTLE DOWN TO THE SIMPLE LIFE FOR KEEPS SOME DAY

HE ALWAYS TRAVELS BY AEROPLANE AND SOMEDAY HOPES TO PILOT HIS OWN.

THE SENTIMENTAL GENTLEMAN OF SWING.

Usually there will be many roots and branches, and dozens of different reasons why.

But history demands a place, a name. As far as big bands are concerned the name is Paul Whiteman. And the place – New York City. Whiteman initially had a dire band. It plodded, was stodgy and seemed indistiguishable to many of the other outfits that kept America dancing in the years that followed World War I. But the rotund one was a showman, the P.T. Barnum of that postwar scene. By the early 20s he controlled nearly 30 East Coast bands. And it was he who put jazz on the map one glitzy night in February 1924 when he presented a 'jazz' concert at New York's Aeolian Hall.

Naturally, few of today's hipsters would have recognised it as such.

Not unless compositions by Elgar, Friml and Gershwin (playing his 'Rhapsody In Blue' for the first time) could be considered candidates for any Hot Discography. But jazz seemed a handy sobriquet to hang around the neck of Whiteman's music and so he became the self-styled King Of Jazz, the most uncool ruler ever to wave a baton in search of a dollar.

Later, he relented to some extent, began employing musicians like trumpet genius Bix Beiderbecke, reedmen Frankie Trumbauer and Jimmy Dorsey, plus pianist/arranger Bill Challis, sidemen who knew in which direction New Orleans lay, But the emphasis was always on being Big. Having more musicians than any of

Tommy and Jimmy Dorsey brought swing right into the showbusiness mainstream with hit records, movie appearances, and later – in the 50s – even a Hollywood bio-pic, *The Fabulous Dorseys*; and their own TV series, which had the distinction of broadcasting the first-ever television appearance of one Elvis Aaron Presley in 1955

his rivals. And right to the end he'd rather borrow Borodin than barter with Basie.

Fletcher 'Smack' Henderson however, was to provide a whole different bundle of riffs.

With the help of arranger Don Redman, he shaped a big band that roared, turned charts into live things, did the black and proud bit years before others got around to using the phrase to win friends and influence whole communities. What once was tepid became torrid. Remembered trumpet player Leora Henderson: 'We prepared for the Battles of Jazz with the bands that were playing at the Roseland – The Dorsey Brothers, Casa Loma, Vincent Lopez, Jean Goldkette and The Buffalodians, who had Harold Arlen playing piano. But nobody could beat our band, not with people like Don Redman and Louis Armstrong, Bobby Stark, Joe Smith, Coleman Hawkins, Buster Bailey, Benny Carter, John Kirby and all the rest of the musicians that Fletcher had in those years.'

And as Henderson became successful, he inspired many white imitators. The most potent of these being Benny Goodman, a Chicago-born reedman who had joined the musicians' union at the age of 13.

Benny Goodman filled the bill as the great contender. Somehow he looked right for the part. Place him in a line-up alongside Tommy Dorsey and Glenn Miller, other bandleaders who came out of the same New York session scene as Benny, and you could hardly tell the difference. A fine clarinetist, perfectly able to handle himself if someone stuck one of Mozart's hits under his nose, he could appeal equally to dance-daters or those who liked to to intellectualise while their shoes remained nailed firmly to the library floor.

Nobody could accuse Benny of not being musically ofay. Smart as a tack he bought Henderson arrangements by the ream. He also employed the best musicians around, be they black or white, employing black pianist Teddy Wilson as part of a famed trio in 1935 and adding vibesman Lionel Hampton a year later. When he proclaimed himself King Of Swing, nobody complained. But the rivals

developed thick and fast. In May 1938 twenty six bands performed for seven hours at a Carnival Of Swing held at Randall's Island in New Yorks' East River. And 25,000 people came to see and hear.

To be top of the heap required an identity, a trademark. Tommy Dorsey featured his own smooth-toned trombone, Artie Shaw had a distinctive clarinet style that set him apart from that Goodman, the urbane Duke

The Sentimental Gentleman

Coming IN PERSON

TOMMY DORSEY and his ORCHESTRA

FEATURING

PRESENTED BY MCA

YOUR AD COPY HEP

Above: The Goodman band in full swing
Left: Big band vocalist Helen Humes serenades her pianist boss Count Basie

Ellington developed his 'jungle sound', by association emphasising that he led a black band, the ploy proving an instant come-on at various Harlem hotspots where downtown whites came slumming.

But, up there grabbing the headlines was Benny Goodman. And Benny knew what it took to make the news. If Whiteman could play Aeolian Hall, he could play Carnegie. So, one day in January, 1938, he did that very thing. The show proved a celebration of the whole Swing phenomenon. He tossed in the riff to end all riffs that forms Count Basie's 'One O'Clock Jump', and a 'Life Goes To A Party' that had the Goodman band jamming with members of the Basie Orchestra.

Musicians from the Ellington band arrived to provide a tribute to the Duke, elsewhere Benny unfurled a history of jazz through nods in the direction of the Original Dixieland Jazz Band, Bix Beiderbecke and Louis Armstrong, the event was, thankfully, being recorded by CBS by means of a single overhead mike.

But success in this instance, bred success for others. Within months such Goodman stars as hot toned trumpeter Harry James and drummer Gene Krupa, a prototype for the Keith Moons of the future, moved off to form

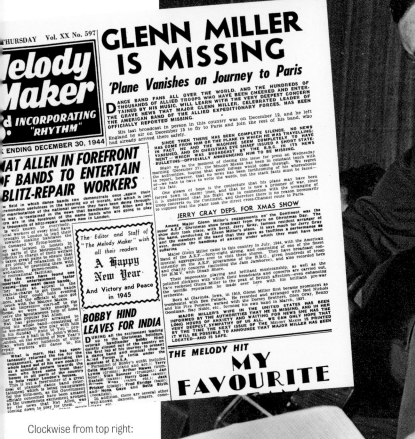

Clockwise from top right:
Glenn Miller in full uniform,
Cab Calloway in the film
Stormy Weather, Artie Shaw

highly successful big bands of their own. Goodman had demonstrated that there was a huge audience just waiting to hug swing to its heart. At which point new bands virtually queued up to get into such a clinch.

There was Basie, doing all the simple things and getting them right – minimalism used to provide power. Glenn Miller, success guaranteed by a clarinet-led reed section that provided a unique sound, did the whole show-biz bit. Woody Herman rose to fame as the reed-playing leader of 'The Band That Plays The Blues', Bing Crosby's younger brother Bob turned small-band Dixieland jazz into a more heavily populated affair, Jimmy Lunceford headed a fantastically disciplined band that still swung more than most, thanks partly to Sy Oliver's incredible scores, while Lionel Hampton fronted an outfit that was a bit ragged round the edges but compensated by being the most exciting crew ever to pound dancers into sheer exhaustion.

'I like to think that I helped bring black music to white audiences' Hamp claimed in his autobiography 'I stayed in the black groove. You'd know my band was black by just listening to it.'

Hamp was hardly alone. There were plenty of others ready to induce media-grabbing amounts of torrid terpsichore at venues like Harlem's Savoy Ballroom and its Chicago namesake, a one-time roller rink, where, in 1936, Dr Jive Cadillac's big band dance policy turned the venue's fortunes around, thanks to a programme that included the names of Andy Kirk and His Clouds Of Joy, Tiny Bradshaw, Erskine Hawkins, and Chick Webb, a diminutive drummer whose feet could hardly reach the foot-pedals, but nevertheless still led a jumpin' outfit that was ever-anxious to take on all comers.

Not that it was all jazz. No swing band of the 30s and 40s could survive without its fill of pops. For every Goodman killer-diller like 'Bugle Call Rag' or 'King Porter Stomp' (both top 10 singles), there were others like 'Is That The Way To Treat A Sweetheart?' and 'I've Got A Date With A Dream', two soft-focus examples of the 164 major hits that Benny logged before the lights went out on the jazz ballroom. Others were equally as prolific in the manner in which they shoved singles into the best-selling listings. Tommy Dorsey amassed over 180 hits with his own band in his lifetime, while his brother Jimmy notched a straight century of winners.

Glenn Miller, whose bandleading career with his 'trademark' band lasted a brief three years, nevertheless tallied over 100 hits during that time, including 23 chart toppers.

Lester Young

Name: Lester Willis Young
Checked In:
27 August 1909 Woodville, Mississippi
Checked Out:
15 March 1959, New York City
Instruments:
Tenor sax, clarinet.
Famous for :
His cool-toned tenor, his pork pie hat and being the Hipster role model who anticipated the bop movement. Not only did Pres inspire Bird but also an entire generation of 'grey-boy' acolytes headed by Stan Getz, Zoot Sims, Al Cohn, Allan Eager and Brew Moore (the latter insisting 'anyone who doesn't play like Lester Young is wrong').
Nicknamed:
'Pres' ('Prez') by Billie Holiday - the President of the tenor sax.
Inspired:
In the *Round Midnight* movie, the Dale Turner character as portrayed by Dexter Gordon, was as much based on Pres as it was on pianist Bud Powell.
Catch him at his best:
In Gjon Mili's jazz movie short *Jammin' The Blues* and on record with Billie Holiday, Count Basie and Jazz At The Philharmonic.
Famous for saying:
Many things, for Pres - like vout vendor Slim Gaillard - invented his own hipster vocabulary. Introduced the term 'bread' (money) into mainstream English slang and referred to other musicians as 'Lady'. Talking about the 'grey boys' Lester exclaimed: 'A lot of the ladies are playing me and making the money.'

Above: The Ellington 'Famous Orchestra' gather round the Duke, drummer Sonny Greer in the foreground

Right: His signature 'Take The "A" Train', referring to the 'A' line on the New York Subway which runs from downtown Manhatten up to Harlem

In Britain, where bands such as those headed by Ambrose and Lew Stone made an early impact, Ted Heath and His Music packed the London Palladium every time they chose to play Sunday Swing Shifts at the venue, prompting others, such as Johnny Dankworth, Vic Lewis, Geraldo, and Teddy Foster to add concert gigs to their heady number of dance dates. Swing ruled okay. And the record companies had the sales figures to prove it.

The passing of time brought about change. Just as rock moved from the simplicity of rockabilly to the mild complexities of the 60s beat groups and then further on to the myriad influences of the 'progressive' bands of the late 60s and early 70s, so too did the approach of some big band leaders and their arrangers.

Stan Kenton of Kansas was among the forerunners. Initially, he stuck to the code of the riff but recorded in such a powerhouse manner, by using an echo-chamber that Eddie Condon once wrote: 'Every Kenton record sounds to me as though Stan signed on three hundred men for the date and they were all on time.' By the latter part of the 1940s, many of his scores were as complex as a three-dimensional crossword. He'd realised that the swing-dance scene was reaching its end and that concert halls would provide the main source of future income. Purists argued that what Kenton was playing was no longer jazz and he added fuel to the fire by recording soundscape suites like Bill Graettinger's 'City Of Glass' and even an album dedicated to the music of Wagner.

In some ways, it was seen as a return to the pomposity of Paul Whiteman. Yet the Kenton band, fuelled by some of the finest musicians ever to grace the California surfline, produced

Above: The classic Benny Goodman Quartet with (left to right) Lionel Hampton on the vibes, pianist Teddy Wilson, Goodman on clarinet and drummer Gene Krupa

some of the most diverting and original sounds to emerge from the kingdom of Swing. There were others who took a similar path. Boyd Raeburn also devised a listening band rather than a dancer's delight. His scores echoed shades of Bartok and Ravel, and his singles included 'Boyd Meets Stravinsky' and 'Tonsilectomy'. Then there was Claude

Thornhill, the pianist who led what was most probably the best-sounding band never to really capture the public ear. It floated on a gorgeous pastel basis, all sustained chords and french horns. Sparked by arrangements by such up and comers as Gerry Mulligan and Gil Evans, who would forward to help shape the future of jazz. According to Evans: 'It was

First Results of Down Beat's
3rd Annual All-American Band Contest

CONTEST

Chicago, November, 1938

Tisket A Tasket Leads Favorite Records of '38

FLETCHER HENDERSON LEADS ARRANGERS

Altho the first returns are very incomplete, and subject to many upsets, last year's favorites are leading almost to a man except in one or two instances.

Goodman again leads favorite swing bands, with Bob Crosby squeezing out Tommy Dorsey for 2nd place. The surprise bands are Artie Shaw, who is third and Count Basie, who is fourth. Last year Count Basie was eighth and Shaw didn't even get in the first dozen.

Among the sweet bands, Tommy Dorsey replaces Hal Kemp, who has slipped to third place.

Tommy Dorsey, altho he slipped from 2nd to 5th among swing bands, while gaining first place among swing bands, is the most popular all-round band.

Heller Upsets Guitarists

Benny Heller, Goodman's guitarist, who wasn't even in the running last year, is leading last year's winner, Carmen Mastren, by a wide margin.

Bud Freeman and Eddie Miller on tenor are both running ahead of last year's winner, Chu Berry.

The rest of last year's winners in the All-American band are again leading.

Among the arrangers, Fletcher Henderson, the excellent colored arranger and leader, is leading Larry Clinton and Edgar Sampson, while in the vocal line, Ella Fitzgerald again leads her white rival, Mildred Bailey.

Sing Sing Gets Most Votes in Error

By mistake, some of the voters have cast their ballot for last year's

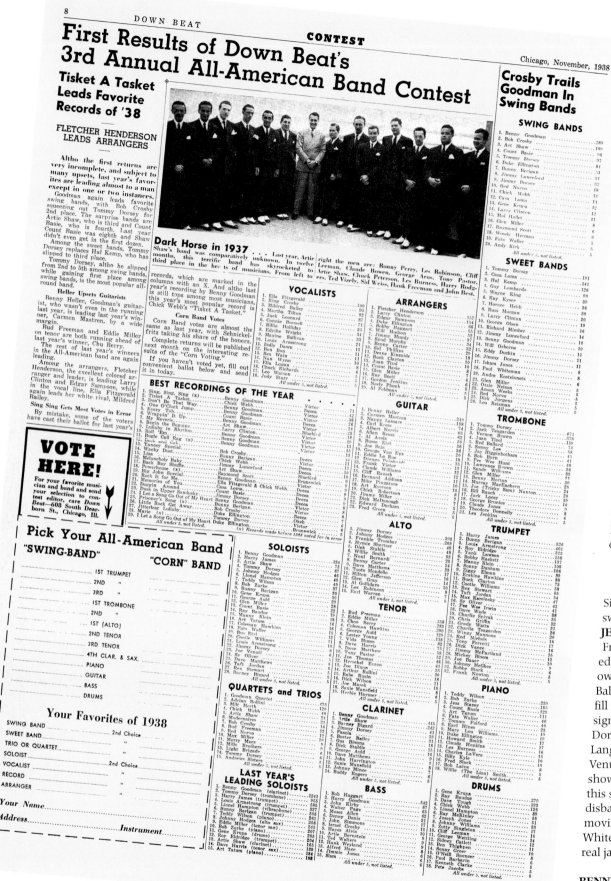

Dark Horse in 1937 . . .

Shaw's band was comparatively unknown. In twelve months, this terrific band has skyrocketed to third place in the hearts of musicians. From left to right the men are: Ronny Perry, Les Robinson, Cliff Leeman, Claude Bowen, George Arus, Tony Pastor, Artie Shaw, Chuck Peterson, Les Burness, Harry Rodgers, Ted Vizely, Sid Weiss, Hank Freeman and John Best.

records, which are marked in the columns with an X. And altho last year's recording by Benny Goodman is still tops among most musicians, this year's most popular record is Chick Webb's "Tisket A Tasket."

Corn Band Votes

Corn Band votes are almost the same as last year, with Schnickel-fritz taking his share of the honors.

Complete returns will be published next month on the interesting results of the "Corn Voting."

If you haven't voted yet, fill out it in today.

VOTE HERE!

For your favorite musician and band and send your selection to contest editor, care Down Beat—608 South Dearborn St., Chicago, Ill.

Pick Your All-American Band

"SWING-BAND"	"CORN" BAND
1ST TRUMPET	
2ND "	
3RD "	
1ST TROMBONE	
2ND "	
1ST (ALTO)	
2ND TENOR	
3RD TENOR	
4TH CLAR. & SAX.	
PIANO	
GUITAR	
BASS	
DRUMS	

Your Favorites of 1938

SWING BAND ....
SWEET BAND .... 2nd Choice
TRIO OR QUARTET .... "
SOLOIST .... "
VOCALIST .... 2nd Choice
RECORD .... "
ARRANGER .... "

Your Name ....
Address ....
.... Instrument ....

VOCALISTS

1. Ella Fitzgerald	190
2. Bing Crosby	
3. Mildred Bailey	95
4. Martha Tilton	92
5. Jack Leonard	87
6. Connie Boswell	71
7. Billie Holliday	
8. Edythe Wright	35
9. Maxine Sullivan	34
10. Louis Armstrong	33
11. Dolly Dawn	21
12. Bon Bon	13
13. Ben Wain	
14. Nan Wynn	
15. Ella Logan	
16. Chuck Richards	
17. Leo Watson	
18. Judy Starr	

BEST RECORDINGS OF THE YEAR

1. Sing, Sing, Sing (x)	Benny Goodman	.71
2. Tisket A Tasket	Chick Webb	
3. Don't Be That Way	Benny Goodman	Victor .42
4. One O'Clock Jump	Count Basie	Decca .36
5. Every Tub	Count Basie	Victor .35
6. Wrappin' It Up	Larry Clinton	Victor .24
7. My Reverie	Larry Clinton	Victor .23
8. Begin the Beguine (x)	Artie Shaw	Bluebird .18
9. Lullaby in Rhythm	Benny Goodman	Victor .18
10. Roll 'Em	Benny Goodman	Victor .13
11. Bugle Call Rag (x)	Benny Goodman	Victor .10
12. Yancey Special		
13. Wacky Dust	Bob Crosby	Decca
14. Liza	Bunny Berigan	Victor
15. Melancholy Baby	Chick Webb	Decca
16. Back Bay Shuffle	Jimmy Lunceford	Victor
17. Powerhouse	Art Shaw	Decca
18. Big John Special	Benny Goodman	Decca
19. Rock It for Me	Raymond Scott	Decca
20. Memories of You	Benny Goodman	Bluebird
21. Doggin Around	Casa Loma	Victor
22. Dusk in Upper Sandusky	Ella Fitzgerald & Chick Webb	Decca
23. I Let a Song Go Out of My Heart	Jimmy Dorsey	Decca
24. Prisoner's Song (x)	Tommy Dorsey	Victor
25. Hold It, Rock Get Away	Bunny Berigan	Victor
26. Jitterbug Lullaby	Bob Crosby	Victor
27. Marie (x)	Duke Ellington	Okeh
28. I Let a Song Go Out of My Heart	Duke Ellington	Victor

(x) Records made before 1938 voted for in error

ARRANGERS

1. Fletcher Henderson		157
2. Larry Clinton		71
3. Edgar Sampson		66
4. Duke Ellington		55
5. Will Hudson		52
6. Jimmy Mundy		47
7. Spud Murphy		37
8. Benny Carter		34
9. Sid Phillips		13
10. Deane Kincaide		12
11. Buck Clayton		10
12. Juan Tizol		8
13. Count Basie		8
14. Glen Miller		7
15. Ray Scott		
16. Gordon Jenkins		
17. Neely Plumb		
18. Al Feldman		

GUITAR

1. Benny Heller		.240
2. Carmen Mastren		.158
3. Nappy Lamare		74
4. Carl Kress		63
5. Albert Norris		50
6. Allan Reuss		50
7. Al Avola		36
8. Eddie La Rue		26
9. Django Reinhardt		19
10. Frank Victor		16
11. Claude Williams		11
12. Cliff Rausch		10
13. George Van Eps		10
14. Jimmy Miller		10
15. Dick McDonough		8
16. Fred Green		

ALTO

1. Jimmy Dorsey		.393
2. Johnny Hodges		.209
3. Frankie Trombar		78
4. Hymie Shertzer		49
5. Dick Stabile		44
6. Willie Smith		33
7. Noni Bernardi		28
8. Benny Carter		24
9. Dave Matthews		28
10. Toots Mondello		18
11. Hilton Jefferson		14
12. Glen Gray		12
13. Al Gallodaro		10
14. Les Robinson		
15. Earl Warren		

TENOR

1. Bud Freeman		.358
2. Eddie Miller		.283
3. Chu Berry		282
4. Coleman Hawkins		280
5. George Auld		129
6. Lester Young		118
7. Vido Musso		75
8. Dave Matthew		58
9. Dave Harris		52
10. Tony Pastor		28
11. Joe Thomas		21
12. Herschel Evans		19
13. Joe Dixon		14
14. Arthur Rollini		
15. Dick Wilson		
16. Joe Masek		
17. Saxie Mansfield		
18. Herbie Haymer		

CLARINET

1. Benny Goodman		.445
2. Artie Shaw		.242
3. Barney Bigard		43
4. Jimmy Dorsey		33
5. Fazola		18
6. Buster Bailey		17
7. Gus Bivona		14
8. Dick Stabile		
9. George Auld		
10. Dave Matthews		
11. John Harrington		
12. Saxie Mansfield		
13. Johnny Mince		
14. Buddy Morrow		

SOLOISTS

1. Benny Goodman	
2. Harry James	184
3. Artie Shaw	
4. Tommy Dorsey	67
5. Johnny Hodges	45
6. Lionel Hampton	40
7. Teddy Wilson	40
8. Bob Zurke	30
9. Bunny Berigan	30
10. George Auld	
11. Count Basie	
12. Glen Miller	
13. Ray Bauduc	
14. Mannie Klein	
15. Art Tatum	
16. Coleman Hawkins	
17. Fats Waller	
18. Bus Etri	
19. Cootie Williams	
20. Louis Armstrong	
21. Jimmy Dorsey	
22. Joe Venuti	
23. Sy Oliver	
24. Dave Matthews	
25. Taft Jordan	
26. Rex Stewart	
27. Rex Stewart	
28. Barney Bicard	

QUARTETS and TRIOS

1. Goodman Quartet	
2. Adrian Rollini	
3. Milt Herth	120
4. Chick Webb	
5. Artie Shaw	
6. Modernaires	
7. Bob Crosby	
8. Bud Freeman	
9. Red Norvo	
10. Max Miller	
11. Merry Macs	
12. Mills Brothers	
13. Light Brigade	
14. Tommy Dorsey	
15. Andrews Sisters	

LAST YEAR'S LEADING SOLOISTS

1. Benny Goodman (clarinet)	
2. Tommy Dorsey (trombone)	1241
3. Harry James (trumpet)	955
4. Louis Armstrong (trumpet)	585
5. Lionel Hampton (trumpet)	327
6. Bunny Berigan (trumpet)	305
7. Teddy Wilson (piano)	261
8. Johnny Hodges (alto sax)	256
9. Eddie Miller (tenor sax)	245
10. Bob Zurke (piano)	207
11. Gene Krupa (drums)	205
12. Roy Eldridge (trumpet)	204
13. Artie Shaw (clarinet)	165
14. Dave Harris (tenor sax)	189
15. Art Tatum (piano)	108

BASS

1. Bob Haggart		.542
2. Harry Goodman		87
3. John Kirby		68
4. Walter Page		62
5. Moses Allen		21
6. Deane Denis		21
7. John Simmons		11
8. Israel Crosby		
9. Hayes Alvis		
10. Artie Bernstein		
11. Ted Walters		
12. Hank Weylond		
13. Alfred Hace		
14. Jimmie Jones		
15. Slam		

SWING BANDS

1. Benny Goodman	.289
2. Bob Crosby	
3. Art Shaw	100
4. Count Basie	98
5. Tommy Dorsey	97
6. Duke Ellington	81
7. Bunny Berigan	51
8. Jimmy Lunceford	34
9. Jimmy Dorsey	32
10. Red Norvo	18
11. Chick Webb	14
12. Casa Loma	11
13. Gene Krupa	12
14. Larry Clinton	12
15. Mal Hallet	11
16. Glen Miller	8
17. Raymond Scott	6
18. Woody Herman	6
19. Fats Waller	5
20. Andy Kirk	5

SWEET BANDS

1. Tommy Dorsey	.191
2. Casa Loma	.141
3. Hal Kemp	.126
4. Guy Lombardo	96
5. Wayne King	39
6. Kay Kyser	36
7. Horace Heidt	30
8. Russ Morgan	
9. Larry Clinton	20
10. George Olsen	19
11. Richard Himber	16
12. Jimmy Lunceford	14
13. Benny Goodman	12
14. Will Osborne	11
15. Eddy Duchin	11
16. Jimmy Dorsey	11
17. Isham Jones	11
18. Paul Whiteman	8
19. Andre Kostelanetz	6
20. Glen Miller	6
21. Ozzie Nelson	5
22. Anson Weeks	5
23. Dick Jurgens	5
24. Leo Reisman	5

TROMBONE

1. Tommy Dorsey	.671
2. Jack Teagarden	.378
3. Vernon Brown	159
4. Juan Tizol	
5. Red Ballard	72
6. Glen Miller	61
7. Jay Higginbotham	58
8. Bob Byrn	45
9. Buck Clayton	41
10. Lawrence Brown	40
11. Sandy Williams	36
12. Glen Miller	33
13. Benny Morton	31
14. Murray MacEachern	26
15. Joe (Tricky Sam) Nanton	25
16. Bill Rauch	20
17. Jack Lacey	
18. George Brunies	19
19. Claude Jones	18
20. Theodore Donnelly	8
21. Les Jenkins	6

TRUMPET

1. Harry James	.526
2. Bunny Berigan	.401
3. Louis Armstrong	.312
4. Roy Eldridge	.212
5. Yank Lawson	.158
6. Bobby Hackett	.137
7. Manny Klein	108
8. Sonny Dunham	.106
9. Ziggy Elman	89
10. Erskine Hawkins	85
11. Buck Clayton	78
12. Cootie Williams	55
13. Rex Stewart	54
14. Taft Jordan	42
15. Max Kaminsky	41
16. Sy Oliver	38
17. Pee Wee Irwin	38
18. Dave Wade	31
19. Charlie Spivak	26
20. Chris Griffin	24
21. Gordy Watts	18
22. Charlie Teagarden	16
23. Wingy Mannone	15
24. Red Nichols	15
25. Tony Ferrett	
26. Jimmy McPartland	
27. Dick Vance	
28. Mickey Bloom	
29. Joe Bauer	
30. Johnny McGhee	
31. Bobby Stark	
32. Frank Newton	

PIANO

1. Teddy Wilson	.289
2. Bob Zurke	.185
3. Jess Stacey	
4. Count Basie	.120
5. Art Tatum	.129
6. Fats Waller	73
7. Tommy Fulford	46
8. Earl Hines	40
9. Mary Lou Williams	23
10. Duke Ellington	19
11. Howard Smith	19
12. Claude Hopkins	17
13. Les Burness	16
14. Charles LaVere	16
15. Billy Kyle	10
16. Fred Slack	10
17. Bob Laine	5
18. Willie (The Lion) Smith	

DRUMS

1. Gene Krupa	.279
2. Ray Bauduc	.193
3. Dave Tough	.126
4. Chick Webb	.126
5. Lionel Hampton	
6. Ray McKinley	89
7. Joseph Jones	55
8. Johnny Williams	51
9. Zutty Singleton	20
10. Cliff Leeman	17
11. George Wettling	14
12. Sidney Catlett	12
13. Ben Thigpen	11
14. Sonny Greer	10
15. O'Neill Spencer	8
16. Paul Barbarin	6
17. Kenneth Clarke	5
18. Pete Jacobs	5

Crosby Trails Goodman In Swing Bands

one of the first bands to play without vibrato and that's what made it compatible with bebop – because the bebop players played with no vibrato. And they were also interested in the impressionistic harmony that I used with Claude – the minor ninths and all of that.'

Such beauty should really have lasted forever. But, sadly, time ran out for big band swing. Just as, at the beginning, there had been a myriad of contributory factors, so it was at the end. Recording bans, during which only vocalists could make records, the use of jukeboxes where formerly combos had played, the rise of a generation that was now desperate to dump anything and everything which even suggested they were still wearing their parents under-pants. All served to erode. Meanwhile, the riff went on to other things.

Six others who helped things swing:

JEAN GOLDKETTE: French born, Greek raised and educated in Russia, Jean became owner of Detroit's Greystone Ballroom in the 20s. He opted to fill it with a band of his own and signed Jimmy and Tommy Dorsey, Pee Wee Russell, Eddie Lang, Bix Beiderbecke and Joe Venuti. But, in the wake of a 1927 show at the Roseland, New York, this star-studded but costly outfit disbanded, several of its members moving on to provide Paul Whiteman's orchestra with some real jazz credibility.

BENNIE MOTEN: Moten's band hardly moved out of Kansas City. But whenever the sound of Basie is heard, the Moten influence is

THE CATS ARE CALLING! THE SKINS ARE SIZZLING! IT'S PARAMOUNT'S HEAT RAVE OF SOLID SENDING!

BOB HOPE
SHIRLEY ROSS
GENE KRUPA AND HIS ORCHESTRA

SOME LIKE IT HOT

invoked, his band boasting a line-up that, at one point or another, included Ben Webster, Jimmy Rushing, Hot Lips Page, Walter Page and Basie himself.

BEN POLLACK
A fiesty drummer, Pollack led a band that almost acted as a preparatory school for future swing stars. His first outfit, in 1925, had Glenn Miller on trombone and Benny Goodman on clarinet. Another stellar line-up just quit on him, virtually intact, and became

Duke Ellington

Name: Edward Kennedy 'Duke' Ellington
Checked In: 29 April 1899, Washington, D.C. USA
Checked Out: 24 May 1974, New York City
Instrument: Piano
Famous for:
Arguably the greatest contemporary American composer of the 20th Century, and certainly the most prolific.
Appearance:
Sartorially elegant. The original brown-eyed (tall, dark and) handsome man. Epitome of sophistication and charm.
Worthy works:
Hundreds, including 'Sophisticated Lady','Mood Indigo', 'Satin Doll', 'Black & Tan Fantasy', 'In A Sentimental Mood', 'Black, Brown And Beige', 'Creole Love Call', 'Rocking In Rhythm', 'I Got It Bad And That Ain't Good', 'Prelude To A Kiss', 'Do Nothin' Till You Hear From Me', 'Cottontail', 'Don't Get Around Much Anymore,' 'Take The "A" Train','I'm Beginning To See The Light' and the marathon Newport Festival showstopper 'Diminuendo And Crescendo In Blue'.
Modus Operandi:
Used orchestra as instrumental paintbox – staffed with highly colourful stylists including Bubber Miley, Tricky Sam Nanton, Harry Carney, Juan Tizol, Cootie Williams , Johnny Hodges, Ben Webster, Jimmy Blanton, Paul Gonsalves, Ray Nance, Cat Anderson, Britt Woodman and Lawrence Brown.
True Confession:
He wrote in his autobiography *Music Is My Mistress* 'Music is my mistress and she doesn't play second fiddle to anyone.'
Famous for saying:
'Love you, madly.'

49

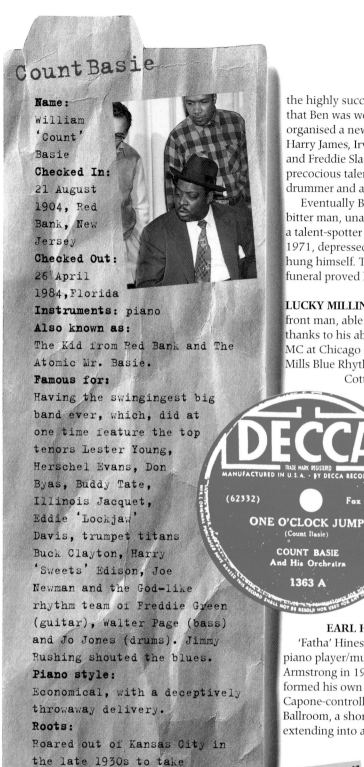

Count Basie

Name:
William 'Count' Basie
Checked In:
21 August 1904, Red Bank, New Jersey
Checked Out:
26 April 1984, Florida
Instruments: piano
Also known as:
The Kid from Red Bank and The Atomic Mr. Basie.
Famous for:
Having the swingingest big band ever, which, did at one time feature the top tenors Lester Young, Herschel Evans, Don Byas, Buddy Tate, Illinois Jacquet, Eddie 'Lockjaw' Davis, trumpet titans Buck Clayton, Harry 'Sweets' Edison, Joe Newman and the God-like rhythm team of Freddie Green (guitar), Walter Page (bass) and Jo Jones (drums). Jimmy Rushing shouted the blues.
Piano style:
Economical, with a deceptively throwaway delivery.
Roots:
Roared out of Kansas City in the late 1930s to take New York by storm.
Best heard on:
'Jumpin' At The Woodside' plus anything on Columbia, Decca and Verve
Famous for saying:
'....one more time.'

the highly successful Bob Crosby band. Not that Ben was worried at that point He just organised a new unit, packed with talents like Harry James, Irving Fazola, Dave Matthews and Freddie Slack, a later line-up featuring the precocious talent of the 16-year-old singer, drummer and arranger Mel Torme.

Eventually Ben became a disillusioned and bitter man, unable to grasp why his ability as a talent-spotter had never paid off. In June 1971, depressed by financial problems, he hung himself. The subsequent star-studded funeral proved little reward.

LUCKY MILLINDER: Lucky was basically a front man, able to donate kicks and quips thanks to his ability as one-time dancer and MC at Chicago clubs. He took the influential Mills Blue Rhythm Band into Harlem's Cotton, headed the Bill Doggett band, then, following some lean years, formed an R&B-tinged outfit that, at various times featured Dizzy Gillespie, Tab Smith, Eddie 'Lockjaw' Davis, Sam 'The Man' Taylor, Bill Doggett and Sister Rosetta Tharpe. Not bad for a leader who couldn't even read music !

DECCA
TRADE MARK REGISTERED
MANUFACTURED IN U.S.A. • BY DECCA RECORDS, INC.
(62332)
Fox Trot
ONE O'CLOCK JUMP
(Count Basie)
COUNT BASIE
And His Orchestra
1363 A

EARL HINES/BILLY ECKSTINE:
'Fatha' Hines refused to be categorised. A piano player/musical director with Louis Armstrong in 1927, the following year he formed his own big band and opened at the Capone-controlled Chicago Grand Terrace Ballroom, a short-term booking eventually extending into a ten year stay, thanks to a $150 a week contract that he couldn't refuse. It was a band of no consequence, and little happened until 1940 and the boogie boom when Earl's 'Boogie Woogie On The St Louis Blues' brought the band to prominence. Then the blues moved in, and the band's good looking baritone Billy Eckstine proved a prime punter-puller with such records as 'Jelly Jelly' and 'Stormy Monday Blues'. But by now the saxophonist/arranger Budd Johnson was already in the band – and he was shaping charts based on new sounds he'd heard at Minton's, in Harlem. Eventually Hines was leading the first big bebop outfit, boasting such musicians as Parker, Gillespie and Benny Harris, plus singer Sarah Vaughan.

Eckstine quit and formed his own band in early 1944, taking Johnson, Gillespie, Vaughan and others of like-mind with him. His was, arguably, the most star-studded band

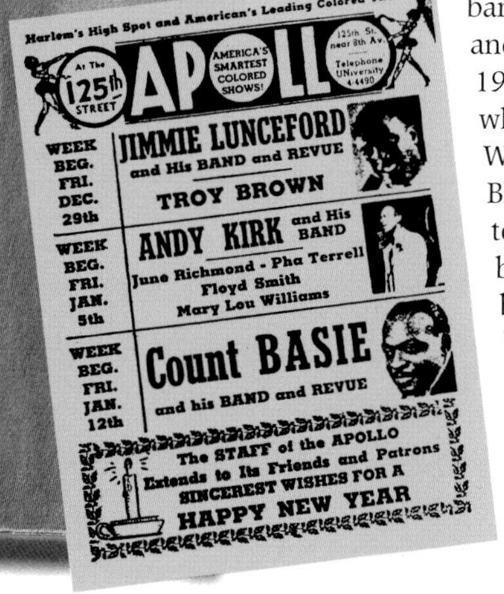
Harlem's High Spot and America's Leading Colored Theatre
At The 125th STREET
APOLLO
AMERICA'S SMARTEST COLORED SHOWS!
125th St. near 8th Av.
WEEK BEG. FRI. DEC. 29th
JIMMIE LUNCEFORD and His BAND and REVUE
TROY BROWN
WEEK BEG. FRI. JAN. 5th
ANDY KIRK and His BAND
June Richmond - Pha Terrell
Floyd Smith
Mary Lou Williams
WEEK BEG. FRI. JAN. 12th
Count BASIE and his BAND and REVUE
The STAFF of the APOLLO Extends to Its Friends and Patrons SINCEREST WISHES FOR A
HAPPY NEW YEAR

Chick Webb Dies In Baltimore

Expires After Operation For Kidney Disorder

Chick Webb's heart stopped beating on June 16 in Baltimore, the place where he was born. The famous drummer and orchestra leader succumbed at the age of 33 after an emergency urological operation at Johns Hopkins hospital. He had been rushed there from the midst of a journey he and his band had been making from Virginia to Alabama. His mates, when informed of their leader's passing, broke down and walked off an Alabama bandstand to rush back to Baltimore.

Sick Long Time

Chick had been seriously ill for almost two years. Physicians announced from time to time that he was suffering from a complicated kidney and bladder disorder. He had been confined to hospitals frequently, but always insisted upon leaving as soon as possible, never completely cured, in order to rejoin his band.

Recovery Impossible

During those two years Chick never looked well. He was drawn, tired, and frequently had to leave the stand because of pain. Few, and least of all Chick, himself, suspected or knew that he had an almost surely fatal disease. Had Chick survived his last operation, he would have been confined to a wheelchair for the rest of his life.

Left: The key man Earl 'Fatha' Hines

Below: Erskine Hawkins and his Orchestra

ever, those who passed through its ranks including Miles Davis, Art Blakey, Fats Navarro, Dexter Gordon, Gene Ammons, Lucky Thompson, Kenny Dorham, Charlie and Leo Parker. It survived rather than thrived on a menu of bebop and ballads but was recorded abysmally and eventually gave up the ghost, leaving Billy to recall later: 'I guess I was a little ahead of my time.'

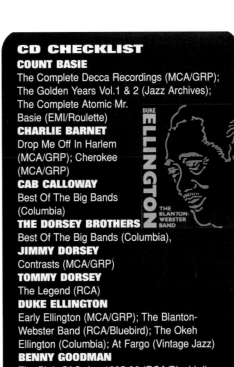

CD CHECKLIST

COUNT BASIE
The Complete Decca Recordings (MCA/GRP); The Golden Years Vol.1 & 2 (Jazz Archives); The Complete Atomic Mr. Basie (EMI/Roulette)
CHARLIE BARNET
Drop Me Off In Harlem (MCA/GRP); Cherokee (MCA/GRP)
CAB CALLOWAY
Best Of The Big Bands (Columbia)
THE DORSEY BROTHERS
Best Of The Big Bands (Columbia),
JIMMY DORSEY
Contrasts (MCA/GRP)
TOMMY DORSEY
The Legend (RCA)
DUKE ELLINGTON
Early Ellington (MCA/GRP); The Blanton-Webster Band (RCA/Bluebird); The Okeh Ellington (Columbia); At Fargo (Vintage Jazz)
BENNY GOODMAN
The Birth Of Swing 1935-36 (RCA/Bluebird); The Harry James Years (RCA/Bluebird); Live At Carnegie Hall (Columbia); Best Of The Big Bands (Columbia)
LIONEL HAMPTON
Lionel Hampton (Giants Of Jazz)
WOODY HERMAN
The V-Disc Years Vol 1 & 2 (Hep); The Thundering Herds 1945-47 (Columbia)
HARRY JAMES
Embraceable You (Conifer)
JIMMIE LUNCEFORD
Blues In The Night (Jazz Roots); Stomp It Off (MCA/GRP)
GLENN MILLER
Greatest Hits (RCA/BMG)
ARTIE SHAW
Begin The Beguine (RCA/Bluebird)

Crooners

Though 'croon' rhymes with 'moon' and 'June', there was much more to it than that. The crooners took some of the finest songs of the century and turned them into simply the hippest sound around.

FOR COMPLETE LIST OF RECORDS BY DICK HAYMES See page 36

DICK HAYMES

Blonde and handsome Dick Haymes, one of the trio of most popular vocalists in the States, is also a he-man. He is proficient at tennis, swimming, sailing, and skiing. He also speaks fluent French, having lived in Paris for ten years. Onetime peddler of his own songs, Dick approached U.S. trumpet star Harry James, who said: "Your songs don't sell, but I'll buy your voice". Having made his name with James, he set out on his own. His recording of "You'll Never Know", with a vocal background instead of an orchestral accompaniment, has sold over a million copies.

THEY CAME, THEY CROONED, and they conquered. But it wasn't meant to happen that way.

The thing was that big band singers were originally thought of as something of a necessary evil, to merely punctuate the proceedings while the bands got on with the real job in hand – providing instrumentals for dancing and demonstrating a show of musicianship.

After all, anyone could sing. But it took something more to play trumpet like Bunny Berigan or trombone like Tommy Dorsey.

Often these singers didn't get paid much. They formed part of no Union and lacked clout. And even when they appeared on chart records, they often did so anonymously. The labels on most of Frank Sinatra's biggest hits while he was band singer with the Tommy Dorsey Orchestra read 'with vocal refrain'. Dorsey made with the wage packet each week. He wasn't into handing out kudos as a bonus.

The singers, as a whole, realised their place in the scheme of things and accepted it. Mostly they regarded the dance and swing band scene as a kind of training ground, a commando course which, if conquered, would set them on their way to becoming star solo acts. Sixteen men swinging plus a couple of singers had to be a bigger attraction than one unknown vocalist clinging to a mike. Or so the reasoning ran.

And virtually every class singer of the 40s and early 50s had endured the course and passed with flying colours. Sinatra spent several years with Harry James and Tommy Dorsey, while one of his main rivals, Dick Haymes, had worked with the same two bands. Doris Day sang with Bob Crosby and Les Brown, Peggy Lee with Benny Goodman, Jo Stafford with Tommy Dorsey, Anita O'Day, June Christy and Chris Connor with Stan Kenton, Perry Como with Ted Weems, Billy Eckstine and Sarah Vaughan with Earl Hines and Ella Fitzgerald with Chick Webb. Even Bing Crosby, the biggest vocal star in the world during the 30s and on through the 40s, had made his initial impact singing with Paul Whiteman during the late 20s. There was little glamour attached to the job. Doris Day claimed in her autobiography: 'The sensation I most vividly recall, working for the Crosby band and later for Les Brown, was that of awakening in a hotel room and not being able to remember what city I was in. It was a constant struggle to

meet a string of little deadlines, and I slept more hours in my bus seat than I did in a bed.'

The bandleaders were right of course. Anyone could sing. But that's exactly why the band vocalists proved so popular. The audiences knew that the musicians were good, but didn't have the expertise to know exactly how good. But when they heard Sarah Vaughan out front with the Earl Hines Band, or maybe Al Bowlly crooning with Ray Noble and his Orchestra, they knew almost instinctively that these people had something special.

Left: Dick Haymes, above: Peggy Lee, below: Mel Torme.   Opposite: Fran

So, in many cases, the singers became an integral part of the band's appeal, sometimes providing a unique point of recognition. Lionel Hampton once recalled: 'We had a smoking band but Dinah (Washington) alone could stop a show.'

Not everyone was a genius like Ellington, not many had a trademark rhythm section like Count Basie's. Many of the bands sounded alike. They often used the same arrangers or near identical arrangements. But a distinctive vocalist could give them an edge. There was little doubt that the Charlie Barnet band was on the air whenever Kay Starr or Lena Horne stepped to the mike. The Barnet aggregation often sounded Ellington-like (Charlie even recorded a single titled 'The Duke's Idea') but nobody sounded like Kay or Lena. Even today they retain a sound that is definitely their own.

And that commando course analogy was an accurate one. A singer touring with a band was fair game for send-ups and other problems less easy to handle. Doris Day twice married musicians from the Les Brown band, one of whom proved to be psychopathic sadist. Anita O'Day was forced to state: 'It's not true about me and the whole Stan Kenton band !', Billie Holiday had accomodation problems while travelling with the all-white Artie Shaw Orchestra, and Dinah Washington, who sang with Lionel Hampton's all-black bunch of crazies, experienced a variation on the same theme, when the musicians headed for digs as soon as they hit a town, leaving her crying on the band bus. And getting out had its own set of rules. When Frank Sinatra attempted to leave Tommy Dorsey, he was only able to split after promising to pay to Dorsey one third of all his future earnings plus

Crooners

Above: Stan Kenton and June Christy
Top right: The dream duo of Billy Eckstine and Sarah Vaughan

another ten per cent of his income to Dorsey's manager !

Looking back it's hard to relate to some of the singers who seemed important during Swing's heyday. Bob Eberle and Ray Eberly (brothers despite the different spelling of the surname) were the crowd-pullers with Jimmy Dorsey and Glenn Miller respectively. They were smooth, good-looking and anonymous. Yet they topped polls and helped sell records by the jeep-full. But the odd thing was that once the big band era ended and they embarked on solo careers, nothing much happened. In their particular cases the band ultimately proved bigger than the outfront crooner in terms of appeal.

Others though – like the bow-tied Sinatra, the delectable Dinah Shore (from the Beasley Smith band), Billy Eckstine, (dubbed 'the Sepia Sinatra'), and Rosemary Clooney, one of the Clooney Sisters who sang with Tony Pastor – moved on to become superstars whose fame often far eclipsed that of their former employers.

And, eventually, the era of the big swing band did come to an end. There was no last riff, and no final jump. But due to a combination of circumstances –

recording bans, the increase in the popularity of small-size but volume-making rhythm and blues combos, and a score or more other things that were to culminate in the rise of 50s pop, rock 'n'roll and a whole new youth culture – the genre slid to what was often a less than graceful death.

Meanwhile, however, the successful singers who had learnt their craft with the big bands were having the last laugh, usually while on their way to impress bank managers.

The most influential song stylist of them all, Frank Sinatra, who later made an album titled 'I Remember Tommy', claimed that if he hadn't gone on the road with Harry James and Tommy Dorsey, he simply wouldn't have made anywhere near the impact that he did. 'If I were starting all over again, I'd get a job with a band and I would sing and sing and sing. If a leader gave me forty songs a night, I'd tell him to give me sixty. There's no teacher like experience.'

Discs

No. 343A

THREE LITTLE MESSERSCHMITTS
Damon-Lasky-Haynes-Layton-Beittel

The United States Army Air Forces Band
Narration: S/Sgt Glenn Darwin

VP 954   Novelty

To the public at large Glenn Miller and the Andrews Sisters were the most popular examples of the military/music alliance during the Second World War, but the V-Discs phenomenon was where the music really got to the front line in the most direct way.

Some armies march on their stomachs.

Uncle Sam was so convinced that his dog-faces campaigned best to a Lindy Hop and A Bop Kick that, in October 1943, the ol' fella went into the record business in a big way.

Victory Records (V-Discs as they became universally known) came into existence during October 1943 as a result of the events of July 31, when the AFM (American Federation Of Musicians) instigated a nation-wide recording ban.

For a number of years, musicians had been incensed with the blatant use of their records by jukebox operators and radio

Just the labels on this page give some idea of the 'Whos Who' of jazz that made up the catalogue of artists on V-Discs during the Second World War

stations without any royalty payments. All efforts by the AFM to secure some sort of satisfactory deal for its members failed, and eventually it became necessary to impose a ban on all domestic recording .

Decca and Capital capitulated in September 1943, while two of the biggest labels Columbia and RCA-Victor held out until November 1944, before reaching a settlement.

A US Senator may have pontificated: 'If the record ban wipes out jitterbug music, jive and boogie woogie, it might be a good thing all round!' but his was a lone voice.

No. 418B

THE SHEIK OF ARABY
Smith-Wheeler-Snyder

Hot Lips Page and the V-DISC All Stars
Hot Lips Page, Trumpet; Jack Teagarden & Lou McGar- ity, Trombones; Ernie Caceres, Clarinet; Bobby Hackett, Cornet; Nick Caiazza, Tenor Sax; Johnny Guarnieri, Piano; Herb Ellis, Guitar; Al Hall, Bass; Specs Powell, Drums

VP 1073   Hot Jazz

This record is the property of the War Department of the United States and use for radio or commercial purposes is prohibited.

No. 404A

VIBE BOOGIE
Hampton

Lionel Hampton and his Orchestra
Featuring Lionel Hampton - Vibraphone and Milt Buckner - Piano

VP 1125   Swing

This record is the property of the War Department of the United States and use for radio or commercial purposes is prohibited.

V Discs

For once, it wasn't so much the U.S. Cavalry to the rescue as The Special Services Division, which, in 1942, established a Radio Section producing top variety shows such as *Command Performance, Jubilee* and *G.I.Jive.*

Concern for the morale of the rookie Kingdom of Swing conscripts escalated as new material for its Armed Forces Radio Service ceased. It was only then that Special Services took the initiative and began producing exclusive-to-overseas-service personnel V-Discs which circumvented the AFM ban with the blessing of AFM President James C. Petrillo.

Material was sourced from recording sessions, from live concerts, radio broadcasts and rehearsals, movie soundtracks, various radio transcription services and alternate/unissued takes of commercial recordings.

Below: A Woody Herman line-up that appeared on V-Discs: (l to r) Terry Pollard (vibes), Bill Harris and Sonny Berman, (trumpets), Flip Phillips (tenor) and Herman on clarinet

WAR DEPARTMENT · MUSIC SECTION · ENTERTAINMENT & RECREATION BRANCH · SPECIAL SERVICES DIVISION · A.S.F.

No. 382A
RED TOP
Herman
Woody Herman and his Orchestra
VP 914   Swing

VDisc

This record is the property of the War Department of the United States and use for radio or commercial purposes is prohibited.

OUTSIDE START · 78 RPM

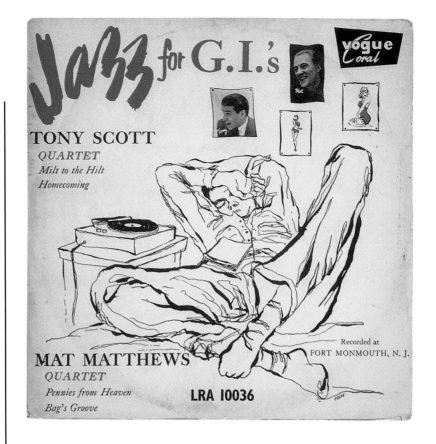

Purpose-pressed by RCA-Victor on unbreakable vinyl so as to withstand the rigours of war, V-Discs released close to 1,000 different 12-inch 78s – a format that doubled the then standard ten-inch playing time to almost a full seven minutes on each side.

Almost every major artist of the day, not only donated their services free, but frequently produced exclusive studio or concert recordings which they fronted with personal words of encouragement.

Comedian Bob Hope when introducing `The Song Is You', wisecracks: 'When Bing Crosby was 14, he had his adenoids removed. And here is one of them now – Frank Sinatra.'

And for Slim Gaillard's `Chicken Rhythm' he rises to the occasion. 'Hi ya lads, this is Bob "V-Disc" Hope, telling you that things are melloroonie, vout and oh dig it! And here's a man who can dig it without asking John L.Lewis. I mean Slim Gaillard, that mad savage boy. You're on, Slim!'

Still tongue-in-cheek, for a 1945 V-Disc release, Sinatra wisely chose to introduce himself: 'Gentlemen Of The Armed Forces, this is the hoodlum from Hoboken,' then upped and crooned `I Have But One Heart'.

It was not uncommon for jump specialist Louis Jordan to invite V-Disc listeners to 'Get groovy and latch onto this jive.' Similarly, after giving himself a name check, Lionel Hampton continues: 'The label on this V-Disc says "Flying Home", and we all hope you'll be flying home soon.'

Count Basie prefaced `Basie's Boogie' thus: 'Hi Men, this is Count Basie. The War Department gave me this opportunity to say hello on V-Disc. So hello – and I sure hope you continue to receive those fine platters.'

And they did - for over 8-million V-Discs were shipped overseas as goodwill gifts - proving just as welcome as soap, cigarettes, chocolate, chewing gum and silk stockings.

In some of the London record stores, the latest V-Discs promptly became under-the-counter specialities for those who were regular jazz hounds.

Due to the nature of the whole V-Disc operation, producers like George Simon could ignore contractual restrictions and put together dream line-ups: in December 1944, an 11-piece V-Disc All-Stars assembled in a New York studio featured Louis Armstrong, Billy Butterfield and Bobby Hackett.

Even after hostilities ceased, the music played on, with band-leader Woody Herman informing peace-keeping forces: 'Now the shooting's all over, the guys and I would like to shoot a V-Disc or two your way.'

In May 1949, the US decided V-Discs no longer served a morale-boosting service and so, after almost six years, the operation was shut down.

STAND-AT-EASE Though, devoid of the same charisma as V-Discs, further post-war efforts to entertain the troops resulted in such one-shot albums as 'Jazz For G.I.s' and PX Store labels such as Stand Easy which used the back catalogue material from ABC-Paramount (now MCA).

The order to destroy all the existing stock was posted; however, the unbreakable nature of these unique discs made this take longer than anticipated!

Meanwhile, the exclusivity of the custom-recorded V-Disc catalogue (Basie, Ellington, Sinatra, JATP, Tristano, Krupa, Rich, Goodman, Kenton plus the 1944 Esquire Concert, etc,) promptly spawned an extremely lucrative black market trade, eventually resulting in the FBI being called in to confiscate vast quantities of wayward mint discs that had somehow fallen off the backs of passing tanks and into the open car boots of waiting racketeers.

At least one of the major label employees involved with the V-Discs operation served time for illegal possession of 2,500 singles. The enterprising music fan's defence wasn't too unreasonable – he had just taken them all home to play for his own amusement!

The Be Bop Revolution

'Bop is no lovechild of jazz. Bop is something entirely separate and apart. It's just music. It's trying to play clean and looking for the pretty notes.' – Charlie Parker

COME UP WITH the most original of concepts and it's almost a given cert that someone else is working on an identical theme at that precise moment.

Perhaps more than at any juncture in the evolution of jazz, this theory certainly applied to the music that would soon be referred to as bebop.

Alto saxman Charlie `Bird' Parker, it is claimed, commenced his truly radical over-haul of rhythm and harmony in a Manhattan chili house between 139th and 140th Street in the December of 1939 when jamming with guitarist Biddy Fleet's quartet on material such as Cherokee' – in particular the deceptive middle section which breaks steps and changes key. 'I kept thinking there's bound to be some-thing else. I could hear it sometimes but I couldn't play it.'

As Biddy Fleet later explained to the writer Ira Gitler 'The voicing of my chords had a theme within themselves. You could call a tune, and I'd voice my chords in such a way that I'd play the original chords to the tune, and I'd invert 'em every one, two, three, or four beats so that the top notes of my inversions would be another tune. It would not be the melody to the tune I'm playing, yet the chords, foundation-wise, is the chords to the tune.'

One of the hotbeds of the bebop revolution was New York's Royal Roost club, seen here in 1948 (l to r) Charlie Parker, Miles Davis, Allan Eager and Kai Winding

The crucible for the biggest-ever shake up in jazz was Minton's Playhouse at 210 West 118th Street and a house band led by the trumpeter Joe Guy that included Thelonious Monk and Kenny Clarke. Heavy action also took place over at Clark Monroe's Uptown House. Almost nightly, trial-by-ordeal jam sessions helped shape this new music which, in it's first manifestation, was for a brief time tagged as 'rebop.'

From the outset, bop proved to be a most demanding experience for both musicians and listeners alike. To begin with, rhythm sections redefined their role, eschewing basic four-beats-to-the bar time keeping that underpinned swing to create what was termed 'comping' – a series of complexities in which piano, bass and drums not only established the momentum but interacted with one another and the horns through a series of on-and-off beats, punctuations and jabs which upped the intensity and spurred on the soloists. Plus, the tempos seemed hell-bent on smashing all speed records.

The format of a typical bop performance commenced with an improvised piano intro that skidded straight into a complex theme played in unison by a front line of no more than three horns and invariably based on the chords and harmonic structures of a familiar popular tune. This gave way to a string of solos, followed by hectic four-or-eight bar exchanges with the drummer, a final return to the original theme and a dead-stop finish.

It was the over-stylisation of swing that suddenly made bop such an attractive shock-of-recognition alternative to those in search of something radically new.

After their first phenomenal flush of success, many top draw swing big bands had become so disciplined and over-arranged in their pursuit of a signature sound that sax and brass sections were reduced to no more than incessantly riffing.

In such regimented environments, solos were extremely brief and usually only played by the leader or a couple of big wage-earning star soloists. The formula was on the verge of losing all potency.

This is why the Jazz At The Philharmonic formula ultimately proved to be successful; for the first time in years, musicians were afforded an opportunity to stretch out and develop an idea far beyond the confines of 16-bars and the time constraints of a ten-inch 78. And it was to be JATP, with its swing-into-bop bias and the inclusion of Bird, Gillespie, Lester Young, J.J. Johnson, Howard McGhee and others, that quickly spread the word from coast-to-coast.

So who beeped the first bop? Who takes the kudos for being the originator?

Aside from the 19-year old Parker, then, between stints with the blues blowin' road band of Kansas City pianist Jay 'Hootie' McShann, a number of young musicians were simultaneously working on the same radical game-plan.

But, if a line has to be drawn in the sand, it's former Basie tenorman Lester Young who was the original source of inspiration closely followed by guitarist Charlie Christian as the first major practitioner. However, it would be the prodigiously talented Parker and his trumpèt playing sidekick Dizzy Gillespie who would forever change the sound of jazz in a manner never experienced before.

.Thereafter, pianists Thelonious Monk and Bud Powell plus drummer Kenny Clarke all made their move soon to be followed by such Young Turks as Miles Davis, Fats Navarro, Little Benny Harris (trumpet), J.J. Johnson, Kai Winding (trombone), Dexter Gordon, James Moody, Jimmy Heath, Allan Eager (tenor), Sonny Stitt (alto), Leo Parker, Cecil Payne (baritone), Al Haig (piano), Milt Jackson (vibraphone), Oscar Pettiford, Ray Brown (bass), Max Roach, Art Blakey (drums) all eager to translate the word-according-to-Bird on their respective instruments.

The basic bop vocabulary evolved during the time of the 1942-44 AFM recording ban and, with few exceptions, was never actually preserved on disc. Furthermore, save for a few precious snapshots, no recorded documentation has surfaced of the pivotal residency that Bird and Diz shared (along with singers Billy Eckstine, Sarah Vaughan and the trumpet player Little Benny Harris) as sidemen with the Earl Hines Orchestra.

Opposite: Piano pioneer Thelonious Monk
Below: Dizzy Gillespie at the Royal Roost

GENE NORMAN PRESENTS

DIZZY GILLESPIE and his orchestra

FEATURING CHANO POZO

While a plethora of both studio recordings and 'live' airshots accurately document Charlie Christian's dazzling work with Benny Goodman's Sextet, were it not for the informal swing-based sessions featuring Dizzy, Monk, Christian and Clarke that obsessive fan Jerry Newman privately captured on his portable recording machine at Minton's during the early 40s, then little first hand evidence would remain of bop's birth pangs.

Thelonious Monk: 'While I was at Minton's, anybody sat in who would come up there if he could play. I never bothered anybody. It was just a job. I had no particular feeling that anything new was being built. It's true modern jazz probably began to get popular there. But as for me, my mind was like it was before I worked at Minton's. It got a little glamorous maybe on Monday nights when Teddy Hill, the manager, would invite the guys who were at the Apollo that week. As a result, all the different bands that played at the Apollo got to hear the original music, and that way it got around, talk started going around, about the fellows at Minton's.'

Early in his life, the impressionable young Charlie Parker suffered the ignobility of being unceremoniously kicked out of a Kansas City jam session in front of his peers. The incident occured when, with a resounding crash, Basie's innovative drummer Jo Jones showed his displeasure by throwing a cymbal across the floor as Bird played.

Though not as drastic, a similar situation took place at Minton's when Kenny Clarke initially didn't want Monk's young friend Bud Powell to sit in on piano. But as events rapidly demonstrated, Bud Powell was to prove himself as much a genuine architect of modern

jazz as Bird, Diz and Monk in drafting a piano-style that continues to be the first primer point of reference.

But in those early days, Monk and Clarke together with Dizzy and Joe Guy regularly worked out new chord progressions, not just to dissuade sitting-in but to see where this direction would lead.

Indeed, such agendas gave rise to the belief that be-bop had almost Masonic-like aspirations; being a self-interested closed society intent on separating the men-from-the-boys or, as Diz frequently insisted, 'separate the sheep from the goats'.

After quitting Earl Hines, Billy Eckstine may have put together bop's first big band (1944-47), but again the AFM ban kept them out of the studio at a crucial period and the only commercial recordings cut for the DeLuxe label are less than hi-fi and give hardly any indication as to why, live, the Eckstine band was a powerhouse outfit.

Only an Armed Forces Jubilee Show radio transcription, issued years later in the UK on Spotlite, partially lifts the curtain. However, by then, due to a rapid turnover of the line-up, Diz, Bird, Fats, Miles, Dexter, Wardell, Lucky Thompson and many others had already pulled up stakes. Nevertheless, their replacements that included tenorman Gene Ammons and Art Blakey still frantically waved the bop banner as if their very lives depended upon it.

Texas-born Eddie Durham, as much a major league arranger as he was guitar stylist, may well have been the first to electrify the guitar, but it was Charlie Christian who

became the instrument's first and arguably most accomplished maestro. However, too much good living killed Christian in March 1942 at the age of 25, while Duke Ellington's equally skilled bass player Jimmy Blanton was felled by TB, four months later, age 23. It had been Blanton, like Walter Page before him, who had first introduced the concept of modern walking bass patterns.

Of course, bop didn't spring fully-realised from just one source. All around, musicians jockeyed for position as these new ideas painstakingly took shape.

Dizzy Gillespie may have secured his place with bandleader Teddy Hill due to his then similarity to Hill's previous trumpet star Roy Eldridge, but it was in Hill's band that Dizzy and Kenny Clarke first began their musical experiments until the former moved to Cab Calloway's band

Elsewhere Bird toured extensively with Jay McShann (1939-42) until meeting up with Dizzy, Eckstine and Sarah Vaughan in the big band led by pianist Earl Hines.

Although things were about to change drastically, it was the era when a musician's stature was still measured by whether or not he possessed the qualities sufficient to successfully fronting a big band.

And, while most saw bebop as two, perhaps three, front line horns firing a frantic fusillade over a jittery hyper-active rhythm section, Dizzy perceived it in terms of the ferocity of the big band: it was a direction he

A publicity shot of Sonny Stitt, and (right) a film poster featuring the seminal Billy Eckstine Band

intermittently pursued with almost kamikaze devotion throughout his entire life.

All that was still in the future. The first bop band on New York's 52nd Street debuted, in 1944, at the Onyx Club; a quintet co-lead by Dizzy Gillespie and Oscar Pettiford (bass) and including Don Byas (tenor sax), George Wallington (piano) and Max Roach (drums). Between them, they earned $310 a week but weren't together long enough to get anything down on record.

According to Diz, many of the originals they performed had no titles to begin with. Seemingly, he'd just call 'dee-pa-pa-n-de-bop' and they were away. Very soon, Onyx Club regulars would make requests for some of that 'bebop' music and the press picked up on it.

With the addition of Vic Coulsen, Ed Vanderveer (trumpet), Leonard Lowry, Leo Parker (alto sax), Ray Abramson (tenor sax), Budd Johnson (baritone sax) and Clyde Hart (piano), Coleman Hawkins expanded the Onyx quintet into a 10-piece and, with the

Apollo label picking up the studio bill, cut the first-ever commercially-released bop records 'Woody'n'You', 'Bu-Dee-Daht', and 'Disorder At The Border'.

Over the next couple of years, this new music quickly made it onto wax, though, to begin with, mainly by way of hole-in-the-wall operations who hedged their bets by often mixing bop horn men with established swing stars, Cootie Williams, Red Norvo (Comet), Clyde Hart (Continental), Tiny Grimes (Savoy) Sir Charles Thompson (Apollo), but it was Norman Granz's Jazz At The Philharmonic all-star package shows, as much as anything, that helped bring bop to the masses.

By 1945, Dizzy and Bird – either in tandem or solo – were undertaking their own dates for Guild, Manor, Dial and Savoy to produce such future classics as 'Ornithology', 'Hot House' 'Groovin' High', 'Salt Peanuts', 'Yardbird Suite', 'A Night In Tunisia' and such.

Having been hired-and-fired by extrovert entertainer Cab Calloway, Dizzy was very much aware that, despite the amount of attention being focused on bebop, if it was to attract a much wider audience, a degree of showmanship was required together with an equally dynamic image. While appreciating his one-time partner's motive, Bird was philosophical.

'The leopard coat and wild hats are just another part of the managers' routines to make him [Dizzy] box office. The same thing happened when they stuck his name on some tunes of mine to give him a better commercial reputation.'

Bop also spawned a new parlance, partly derived from Cab Calloway's *Hipster's Dictionary* (1938) and Slim Gaillard's equally bizarre form of back slang he called 'Vout'. On a more sartorial tip, bop's threads-and-skimmers dress code toned down the more lurid aspects of zoot suit apparel in favour of broad chalk-stripes, wide-brimmed fedoras, french berets, dark shades and goatee beards. Fearful and feeling somewhat threatened by bop, the likes of Cab Calloway derided it as 'Chinese Music', Louis Armstrong

William D. Alexander presents

BILLY ECKSTINE HIS BAND

Rhythm In A Riff

BABE WALLACE
SARAH HARRIS
GARFIELD LOVE
RAY MOORE
ANN BAKER
HORTENSE ALLEN

Produced by
ASSOCIATED PRODUCERS
OF
NEGRO MOTION PICTURES, INC.

A boistrous crowd at San Francisco's Bop City in 1949, which includes Dizzy Gillespie sitting at the piano, with Miles Davis studying his technique, the Heath Brothers Percy (right, in front of the piano) – later of the MJQ – and sax player Jimmy (front, third from right)

denounced it as 'Ju-jitsu music', adding the judgement 'Bop is ruining music', while Eddie Condon took a rather more humorous stance with the characteristic boast: 'We don't flatten our fifths, we drink 'em.'

Years later, once he had become a major international attraction, a Columbia University lecturer had the temerity to ask of Thelonious Monk: 'Would you play some of your weird chords for the class,' only to have Monk retort sharply 'What do you mean weird? They're perfectly logical chords.'

To begin with, the heaviest bop action took place around New York City. A visit to the West Coast, in 1945, by Dizzy Gillespie's Sextet featuring an already wayward Bird may have proved disastrous, but Los Angeles' already informed hipsters headed by saxmen Dexter Gordon, Wardell Gray, Teddy Edwards and Sonny Criss plus trumpet players Howard McGhee, Art Farmer and pianists Hampton Hawes and Dodo Marmarosa, immediately opened up a second front along tinsel town's Central Avenue.

Though early trace elements had been detected, the fact remained that, outside of those aggregations led by Mr. B and Diz, black big bands almost entirely ignored the new music, content to carry on swinging in the style that had fattened the wallet and made them popular with the ladies.

For the moment, these bandleaders didn't encounter problems from their audiences who preferred dancing to familiar music as opposed to trying to fit their movements to bop's often complex tempos.

The first bop outfit to play New York's 52nd Street, soon to be regarded as the bebop centre of the world: (l to r) Max Roach, Don Byas, Oscar Pettiford, George Wallington and Dizzy Gillespie in 1944

Jay McShann's reed section at the Savoy Ballroom, Harlem, in 1941: (l to r) Bob Mabane, Charlie Parker, John Jackson and Freddy Culliver

JAZZ 100 Fact File

Dizzy Gillespie loved a good title. His discography is filled with recordings that boast such nutty names as 'You Stole My Wife, You Horsethief', 'He Beeped When He Should Have Bopped', 'Oo- Pop- A- Da', 'Swing Low Sweet Cadillac' and 'Ool-Ya-Koo'. When it came to books, things didn't change much. Once, in London, while staying at the Mayfair Hotel, Diz decided to have a stroll around the back streets and came across a shop filled with antiques, books, paintings and general what-have-you. Espying a painting of Shakespeare and a related object-d'art, bedecked with a sign that read 'To Be Or Not To Be', the man-with-the-turned-up-trumpet and goatee became enthusiastic and informed the shop-owner that if she changed the last word on the sign, he would buy a whole boodle of goodies from her establishment. She should change the 'Be' to 'Bebop' he informed her. And in the interim, he would go feed the ducks in Hyde Park.

Good to his word, Diz returned within the hour, saw the sign now displaying the words 'To Be Or Not To Bebop' and promptly purchased various trinkets that surrounded it. 'That's how my autobiography got its title', he maintained. 'I wanted "To" printed small, a large "Be" and then, further down, a small "not to" and a huge "Bop" so that when you looked at the book cover it said, "Be-Bop". I thought it was a clever idea.' But, like many of Diz's chunks of hip word-play the ploy proved uncommercial and the book sold dismally. 'Oo-Shoo-Be Doo-Be' as the man once remarked.

Even at the best of times, sustaining a big band can be a thankless, money-draining vocation as both Eckstine and Gillespie would soon experience.

The handsome Mr. B's decision to disband his wild bunch in 1947, to pursue a lucrative career as a Sepia Sinatra, coincided with Woody Herman regrouping with a bunch of predominantly rowdy white beboppers to front his Second Herd.

Simultaneously referred to as the 'Wild Root' band (a nod to the hair oil preparation who sponsored Herman's weekly radio broadcasts) but universally known as the 'Four Brothers' line-up: being a reference to the unique sounding three tenors & baritone sax team of Stan Getz, Zoot Sims, Herbie Steward and Serge Chaloff which enjoyed such a tremendous success with Jimmy Giuffre's chart of the same name.

Though Herman's earlier jukebox smash 'Caldonia' is cited as the first use of hardcore boppery on a hit record, to begin with things didn't run smoothly. This was entirely due to Woody's reluctance to rerun all but a few past glories from his former 'The Band That Plays The Blues' (1936-44).

Left: Tenor giant Gene Ammons with hip vocalist Buddy Stewart and trobonist Kai Winding, Chicago 1948

Below: The Georgie Auld Band with Auld (tenor) George Wallington (piano) Curly Russell (bass) Serge Chaloff (baritone) and Tiny Kahn (drums)

The Earl Hines Orchestra at the Apollo Harlem 1943, including Diz (far left), Bird (far right), trombonist Benny Green next to drummer Shadow Wilson, with Earl Hines and vocalist Sarah Vaughan sharing piano duties

With a brand new line-up of fire-eaters that also included Shorty Rogers, Red Rodney (trumpet), Bill Harris, Earl Swope (trombone), Terry Gibbs (vibraphone), Oscar Pettiford and Chubby Jackson (bass), Don Lamond, Shelly Manne (drums), Herman's bop-crazy Second Herd soon became the toughest of the tough and acutely aware of both their crowd-pulling status and the often grudging respect shown by other musicians. Chubby Jackson: 'In the Herman band the Marines were coming.'

The attitude of be bop may have been anarchic, but most of the repertoire, which Bird once termed, 'advanced popular music,' was based on the chord changes of either swing era chestnuts or contemporary pop material: 'I Got Rhythm' ('Anthropology'), 'Honeysuckle Rose' ('Marmaduke'), 'How High The Moon' ('Ornithology'), 'Indiana' ('Donna Lee'), 'Cherokee' ('Ko Ko'),'What Is This Thing Called Love?' ('Hot House'), 'Whispering' ('Groovin' High'), 'Lover Come Back To Me' ('Bird Gets The Worm'), 'All The Things You Are' ('Bird Of Paradise') and so on.

However, it has been argued that on more than one occasion, Charlie Parker went into a recording session with the intention of cutting standards only to have them re-titled by the label as 'original' compositions to avoid their having to pay publishing copyrights and instead, paying themselves.

Part of bop's earliest appeal wasn't so much the break-neck tempos and quicksilver soloing, but the novelty scat vocal records of Dizzy Gillespie with Joe Carroll ('Oop-Bop-A-Da' selling 700,000 copies in 1947 for RCA-Victor), Babs Gonzales, Eddie Jefferson, King Pleasure, Dave Lambert & Buddy Stewart

Charlie Christian

Name: Charles Christian
Checked In: 29th July 1916
Dallas, Texas
Checked Out: 2nd March 1942
New York City
Instrument: Guitar
Famous for:
Electrifying the guitar for
the purpose of competing as a
front line soloist, and an
architect of bop.
Big Break:
First, pianist Mary Lou
Williams spoke glowingly of
his talents after hearing
him in Oklahoma City. Soon after, record
producer John Hammond brought Christian out to Los Angeles
for his now-famous audition with a sceptical Benny Goodman
with whom he remained for the duration of his tragically
short career.
Blue Plaque Status:
A regular participant at birth-of-bop jam sessions at
Minton's Playhouse up in Harlem involving Thelonious Monk,
Dizzy Gillespie, Kenny Clarke, Charlie Parker and Joe Guy.
Lifestyle:
Addicted to the fast life, Christian finally succumbed to
tuberculosis in mid'41 from which he never recovered.
Gone But Not Forgotten:
Herb Ellis, Grant Green and Jim Hall are but three major
league guitarists to reveal their lifelong debt to the
young tall Texan.
Setting The Record Straight:
Many of the most memorable guitar figures that Christian
improvised in his solos were shamelessly ripped off by
Benny Goodman for the top melody lines for a number of
jazz standards including 'Flying Home', 'A Smo-o-oth One'
and 'Seven Come Eleven'.

with Gene Krupa 'What's This?' while it has to be remembered that Bird's most successful commercial recordings were those that he made with strings for Norman Granz.

In 1948, extrovert swing tenorman Charlie Ventura opted for such a populist stance with his 'Bop For The People' sloganizing and a tight combo that featured the vocal aerobics of Roy Kral & Jackie Cain on 'Euphoria' and the gimmicky 'I'm Forever Blowin' Bubbles'. However, the people did not respond in kind, leading Ventura to snarl, 'Bop is dead.' Then, when the King of Swing, Benny Goodman briefly chanced his luck by playing bop, his former arranger, Fletcher Henderson decried: 'Of all the cruelties in the world, bebop is the most phenomenal.'

Unfortunately, the recurring problem of drugs – Billie Holiday's busts, Fats Navarro's untimely death, Stan Getz's fumbled attempt at an armed stick-up and Bird's high-profile heroin addiction – all conspired to give jazz, and particularly bebop, a bad public image. In short, bop had passed its commercial sell-by date long before Bird's untimely, but not unsurprising, death in 1955.

As other players either died prematurely, were murdered, went into detox, served time or quietly slipped into obscurity, there came a time when many of those surviving players who had originally sworn allegiance to bop became almost unbookable.

Lessons were to be learned, wounds licked as new musical scenes – still using be-bop as their reference point – geared up on both the East and West coasts.

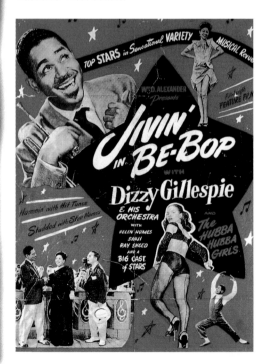

Right: One of the most famous photographic images in jazz, Herman Leonard's celebrated 'smoking' portrait of Dexter Gordon, taken in New York City in 1948

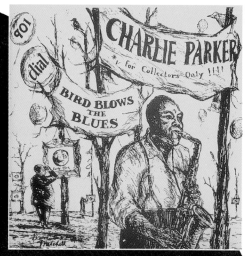

JAZZ OFF THE AIR VOL. 2

fats navarro, bill harris, charlie ventura,
ralph burns, allen eager,
al valente, chubby jackson, buddy rich

play

SWEET GEORGIA BROWN

and

HIGH ON AN OPEN MIKE

L.D. 095

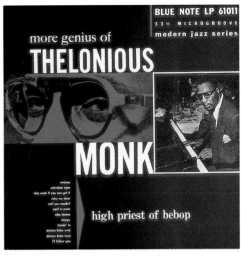

more genius of
THELONIOUS
MONK

BLUE NOTE LP 61011
33⅓ MICROGROOVE
modern jazz series

high priest of bebop

BILLY ECKSTINE
TOGETHER
Spotlite 100

THE FABULOUS FATS NAVARRO

blue note 81531 volume 1

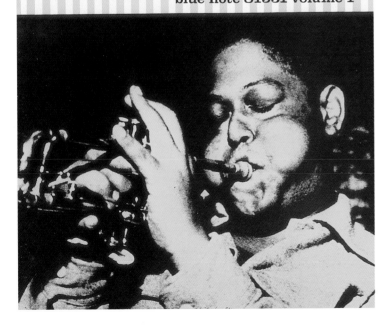

the amazing
BUD POWELL
vol. 2

BLUE NOTE 5041
33⅓ MICROGROOVE
modern jazz series

with GEORGE DUVIVIER, bass · ARTHUR TAYLOR, drums

Jazz World Mourns Loss Of Charlie Parker

New York—Charles Christopher Parker Jr., acknowledged by most of his contemporaries as the greatest jazzman of modern times, is dead.

The alto sax king died of an acute heart seizure at 8:45 p.m. Saturday, March 12. An autopsy revealed that he had lobar pneumonia; he had also been suffering from ulcers and cirrhosis of the liver.

Parker died at the Fifth Avenue apartment of Baroness Nica Rothschild de Koenigswarter. The Baroness, an avid jazz fan and an old friend, told reporters that he had stopped off there the previous Wednesday. That day he complained of difficulty in breathing. A physician summoned by the Baroness recommended immediate hospitalization, but Parker refused to leave. "I did not have the heart to force him to go," she added.

On Saturday evening Parker was watching the Dorsey Brothers' TV show when he began to laugh, then col-

Sudden death of Charlie Parker is irreparable loss to modern music

ALTO-SAXOPHONIST Charlie Parker—the greatest solo genius in American jazz, according to his fellow-musicians—is dead. This tragic news, which several of our national newspapers have already recorded, has fallen as a sombre cloud upon every community of jazz musicians throughout the world.

Charlie passed away, quite suddenly, in the New York apartment of his friend, the Baroness Nica Rothschild de Koenigswarter, last Saturday (12th). He was stricken with what seemed to be a heart attack, and died soon after. Later, the cause of his demise was diagnosed as pneumonia.

Word of Parker's death did not break until Monday night, after his body had been removed to Belle Vue Hospital, New York.

Powell and bassist Charlie Mingus. According to a cable from Hentoff, the alto genius will be laid to rest today (Friday) afternoon. A benefit show for his dependants will be held

GRANZ ISSUING PARKER MEMORIAL RECORD ALBUM

WITH the news of the death of the great altoist

Right: Trumpet supremos Miles Davis and Dizzy Gillespie caught on camera by Herman Leonard while appearing in Paris in 1958

Bird

The Chan Parker Collection | 8th September 1994

Enquiries:

Carey Wallace on (071) 581 7611 ext 3275

Christie's South Kensington
85 Old Brompton Road
London SW7 3LD

Tel: (071) 581 7611
Fax: (071) 321 3321

BOB REISHER Presents
"BIRD"
CHARLIE PARKER
AND HIS ALL STARS

Sunday, June 6
9.30 P.M. to 2 A.M.
OPEN DOOR

CHRISTIE'S

the complete blue note and capitol recordings of
FATS NAVARRO
AND
TADD DAMERON

'Up Jumped The Blues'

ONE MORNING the blues woke up and decided to jump. And jump it did – in the direction of the nearest jukebox. It was genuine, unadulterated blues, as rugged and raunchy as Bessie Smith's great originals. But, this time, it came with an invitation to dance.

Hot-stepping it more than most was stompin' saxman Louis Jordan with a style that was part jazz, part black vaudeville but with the largest portion clearly labelled, pure blues.

Jordan was a one-off original who'd once fronted the Chick Webb big band, had all the personality in the world, a full-of-character alto style to match, and a singing voice

Like with be bop, small combos were the order of the day on the black dance circuit after World War II – and they called it rhythm and blues.

that could win hearts and cause cash-register bells to ring loudly.

As leader of The Tympany Five, Jordan good-humoured his way to the top of the R&B charts in the early-40s, littering the listings with such smashes as 'I'm Gonna Move To The Outskirts Of Town' (1942), 'What's The Use Of Getting Sober (When You Gonna Get Drunk

Again)' (1943), 'Five Guys Named Moe' (1943), 'Is You Is Or Is You Ain't My Baby'/'G.I.Jive' (1944), 'Caldonia' (1945); 'Beware, Brother, Beware' (1946), 'Open The Door, Richard' (1947),'Saturday Night Fish Fry' (1949) and continued without a break, hitting pole position right through to 1950 when his 'Blue Light Boogie' concluded the run. During

Left: The legendary Nat Cole Trio in the 1949 jazz movie *Make Believe Ballroom*

Above & Right: Publicity material for Louis Jordan screen-stealers *Caldonia*, a movie juke box short, and *Swing Parade of 1946*

MONOGRAM PICTURES presents

"SWING PARADE of 1946"

ERE COMES MR. JORDAN

KING OF THE BOBBY SOCK BRIGADE

GLOBAL FAVORITE of 11,000,000 GI Joes

Preachin the Blues IN HIS FIRST BIG SCREEN SHORT

CALDONIA

★ Solid with You
★ Dancin' Prancin'
★ Sepin Beauties
★ 4 Big Song Hits

THE BIGGEST EXTRA ADDED "MONEY" ATTRACTION IN YEARS

this period, his fans appeared to love Jordan equally as much as his music; his popularity was further enhanced by way of 'soundies' (short films for movie juke boxes), regular radio appearances on the Armed Forces Radio Service *Jubilee* show, and finally onto the big screen of the cinema.

Decca Records went so far as to reveal that during the mid-40s, Jordan was second only to Bing Crosby in shifting shellac. Infact, they even cut a couple of duets together ('My Baby Said Yes'/1944). More popular, however, were Jordan's record dates with Ella Fitzgerald that produced 'Stone

Cold Dead In The Market' (1945) and 'Baby, It's Cold Outside' (1949).

Significantly, almost from the beginning Louis Jordan's following had been just as big amongst white record buyers as it was with blacks.

In the 90s, almost two decades after his death, Jordan's music would again be celebrated in the form of the highly successful stage production entitled *Five Guys Named Moe*.

Nat 'King' Cole was lighter, more sophisticated, an easy-breeze cool supplier of silken R&B riffs for the Hollywood lounge trade. But, Cole's songs were as ultimately jivey as those of Jordan, his piano-headed trio vying with Louis in the charts through such opposition slammers as 'That Ain't Right', 'All For You', 'Straighten Up And Fly Right' and 'Gee Baby, Ain't I Good For You', chart-toppers all.

Every year between 1944 and 1947, the King Cole Trio clinched *Downbeat* magazine's coveted Top Small Combo award.

Those who were influenced by his seductive 'club-blues' vocal style (often sung in unison with his two sidekicks) and textured line-up of piano, guitar and bass, included Johnny Moore's Three Blazers with Charles Brown, Private Cecil Gant,

Ray Charles, Floyd Dixon and Ivory Joe Hunter. And there were scores of others: piano giants Art Tatum and Oscar Peterson, to be specific, found public favour replicating the instrumentation that was once unique to Cole.

If Cole hit the escalator button to the penthouse suite, Wynonie 'Mr. Blues' Harris, like Louis Jordan a one-time singer with the Lucky Millinder big band, headed for the basement bedroom.

From 1947 until the early 50s, Mr. Harris — one in a succession of hit-making brown-eyed handsome men — dispensed sex-filled singles that needed little but their titles to provide a cash-generating come-on to record consumers.

'I Want My Fanny Brown', 'Sittin' On It All The Time', 'Lovin' Machine', 'Playful Baby', 'Bloodshot Eyes' all proved products of the Harris hit production line, as was the culinary cutie, 'I Love My Baby's Pudding'.

Just as subtle was 'All She Wants To Do Is Rock', a 1949 biggie that some now see as a landmark in rock'n'roll history.

There is always a joker in the pack, and in this instance it was proto-hipster Slim Gaillard.

Immortalised by Jack Kerouac in *On The Road* ('To Slim Gaillard the whole world was just one big orooinie!'), hip hits 'Flat Foot Floogie' and 'Cement Mixer', regular guest shots on Frank Sinatra's CBS radio show, appearances in Hollywood movies (*Hellzapoppin*), disc dates with Bird and Diz, and inventing his own nonsensical backslang lingo ('vout-o-roonie') as published in his 25-cent *Vout Dictionary* and recorded under the title, 'Opera In Vout' (1946) during a JATP gig, kept

him high-profile when it mattered. Much to the chagrin of a number of scandal-fearing movie moguls, the debonair Gaillard also answered to the name 'Dark Gable' on account of the deep affection many top Hollywood actresses willingly imparted on this Cuban-born adventurer. It was such after-hours 'entertainment' that ultimately hampered Slim's career for many years, prompting a successfull re-location to Britain during the last years of his life.

But instrumentally, it was the Tulsa-born alto supremo Earl Bostic who really ran the game.

He blew alto sax like a tough tenor, gritty and gutsy, as if it was about to leap out of his hands. And then he'd apply his exhilarating way of things to nice cozy tunes, standards like 'Flamingo' and 'Temptation', transforming them into musical Mr. Hydes.

But, for every Oklahoman could be counted a score of Texans all

Left: The alto superstar – and in the early 1950s he really was just that – Earl Bostic

Left: Some of the Johnny Otis Show (including Marie Adams and the Three Tons of Joy, and Otis with the guitar) clowning on the bandleader's front lawn

Below: The Viceroy of Vout, a self-made legend in his own colourful lifetime, Slim Gaillard

Much of the heaviest R&B action took place on the West Coast, where a large community, mainly of migrant workers from Texas and the south, had put down roots, as a result of lucrative swing-shift employment on the war effort.

Drummer-vibist Johnny Otis was a white Greco-American who chose to live as a black man and operated the famed Barrelhouse Club in Los Angeles. Otis pioneered big band jazz-based rhythm and blues as the basis of his R&B road show, The Johnny Otis Blues And Rhythm Caravan, and as a launch pad for his discoveries Little Esther Phillips, Jackie Wilson, Johnny Ace, The Robins, Big Mama Thornton, Hank Ballard and Little Willie John.

Other major players working along similar lines included Roy Milton & His Solid Senders ('R.M's Blues') Joe Liggins & The Honeydrippers ('Pink Champagne') and Joe's guitar-playing brother Jimmy Liggins ('Cadillac Boogie').

joining in the beat bonanza. Along with the already mentioned Charles Brown and Floyd Dixon, Lone Star State showmen of the stature of Amos Milburn, T-Bone Walker, Pee Wee Crayton, Eddie 'Cleanhead' Vinson, Joe Houston, King Curtis, Clarence 'Gatemouth' Brown, Walter Brown and 'Good Rockin' Tonite' hit-maker Roy Brown, all fronted blazing R&B sax and guitar flavoured bands, yet stayed relatively true to the tradition of such larger-than-life blues shouters as Jimmy Rushing ('Goin' To Chicago'), Joe Turner ('Roll 'Em Pete') and Jimmy Witherspoon ('Ain't Nobody's Business').

Just as, studiowise, much of what took place on the West-Coast rhythm and blues scene was the creation of tenorman/producer Maxwell Davis, similarly the familiar second-line sounds to come rockin' out of New Orleans were created under the auspices of the trumpeter, bandleader and composer Dave Bartholomew, whose greatest find was Fats Domino.

And it was not only solo singers and instrumentalists who were out to catch the new golden ring. Vocal groups made the switch as well. Where once black vocal outfits such as the Ink Spots and the initially jazz-happy Mills Brothers aimed at white audiences, their music safe and unlikely to contaminate, The Ravens and The Orioles began to bridge the gap, establishing a blues-based bridgehead that would result in a zillion doo-wops.

Eventually, white singers and musicians would catch on, renaming Rhythm and Blues 'Rock'n' Roll', with the thus-invigorated record business even suggesting that the world would never have changed had it not been for the disc-jockey and pioneering promoter Alan Freed (who, to be fair, championed black R&B along with its white offspring).

However, those in the know were aware that as far back as 1948, extrovert Texas-born d.j. Hunter Hancock's 'Harlem Matinee' R&B show on Station KFVD (Los Angeles) predated Freed, Wolfman Jack and other white Knights of the turntable in programming almost nothing else but 'youth-corrupting' jumping jive and rockin' blues. But, during the 40s and early 50s, R&B shouted that it was black and proud. Just around the corner, James Brown was waiting.

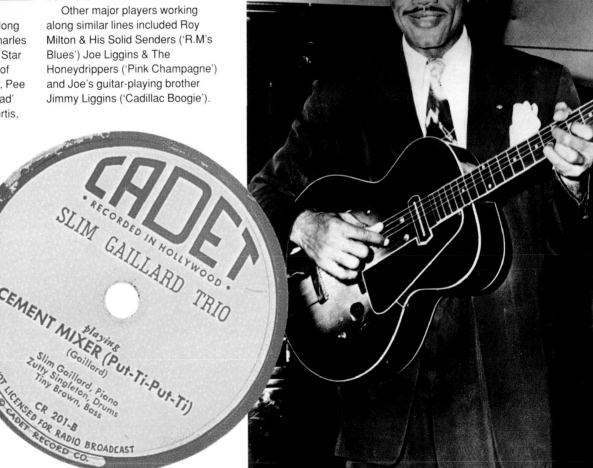

Progressive Big Bands

With 'Progressive Jazz', orchestrally ambitious bandleaders took post-bop arrangements out of the dance halls and onto the stages of 'serious' concert halls.

WHILE IT WAS becoming apparent that big bands were no longer central to the popular end of swing and jazz, there were those who not only blatantly ignored the signs but also challenged the cruel economics by further broadening the brand of music they performed as well as musician quotas. 'This is the way music will be played from now on by the really hip and talented and profound and musically healthy,' noted critic Barry Ulanov once wrote of the Boyd Raeburn band. Another pundit slyly added: 'But not by the wealthy.'

And that was the way of things in the immediate post World War Two

The Stan Kenton Orchestra in full concert flight and (right) the programme for a 1953 show in Dublin

Stan Kenton
souvenir programme

THEATRE ROYAL, DUBLIN, SUNDAY, 20th SEPTEMBER 1953

WOODY HERMAN
and the New
THIRD HERD

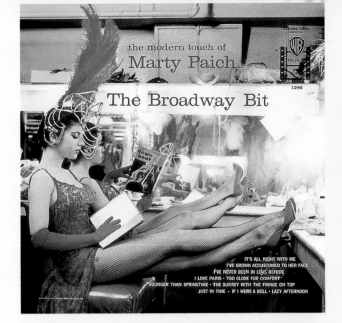

Clockwise from left: A press release for the Woody Herman Third Herd, Marty Paich album cover, the Boyd Raeburn band in action, and Stan Kenton's 'Viva Kenton' LP

years. With the big band dance scene diminishing rapidly, several leaders opted for the final flourish, one last grand gesture before the lemming dive.

In some instances it was really all down to testing the listening public's tolerance.

The big bands played mainly for dancers, but the determination of the major league player Stan Kenton to move his music into a seated 'concert' environment may have secretly appealed to the likes of Woody Herman's Third Herd, the Sauter-Finegan Orchestra, Claude Thornhill, Pete Rugolo, Johnny Richards, Terry Gibbs, Maynard Ferguson and Buddy Rich, but most left their options open. And somewhere, in a far off universe, Sun Ra

An agency publicity shot of 'progressive' pioneer bandleader Claude Thornhill

boldly went where no band had ever gone before.

Raeburn, for instance, began his career as a leader of something of a Mickey-Mouse outfit but generally acquired a taste for better sounds, in 1945 creating an outfit that sported French horns and paid due homage to Stravinsky ('Boyd Meets Stravinsky') as well as Debussy, Ravel and Bartok in its grandiose arrangements. Eggheads loved what was going on. Not that there were enough of them.

Thankfully for the sharp-dressed bass-sax blowin' Raeburn, Duke Ellington was among his admirers and offered financial support. Which was much needed. However, Raeburn wasn't the first to dabble in

highbrow hybrids; Igor Stravinsky had created 'Concerto In Ebony' for Woody Herman who, in turn, had forged a mutual admiration society with Leonard Bernstein.

However, as undisputed leader of the progressive pack, Stan Kenton simply refused to extend his invitation to the dance, making the point clearly: 'Everybody can blame Woody Herman and Dizzy Gillespie and me for ruining the dance band business. We ruined it because we were determined to play the kind of music we wanted to play.'

At a time when the magazine *Metronome* ran an article headed 'Bands Busting Up Big', Kenton began planning line-ups that only someone interested in trying out a

breadline existence could even begin to envisage.

With charts that included the Stravinsky-influenced 'Artistry In Percussion' and the Ravel-riffed 'Aristry In Bolero' already in his library, Kenton launched his 'Innovations In Modern Music Orchestra', during the early 1950s. A 43-piece affair that included strings and woodwinds performed quasi-classical constructions such as Bob Graettinger's controversial 'City Of Glass' which severely tested the goodwill of even the most loyal fans of the Kenton sound.

AMAZINGLY, despite the loss of $125,000 on one six month tour, Kenton survived and, after making it into the 60s, attempted what seemed like musical suicide yet again with a brass-dominated 23-piece outfit that sported a fine line in mellophoniums. The much-maligned offspring of the bizarre mating of mellophone and trombone, it was aimed at trumpet players in search of an instrument on which to double, but failed in the attempt. Almost to a man, the mellophonium was hated by everyone in the band, featuring on non-selling albums such as a bunch of grandiose Wagner themes. This led to the formation of the

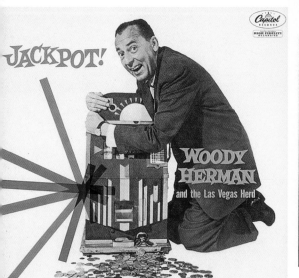

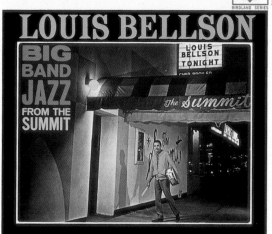

'Neophonic' orchestra in 1965, yet another over-stocked aggregation that involved five extra players and a guaranteed dive into the red of around $15,000 each year.

Admittedly, Kenton did resort to what he felt was a commercial ploy from time to time: 'Like when Jimmy Smith was a guest artist and played "Slaughter On Tenth Avenue".'

But this inevitably offended the minute legion of 'Neophonic' fans who complained to Kenton that they 'could hear that crap on television.' And there were others – visionaries, nutters, call 'em what you will – all ready to do things big and, in doing so, scare the very life out of the music biz accountants.

Eddie Sauter and Bill Finegan were two such men. Arrangers who, respectively, had made their names with Benny Goodman and Glenn Miller but, in 1952, teamed up to create what was considered an out-of-leftfield orchestra, that utilised unusual percussion effects such as sleigh bells and diverse instruments that included oboe, piccolo, harp and English Horn. Surprisingly, the Sauter-Finegan Orchestra, as it was dubbed, made some beautiful and descriptive noises that included 'Doodletown Fifers' and their highly evocative adaptation of 'Troika' from Prokofiev's 'Lieutenant Kije' which was retitled, 'Midnight Sleigh Ride'. The band survived for around five

Opposite: Centre, UK bandleader Vic Lewis showing off his LP of Mulligan arrangements to the master himself. Below, the Peter Rugulo Orchestra

Right: Igor Stravinsky and Woody Herman working on 'Ebony Concerto' with Columbia Records' Bill Richards. Far Right: Leonard Bernstein and Woody Herman

years. But survival it was, and the creative twosome found it more profitable when, after some years apart, they linked together, in the 60s, to produce jingles for radio and television. And it was in 1961 that Saunter masterminded 'Focus' – a perfectly realised fusion of pop jazz and contemporary classical forms that revolved around the inventive tenor saxophone of Stan Getz and a chamber string ensemble.

Pianist Claude Thornhill was one leader who actually bucked the trend. After heading fine bands for many years, in 1946, he pieced together something of a ground-breaker. As with Raeburn, there were two French horns in the line-up plus a tuba, an eye-brow raiser for those instantly hip to the ways of those seeking to concertize jazz. But the band, though as big as most, moved and sounded like a small group, with power implied rather than utilized. Arrangers such as Gil Evans, Bill Borden and, later, Gerry Mulligan, provided some joyous arrangements of such standard be-bop anthems as 'Anthropology', 'Donna Lee' and 'Yardbird Suite' while the ballads came both gorgeous and certainly danceable. Thelonious Monk described the Thornhill outfit as 'the only really good big band I've heard in years.'

And, maybe this was one that would have lasted. However, ill health rather than any cash-flow problems proved a terminator for Thornhill, though his sounds, as remembered by Evans and Mulligan, were once more utilised when Miles Davis and Mulligan began looking around for something different to launch – which soon become known as the Birth Of The Cool. For if Miles' pioneering 'Birth Of The Cool' line-up was indeed a scaled-down version of Claude Thornhill's much larger aggregation, then the equally short-lived tentette assembled by the 'cool' crew's prime architect Gerry Mulligan (which was also released by Capitol) was, by the baritone star's own admission, 'my original quartet with Chet Baker combined with the instrumentation of the Miles Davis nonet.'

Jazz At The Phil

There were always club promoters and record company hustlers ready to exploit jazz without a care for the music, but a nucleus of enlightened entrepreneurs helped it survive and grow – no more so than 'Mr JATP' Norman Granz.

> Mission Statement:
> **'I ENDEAVOUR TO PRESENT THE BEST POSSIBLE JAZZ TO THE WIDEST POSSIBLE AUDIENCE'**
> Norman Granz

THE SLOGAN 'supervised by Norman Granz' was, for many years, a guarantee of excellence. Few entrepreneurs working in either movies or music (Granz had experience in both) possessed his breadth of vision. He knew how to coax the best out of even the most difficult artist, or gather a bunch of seemingly incompatible talents in the same studio and produce exciting and coherent music. By doing so, he demonstrated that there is very little that separates great players and prevents interaction other than non-player preconceptions.

Granz' greatest contribution was his pioneering Jazz At The Philharmonic roadshow.

Working along a swing-into-bop bias, Granz assembled a cast of a dozen or so of the biggest stars of the day to recreate, on the stages of the world's major concert halls, the intimacy of those competitive jam sessions that took place in after-hours basement clubs and then released the highlights on a succession of discs for which David Stone Martin supplied innovative sleeve art graphics.

From the very beginning, the format seldom altered.

Interestingly, a watertight case for the genesis of rock 'n' roll taking place in Los Angeles on Sunday, 2 July 1944, during a fund raiser – organised by Norman Granz – for Mexican youths wrongly jailed for a killing following the 'Zoot Suit' riots, can be supported by a recording of a sensational jam entitled 'Blues'.

Suddenly, tough tenor players Illinois Jacquet and Jack McVea square off against one another, cutting contest style, for an almighty blowing showdown of skill, excess and endurance.

DOWN BEAT presents
10th National Tour of
THE WORLD'S GREATEST JAZZ CONCERT
norman granz
Jazz at the Philharmonic
featuring ELLA FITZGERALD
Buddy Rich   Bill Harris
Flip Phillips   Harry Edison
Lester Young   Ray Brown
Coleman Hawkins   Hank Jones
and OSCAR PETERSON
his first U S concert tour

only appearance here this year

Added Attraction!
CHARLIE PARKER
with Strings

National Guard Armory—Sunday, Sept. 17, 8:30 P.M.
Tickets on Sale at Quality Music Store 1836 7th St., N.W.
Also at Willard Hotel Ticket Agency
Prices: $2.00, $2.50, $3.00 and $3.60—All Seats Reserved

HAROLD DAVISON
presents
NORMAN GRANZ'
JAZZ AT THE PHILHARMONIC
FOURTH BRITISH TOUR

SOUVENIR PROGRAMME
PRICE · TWO SHILLINGS

Left: The programme for the fourth 'Jazz At The Philharmonic' tour of the British Isles, and tenor star Illinois Jacquet seen wearing a sensational zoot suit and tie during a JATP concert in New York City in 1946

The crowd goes wild reacting more like spectators at a Main Event boxing match than a jazz show.

Originally recorded by the American Forces Radio Service (AFRS), 'Blues' was not released commercially by Granz until two years after it was first broadcast.

And it paid dividends. 'Blues' became a big hit record, as did the very first Jazz At The Philharmonic album which sold a phenomenal 150,000 copies and, in doing so, heralded the advent of genuine 'live' recordings (complete with announcements, applause and the rest) as a legitimate accepted form.

Granz regarded his presentations as 'A variety show of the finest jazz', for nowhere else could the public witness tenor titans Coleman Hawkins, Lester Young, Illinois Jacquet and Flip Phillips holding centre stage, trumpet top-guns Dizzy Gillespie and Roy Eldridge in nightly confrontational mood, or that magic occasion in the mid-40s when Bird met his mentor Lester Young in a single spotlight.

By transversing the States twice yearly and thereafter rolling across Europe (and later, Japan), Jazz At The Phil' hit the road with a basic repertoire including 'Lester Leaps In', 'Perdido' and 'How High The Moon' (the JATP anthem).

By recording these events and releasing them commercially in a blaze of publicity, Granz built himself a multi-million dollar empire to rival anything in pre-Beatles pop.

In 1944, Granz also produced *Jammin' The Blues* an atmospheric black and white film short photographed by Gjon Mili which received an Oscar nomination.

And as early as 1941, Granz was organising ground breaking shows in local clubs in the Los Angeles area for desegregated audiences, which were headlined by all-time giants of jazz Billie Holiday, Duke Ellington and Lester Young.

Norman Granz· 'I remember once Billie was complaining that some of her friends had come to see her and they weren't allowed in. She was crying and everything.' It was incidents such as this that prompted him to adopt a confrontational stance when faced with racial segregation. Granz once threatened litigation against a ballroom that refused Count

Basie admission to see a Harry James show, staged the first lunch-counter sit-down in 1947, and even sued Pan-American airlines over their unforgivable behaviour towards Ella Fitzgerald during a flight. Pan-Am settled out of court.

Years later, Norman Granz admitted that in the beginning, his motives were primarily sociological as opposed to musical.

Nat King Cole, who'd befriended Granz in '41, insisted, 'Even in those days he wouldn't knuckle under. A lot of people disliked him, but I understood his attitude: he just knew what he wanted and exactly how he was going to get it. He always had the interests of his artists at heart.'

Truncated from 'A Jazz Concert At The Philharmonic', to 'Jazz At The Philharmonic', the first Norman Granz tour was a financial disaster. However a second attempt, in 1946, which featured the two greatest pioneers of the tenor saxophone Coleman Hawkins and Lester Young, proved a tremendous success.

Twice yearly, until 1957, Granz undertook a 10-week tour playing up to 60 different cities. In Europe, JATP toured up until 1960.

JATP was the premier jazz attraction and, at the peak of popularity, each tour would open with a midnight matinee at New York's Carnegie Hall featuring a dozen or more stars permutated from a talent pool that over the years included: Dizzy Gillespie, Roy Eldridge, Charlie Shavers, Howard McGhee (trumpets), Illinois Jacquet, Flip Phillips, Lester Young, Coleman Hawkins, Ben Webster, Charlie Ventura, Stan Getz, Zoot Sims (tenor saxes), Benny Carter, Charlie Parker, Sonny Criss, Willie Smith (altos), Bill Harris, J.J. Johnson (trombones), Buddy Rich, Gene Krupa, J.C.Heard, Louie Bellson (drums) with first Nat Cole's trio and later, Oscar Peterson's threesome (Ray Brown, bass and Herb Ellis, guitar) doubling as both the house rhythm section and star attraction in their own right.

It was always extremely combative and that's what drew highly demonstrative

crowds. The tenors locked horns, trumpet players eyes popped out like chapel organ stops and between them Gene Krupa and Buddy Rich kicked up more noise than a midtown construction site. And, it's for such crowd-pulling, pitched-battles that the JATP 'circus' is often remembered and criticized.

'I may give the audience honking, but it's the best honking there is.' once boasted the impresario. In the heat of the moment, many overlooked the standard ballad medleys, the deep-soul blues blowin' or the fact that the likes of Hawkins and Young were afforded their own mid-show sets.

What should be remembered, is that these all-star jazz revues delivered far more than any other touring show; being a celebration of the true essence of the music.

Norman Granz: 'Jazz has always been, to me, fundamentally the blues and all the happy and sad emotions it arouses, I dig the blues as a basic human emotion, and my concerts are primarily emotional music. I've never put on a concert that didn't have to please me, musically, first of all.'

In the early days, Billie Holiday was the featured vocalist, a role soon taken over by Ella Fitzgerald, who invariably closed each show with everyone regrouped on stage for a grand slam finale of 'How High The Moon'.

Granz ensured artists received guaranteed top dollar salaries, clothing, with quality

Left: Over the years he was Norman Granz' most frequent JATP drummer, the inimitable Gene Krupa

P2559-37

BILLIE HOLIDAY
AT JAZZ AT THE PHILHARMONIC

SUPERVISED BY NORMAN GRANZ

Left: Billie Holiday with backstage dresser, in Hollywood in 1953.

Below: Ella Fitzgerald on stage with Roy Eldridge

Bottom: Tenor star and JATP regular Flip Phillips

accommodation and blue chip travel. Ella received a then astronomical $5,000-a-week.

As far back as 1954, JATP Inc, grossed four-million dollars and by 1956, Granz could guarantee his main line artists $50,000 a year. Under his guidance, Coleman Hawkins, Charlie Parker and Lester Young where not only handsomely paid for their work but probably performed before more appreciative people on one coast-to-coast tour than in a decade of club appearances.

And often Granz recorded artists that most other labels considered past their sell-by date.

When, after two years of leading half-pint combos, Count Basie re-organised a big band, in 1952, it was a succession of Norman Granz supervised albums – including the great 'Dance Sessions' plus 'Count Basie Swings And Joe Williams Sings' – that restored him to greatness and, a highly bankable proposition.

With practically all of the JATP cast pacted to such customized Granz recording labels as Clef, Norgan, and finally Verve, his proved to be without doubt the most successful jazz based organization for artists and owner alike.

Who else but Granz had the vision to undertake marathon recording projects such as Ella Fitzgerald's series of 'American Songbooks' (now transferred to18 CDs), or Art Tatum's monumental 'Solo Masterpieces' and 'Group Masterpieces'. Similar endeavours focused on the artistry of Oscar Peterson, Charlie Parker and Billie Holiday.

Out on the road, the JATP value-for-money format was designed to give everyone a 20-minute showcase: Oscar, Stitt, Krupa, Eldridge, while Ella was afforded a full 40 minutes in her role as headliner.

With JATP, Granz brought jazz to a public which otherwise might not have ventured into late-night haunts. And then sold them records of the event to remind them of what an enjoyable experience it had been.

In later years, a question of economics and a thinning of the ranks forced Granz to all but scrap his original format, to tour self contained star-led units. In 1960, he toured three separate JATP packages throughout Europe.

The first had Ella headlining while Roy Eldridge, Shelly Manne & His Men and the Jimmy Giuffre Trio rounded out the bill. A second promised the hot ticket of Oscar Peterson, Stan Getz and what proved to be the last tour of the Miles Davis-Coltrane Quintet.

The third package hosted the quintets of

Dizzy Gillespie and Cannonball Adderley plus a supporting cast of J.J. Johnson, Candido, Roy Eldridge, Benny Carter, Coleman Hawkins, Don Byas and Jo Jones. On other occasions, the orchestras of Basie and Duke Ellington were the attraction, though proving 'not the ideal format for JATP'.

'Star musicians tend to have their own groups and are no longer inclined to jam.' observed Granz. 'A tour today could embrace Ornette Coleman, Dizzy and Illinois all in the same group, but half the men I want to hire are all leading their own groups and won't give them up even for a couple of weeks. Worse, they don't seem to care about the experience which the JATP guys used to find stimulating...playing in new contexts rather than just repeating what they've played on records. The jam session is dead.

'And, I had no interest in simply presenting ready-made shows.'
Then there was the unavailability of some artists: 'Stitt versus Carter...fine, possible. Dizzy versus Miles - impossible!'

The writing was on the wall.

A one-off Jazz At The Philharmonic Revival was organised for a European tour in 1966, dusted off to create the original format, when Granz gathered together Dizzy Gillespie,

Above left: The horn section for Granz' legendary 'Jam Session' LPs with (l to r) Johnny Hodges, Benny Carter, Flip Phillips, Charlie Shavers and Charlie Parker
Below: The Oscar peterson Trio with Ray Brown on bass, Peterson at the piano and Herb Ellis on guitar

Clark Terry, Coleman Hawkins, Zoot Sims, James Moody, Teddy Wilson, Bob Cranshaw, Louie Bellson and T-Bone-Walker, but it lacked some of the earlier excitement which the brand name was famous.

Come 1967, even touring Ella Fitzgerald, Duke Ellington and Oscar Peterson was no longer a watertight box office guarantee, Granz had to reluctantly admit.

'It's too much of a risk. In the decade following World War II – until 1957, there was very little competition and the jazz was an extension of the swing era, with most people understanding what we were doing.'

Financially, overheads soared annual.

In 1954, a Hollywood Bowl Show took a record-breaking $31,000. In 1967, the same show needed to take $35,000 just to be able to break even.

Similarly, back in 1957, expenses were $4,000-a day, by 1967 they were $10,000.

But before that time arrived, Norman Granz had sold off his portfolio of record labels to Polygram in 1961 for $2.5 million: though he later inaugurated the Pablo label to re-launch his recording activities with Ella, Oscar, Dizzy, Duke, Count Basie and guitarist Joe Pass as his premier attractions.

A collector of fine art , in May 1968 Granz also auctioned off a personal collection no less than 47 modernist and impressionist paintings by artists that included Klee, Picasso and such, for just under two million dollars.

The music may have frequently been less than subtle, but Jazz At The Philharmonic was never the abberation that some purist critics made it out to be.

The fact is that on a good night, nothing in music quite equalled a JATP blow-out for the raw excitement that is the essence of jazz.

Just Jazz

GENE NORMAN, like many disc jockeys, used his popularity to promote concerts, release records and run nightclubs (The Crescendo).

Looking to Norman Granz for inspiration, on 29 April, 1947 he instigated 'Just Jazz'; an all-star package show not dis-similar to Granz's JATP blueprint that sold out Pasadena's 2,978 seater Civic Auditorium with a bill comprised of a bop group led by Howard McGhee that included Wardell Gray and Sonny Criss plus the Benny Goodman Sextet, Peggy Lee and an all-star jam fronted by Benny Carter and including Charlie Barnet, Errol Garner etc.

Ironically, there were occasions when Just Jazz would do better box office business than JATP. But whereas Granz trail-blazed from coast-to-coast, Gene Norman, for the most part, staged his gigs in Pasadena or at L.A's Shrine Auditorium.

And it was live takes made during such shows that made possible some classic in-concert recordings including Lionel Hampton's 'Stardust', Wardell Gray & Dexter Gordon's 'The Chase' and 'Steeplechase', Wardell, this time with Errol Garner 'Blue Lou', Dizzy Gillespie's Big Band with Chano Pozo plus Charlie Ventura's 'Bop For The People' Septet.

Norman was also the prime mover behind securing Shorty Rogers' first recording contract with Capitol and Gerry Mulligan's Tentette sessions for the same label, as well as persuading Max Roach to front his own group with Clifford Brown and recording the result in concert.

Below: Tough tenors Wardell Gray and Dexter Gordon at the time of Gene Norman's 'Chase' LP

CD CHECKLIST
MAX ROACH/CLIFFORD BROWN
In Concert (GNP)
SHORTY ROGERS/GERRY MULLIGAN
Tentette (Capitol)
WARDELL GRAY-DEXTER GORDON
The Chase (MCA)
GENE NORMAN
Presents A Charlie Ventura Concert (MCA)
WARDELL GRAY
Way Out Wardell (Crown)
LIONEL HAMPTON
Just Jazz (MCA)

Dixieland Revival

From an earnest search for the 'genuine article' to opportunist band-waggoning, Dixieland jazz could be all things to all men.

JAZZ IN THE 40s saw a New Orleans revival and bebop running concurrent to one another. The latter was the avant garde of its day, while the former concerned itself with a back-to-basics restoration of the music's original style.

From the mid-30s almost up until the mid-40s, Swing had overshadowed most everything else. In the process, it had become so stylised that incessant section riffing and the rise of the featured vocalist had all but sidelined instrumental soloists. It didn't come as any surprise that in such a climate, there were those who yearned for the uncluttered music of the early days of New Orleans jazz.

In the wake of John Hammond's yuletide 'Spirituals To Swing' celebration at New York's Carnegie Hall in 1938, all manner of wishes would soon be granted as small independent record labels emerged devoted exclusively to jazz releases.

Commodore and HRS (Hot Record Society) were both Manhattan store-front operations expertly run by Milt Gabler and Steve Smith respectively. They were joined, in 1939, by Alfred Lion's Blue Note trade mark. However, they had all been beaten to the post by French jazz critics Charles Delaunay and Hugues Panassie, who had inaugurated the Swing label in Paris, in 1937.

Amid all this activity, it was the discovery, by music researchers Frederic Ramsey Jr and William Russell (for their book *Jazzmen*) of the long-retired New Orleans trumpet player Bunk Johnson, that secured this specific jazz revival a focal point and drew solid support, most notably from the left wing intellectuals. Born in 1889 (not ten years earlier as he claimed), Johnson didn't record until 1942, by which time he was 53. His style was akin to a slightly faded, dog-eared photograph of a bygone era. Whatever youthful prowess Johnson had once possessed had been somewhat eroded by years of hardship and the fact that he was toothless. He eventually acquired much-needed dentures through the philanthropy of Sidney Bechet's dentist brother.

These obstacles aside, it was what Johnson represented that had him canonized; for many his rehabilitation was of Holy Grail-like importance. Though later there was some doubt about many of his claims, here was the man who had played alongside of Buddy

From a publicity shot for the Good Time Jazz label, trumpet revivalist Bob Scobey

BUNK JOHNSON
THE LAST TESTAMENT
OF A GREAT NEW ORLEANS JAZZMAN

COLUMBIA RECORDS

GD GL 520

LP

The San Francisco Style
LU WATTERS' YERBA BUENA JAZZ BAND
VOL. 2 WATTERS' ORIGINALS & RAGTIME L 12002
GOOD TIME JAZZ.

Bolden at the turn of the century and had worked extensively in New Orleans. The fact that he had never been recorded until the 40s further added to the mystique and supported the verbal testimonies of people like Louis Armstrong that Johnson was indeed the real thing – the musical primitive, untarnished by trite commercialism or passing musical trends.

It was these frayed edges and the genuine passion of his horn playing when framed by George Lewis (clarinet) and Big Jim Robinson (trombone) that further enhanced the mythology and enabled Johnson to front his own band and record prolifically for the remaining seven years of his life.

Just prior to all this, trumpet man Lu Watters' Yerba Buena Jazz Band featuring stars-in-the-making Bob Scobey (trumpet) and Turk Murphy (trombone) became the focal point of the 'San Francisco Revival'. Having taken up residency at the Bay Area Dawn Club in 1940, the Yerba Buena Jazz Band cut its first sides in December 1941. Though World War II disrupted their activities, it wasn't long before their honest hand-on-the-heart directness spearheaded fanatical interest amongst impressionable musicians the world over.

For all their commitment, the sound of the banjo all too soon became something of a

signature trademark that ultimately gave way to a form of vaudevillian Dixieland.

Elsewhere, Muggsy Spanier's Ragtimers, Bob Crosby's Bobcats and trumpeter Jimmy McPartland performed a more individual take before wise-cracking Eddie Condon's radical decision of having a front line – that often included the likes of Bobby Hackett, Wild Bill Davison, Billy Butterfield, Jack Teagarden, Pee Wee Russell, Bud Freeman and others – supported by a much looser swing-style rhythm section usually driven by the fiery drummer George Wettling. In fact, before long, Condon had become something of a national phenomenon, unusual for a jazzman both a television and radio personality.

For some, the reactionary brand of New Orleans revivalism quickly became preserved in aspic, with many of its purist practitioners disparagingly branded 'mouldy fygges'. For others, post-Revival jazz expanded naturally and, by the early 50s, musicians who had pioneered small group swing during the late 30s and early 40s were central to the newly christened 'Mainstream'. All-star sessions for Vanguard and Felsted centred around such former Basieites as Vic Dickenson, Jo Jones, Buddy Tate and Dickie Wells, while Buck Clayton's now-legendary Jam Sessions recorded by Columbia set the style in stone.

Europe also became a base for revivalism,

Top: UK revivalists George Webb (piano) and his Dixielanders with Humphrey Lyttelton (trumpet)

Above: American Dixieland favourites The Firehouse Five Plus Two

Left: British stars (l-r) Nat and Bruts Gonella, here in wartime uniform

Right: Dixie versus bebop; Jimmy McPartland crosses trumpets with Dizzy Gillespie

BLUE NOTE LP 7008
33⅓ MICROGROOVE

days BEYOND RECALL

milenberg joys
days beyond recall
lord, let me in the lifeboat
up in sidney's flat
blame it on the blues
weary way blues

sidney bechet-bunk johnson

Top right: The great Sidney Bechet, with Red Allen's Kenneth Kersey at the piano

Bottom Right: Backstage refreshments for Wild Bill Davison (left) and Eddie Condon

the fabulous
SIDNEY BECHET with
sidney de paris
and jonah jones
Blue Note 1207

both in France – where players like Claude Luter (clarinet) headed a Paris scene which eventually became the home of veteran soprano man Sidney Bechet – and in Britain, where a purist movement in the early 50s led initially by trumpeters Ken Colyer and Humphrey Lyttelton mushroomed into the unprecedented 'trad boom' of the early 60s, with Top Ten chart hits for the bands led by Chris Barber (trombone) Kenny Ball (trumpet) and clarinetist Acker Bilk.

CL 616   COLUMBIA

JAMMIN' AT CONDON'S

EDDIE CONDON and his ALL-STARS

The Cool on the Coast

America's sun-soaked West Coast produced the coolest sound around in the early years of the '50s

W**HILE AN ACTIVE** music scene has always existed along the entire length of America's western seaboar, it was initially localised, but as with the movie and television industries with which it shared geographical space, any noticeable expansion occurred amid the urban sprawl of Los Angeles.

Once viewed as possibly the Last Frontier, Southern California vividly reflects successive generations of optimistic young Americans who accepted the challenge to Go West. No more so was this true than at the time of the Second World War, when two million, predominantly black migrants, moved from Texas and other surrounding locales to the West Coast to work on the US war effort.

In their wake, R&B, club blues and, soon after, bebop put down its roots among the numerous hedonistic hot spots that lined L.A.'s Central Avenue; a district where locals such as Dexter Gordon, Wardell Gray, Teddy Edwards, Charlie Mingus, Buddy Collette, Roy Porter and others held sway.

Often referred to as the Pacific Coast Harlem, it was along Central Avenue that the kind of round-the-clock activity once only found in Kansas City prevailed. However, at the time, few people outside of the city limits knew this to be fact.

It was to take 'The Chase', a self-explanatory head-to-head featuring the duelling tenors of Dexter and Wardell – which had been recorded on 12 June 1947 for the Dial label – to alert the rest of the nation to the fact that, in the late 40s, things were not necessarily cool on the coast.

'The Chase' and its subsequent follow-ups was to firmly establish the two protagonists' credentials while at the same time heralding the insatiable public demand for death-or-glory gladiatorial two-tenor tag teams.

Left: From the 1958 movie *I Want To Live*, (l to r) Shelly Manne, Art Farmer, Gerry Mulligan, Frank Rosolino, Bud Shank. Right: Chet Baker in typical cool mood

As early as 1944, Norman Granz staged his first JATP shows at L.A.'s Philharmonic Auditorium with tough tenors Illinois Jacquet and Jack McVea and pianist Nat 'King' Cole, while, a few months later, Coleman Hawkins blew into town and, with trumpeter Howard McGhee, fronted the area's first bop combo. All this action would be followed by Diz and Bird for what proved to be an ill-starred stint opposite Slim Gaillard at Billy Berg's celebrated Hollywood niterie on Vine Street.

Prior to Ross Russell setting up his Dial label to record Bird, bebop records arrived in L.A. via the most unorthodox distribution methods; enterprising Pullman car attendants outward bound from the Big Apple and Bird's notorious wheelchair-bound dope supplier Moose The Mooche (Emery Byrd) proved to be both the best and most reliable sources if not the costliest.

With the post-World War Two expansion of movies and then TV, together with its monopoly on good weather, California – and in particular Los Angeles – proved to be a magnet for musicians in search of the good life. And, for an elite few, their wish was granted way beyond all expectations. Yet, much of what was about to take place on the coast had its roots back East in the Big Apple.

Both Thelonious Monk and Dizzy Gillespie had openly praised George Shearing's unique-sounding quintet, insisting that the British-born/ New York-resident pianist was 'the greatest thing to happen to bop in the last year.'

The year in question was 1949, and Shearing's highly melodic take on bebop was derived from lock-handed keyboard voicings in which vibraphone doubled the top note while guitar doubled the bottom note. A noticeable absence of break-neck tempos, front-line horns and a stick-wielding drummer, produced a rhythmically soft yet detailed texture which, when augmented by subtle latin percussion, was viewed with suspicion by some as cocktail hour musings.

This somewhat cooler approach was, for the time being, one of a number of new directions that bop-driven modern jazz was seen to be moving. Elsewhere in Manhattan, the reclusive pianist Lennie Tristano and alto player Lee Konitz were exploring a somewhat atonal cerebral alternative to bop which concentrated on linear improvisation and interweaving rhythmic complexities while, in Hollywood, Capitol were releasing the first recordings by the pioneering Miles Davis Nonet with it's richly textured line-up of six horns and three rhythm.

Later to be known as the Birth Of The Cool band, this nine-piece unit was in reality a scaled-down version of the progressive Claude Thornhill Orchestra complete with French horn and tuba. Unsurprisingly, half of the personnel comprised Thornhill alumni – most notably Lee Konitz and arranger Gil Evans. Of the five arrangers involved on the project, baritone saxman Gerry Mulligan accounted for almost half the charts ('Jeru', 'Godchild', 'Venus De Milo', 'Rocker' and 'Darn That Dream'), Gil Evans penned two ('Boplicity' and 'Moon Dreams'), pianist John Lewis scored three ('Move', 'Budo' and 'Rouge'), while John Carisi ('Israel') and Miles Davis ('Deception') contributed one each.

It was only in later years that these sessions were seen for their true value. But, at the time, apart from a solitary two week club date in New York at the Royal Roost (September 1948), three recording dates proved to be the extent of the nonet's working life. Personal involvement with the nonet not only greatly influenced the future direction of Miles Davis and Gil Evans who would later convene in 1957 for the purpose of producing such landmark orchestral masterpieces as 'Miles Ahead',

Gerry Mulligan's US Pacific Jazz sides were released in Great Britain – the singles on 78rpm – on the then-familiar red and white label of Vogue Records

'Porgy And Bess' and 'Sketches Of Spain', but also two of the most successful soon-to-be-formed jazz combos of the Fifties.

In the east, pianist John Lewis would join forces with Milt Jackson, Percy Heath and Kenny Clarke under the collective title of The Modern Jazz Quartet while out west, Gerry Mulligan (25) turned the jazz world on its ear with a pianoless Quartet which involved trumpeter Chet Baker (22), followed by a Tentette album (also for Capitol), produced by Gene Norman, which further explored some of the ideas he'd introduced at the Davis sessions.

Apart from Lewis' insistence that his cohorts dressed like city gents, what both the MJQ and Mulligan's foursome explored was the joy of collective improvisation and counterpoint.

These were personal success stories whereas the influence trumpeter-cum-arranger/leader Shorty Rogers (who also cut a Gene Norman produced Davis-inspired album for Capitol) would exert over the local scene would, for many years, prove to be of even greater significance

In essence what was emerging was still bebop only that it was now being performed in a slightly more restrained manner, with the tempos less frantic and the arrangements somewhat more bevel-edged. Fundamentally, this new cool jazz was just air-conditioned cool bop.

As part of the Californian make-over, a revised image saw bop stripped of its wild zoot suit threads and put into sophisticated Italian-style Ivy-League jackets, straight-leg pants and college loafers. Day-wear favoured Hawaiian shirts, Chinos and imported sports cars.

1951 in the San Francisco Bay Area, trumpeter Bob Scoby went about the business of spearheading a Dixieland revival, while another local boy, pianist Dave Brubeck expanded his trio to a quartet with the crucial introduction of altoist Paul Desmond.

As with Konitz, Paul Desmond had constructed a seemingly fragile, almost aloof approach that ran counter to bop in that it owed almost nothing whatsoever to Bird in terms of style, sound or blues content. Whereas, Brubeck's bombastic approach was bereft of what one regarded as being the accepted roots of jazz, it revealed more than a passing nod in the direction of Milhaud, Hindesmith, Stravinsky, Schoenberg and various other European forms.

Stylewise both Brubeck and Desmond appeared to be at odds with everything around them. Worse still, they were accused of being unable to swing and therefore branded heretics. Wrong! Within three years, Brubeck would be on the cover of *Time* magazine, his quartet having become one of America's major campus attractions with a string of best-selling albums taped on location at various colleges. Later on, he would scale the pop charts with 'Take Five.'

It wasn't just the popularity of Dave Brubeck and the phenomenal success of Gerry Mulligan's innovative quartet in 1952 with hits such as 'Bernie's Tune', 'Walkin' Shoes', 'Nights At The Turntable' and 'Soft Shoe', that had the jazz world looking to the West Coast. When, in 1951, Stan Kenton chose Los Angeles to disband his star-studded Innovations Orchestra, most of the personnel – some of whom had also served with Woody Herman's Herd – broke out the suntan oil.

It was to be this group of musicians who, led by Shorty Rogers and his sidekick, drummer Shelly Manne, would define the soon-to-become-familiar sound of West Coast cool by permutating an expanded pool of around four dozen musicians that included Conte & Pete Candoli, Maynard Ferguson, Stu Williamson, Jack Sheldon (trumpets); Frank Rosolino, Milt Bernhardt, Bob Enevoldsen (trombones); John Graas (French horn); Bud Shank, Herb Geller, Art Pepper, Joe Maini, Charlie Mariano, Lennie Niehaus (alto sax); Jimmy Giuffre, Bill Holman, Bob Cooper, Buddy Collete, Bill Perkins, Jack Montrose, Richie Kamuca

Shorty Rogers and The Giants certainly lived up to their name, striding the West Coast scene like musical collossi

LOS ANGELES

Dragonwyck: Barney Kessel, opnd. 3/9.
Drift Inn (Malibu): Bud Shank, *tfn*.
Keyboard Lounge (Rosecrans): Curtis Counce, *tfn*.
Lighthouse: Howard Rumsey, *tfn*. Name grps.,
Suns.
Renaissance: Jimmy Witherspoon, Ben Webster,
Jimmy Rowles, Red Mitchell, to 3/26. Miles
Davis, 3/28-4/2. Bessie Griffin, Gospel Pearls,
Sun.
Shelly's Mannie-Hole: Shelly Manne, Ruth Price,
wknds. Frank Rosolino, Mon. Red Mitchell,
Tues. Richie Kamuca-Russ Freeman, Weds. Joe
Maini, Thurs.
Sheraton West: Red Nichols to 4/1.
Zebra Lounge: The Jazztet, Redd Foxx, opnd.
2/21. Horace Silver, 3/30-4/9.

(tenor sax); Hampton Hawes, Claude Williamson, Carl Perkins, Pete Jolly, Lou Levy, Russ Freeman, Andre Previn, Marty Paich, Victor Feldman (piano); LeRoy Vinnegar, Red Mitchell, Curtis Counce, Monty Budwig (bass); Stan Levey, Mel Lewis, Chuck Flores, Lawrence Marable, Larry Bunker (drums).

These and other players appeared to spend most of the day in the recording studio and their nights blowing jazz at such shore-line venues as the Lighthouse Cafe, Hermosa Beach. With the ex-Kentonite bass player Howard Rumsey directing the musical policy, the club was quickly transformed into the area's premier jazz showcase with the introduction of Rumsey's resident house band, the now legendary Lighthouse All-Stars.

Meanwhile, tenorman Brew Moore's opinion 'Anybody who doesn't play like Lester Young is wrong,' had been adopted by a generation of 'Grey Boys' – a term Pres used to describe his mainly white disciples.

One of the great ironies of the jazz life can be seen in the circumstances surrounding Lester Young. So profound was his influence that a situation presented itself whereby the great man was known to have been unable to distinguish his own records from those of his many acolytes. Though, not affiliated to any particular caucus, the lyrically-gifted Stan Getz epitomized this phenomenon even more so than any of the

Above: The Chico Hamilton Quintet in the '57 B-movie *Cool And Groovy*

Left: Shelly Manne with bassist Red Mitchell in the background

'Four Brothers' brigade, emerging with just about the most hauntingly beautiful sound ever achieved by any jazz player on any instrument.

So, if saxmen took their lead from Pres out of Getz, then, as with Miles, trumpet players all but dispensed with vibrato as can be heard in the work of Chet Baker and others. Coupled to a plethora of un-Birdlike altoists – of which star-crossed Art Pepper was without equal (he would run a close second to Bird in the polls) – a signature style which was to infiltrate innumerable Hollywood-produced soundtracks was set in ice.

The international acclaim showered upon both Brubeck and Mulligan offered instant access to Brubeck's vibes-doubling drummer Cal Tjader who went off to work with pianist George Shearing prior to organizing his own immensely popular latin kick combo. Similarly, Mulligan's original sticksman, Chico Hamilton also found fame (and a spot in the movie *The Sweet Smell Of Success*) with a unique sounding chamber-jazz quintet which originally showcased guitar (Jim Hall), sax (Buddy Collette) and cello (Fred Katz).

Long before the term was hi-jacked by 60s progressive rock bands, the initial acceptance of the 12-inch long playing records created an audience for 'concept' albums and, by doing so, greatly upped the sales potential of a number of signature sounding groups most notably the East Coast-based Modern Jazz Quartet with its numerous themed releases ('Fontessa', 'Django' etc) and movie soundtracks (*One Never Knows, Odds Against Tomorrow*) .

These were complemented by a number of projects realised on the West Coast. Shelly Manne's million-plus 'My Fair Lady' (1956) unleashed a succession of jazz interpretations of hit musical scores that

took in *The Bells Are Ringing* (Andre Previn), *West Side Story* (Cal Tjader), *The King And I* (The Mastersounds), *South Pacific* (Chico Hamilton Quintet) while pianist Vince Guaraldi hit paydirt with everything from 'Cast Your Fate To The Wind', the Luiz Bonfa/Antonio Carlos Jobim score for *Black Orpheus,* to his own soundtracks for the popular 'Charlie Brown' TV programmes.

Apart from a few murmurs from Manhattan, mainly rooted in envy of the prosperous California lifestyle enjoyed by some best-selling musicians regarded as lightweights, a virulent East-versus-West campaign started to be waged by critics with the West Coast sound often unfairly stigmatised as being anaemic, over-arranged and soul-less. In the wake of such a stinging assault, many musicians went to extreme lengths to distance themselves from the 'West Coast' tag altogether.

In the same way as emergent Hard Bop was – to some listeners – a more accessible take on Bebop, so too was the small group jazz being blown on the West Coast. As much of the studio work appeared to be handled by white players rumours suggested that black musicians were intentionally excluded from such lucrative employment. However, the fact remains, Harry 'Sweets' Edison, Buddy Collette, Harold Land, Teddy Edwards, Curtis Amy, Carmell Jones, Red Callender and Curtis Counce were regulars on numerous L.A. sessions.

Shorty Rogers vehemently denied accusations of covert racism:

'The studios work on strict budgets and unbelievably tight schedules. It's a world in which you have to be a perfect sight reader and very, very disciplined. The standard procedure is, rehearse a piece of music once, then roll the tapes at which point you've got one crack at it. And, it's got to be right. If, at the end of a session, time's running out, you skip the rehearsal and record a track live just sight reading it.

Ellington had some good readers, but there were other black bands who were just into hitting a groove and where you could more than get by if you were a good soloist. And a lot of great music was made like that. But that's never going to work in a high-pressured studio environment where everything from technical excellence and precision right to your punctuality and behaviour count for everything. And where a piece of music might have to be exactly 23 seconds long!

Another deciding factor, most of these players were musically like-minded having previously played together with Kenton or Herman.'

Even at the best of times, the Los Angeles area has always seemed to support a somewhat fragile club life with venues going dark faster than when they first switched on their neon signs. In the mid-60s, the laws of supply and demand suddenly dictated that as jazz musicians became more engrossed in steady-money studio work, the popularity of such guitar-toting A Go Go club acts as Trini Lopez and Johnny Rivers increased, as America willingly capitulated to The Beatles-led British Invasion and the local offensive that spawned countless Electric-Folk/Psychedelic Acid Rock bands with such colourful names as The Byrds, Jefferson Airplane, The Grateful Dead , Moby Grape and The Doors.

With both young and the not-so-young assuming to have suddenly discovered the elixir of youth, eternal hipness, a new wardrobe and light shows, so the number of clubs showcasing jazz dramatically declined or, more often than not, changed their booking policy to accommodate crowd-pulling shaggy-haired rock acts and mini-skirted caged dancers.

For the time being, jazz couldn't compete on that level.

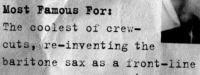

Name: Gerald Joseph Mulligan
Checked In: 6 April 1927, New York City
Checked out: 20 January 1996, New York City
Instruments: Baritone saxophone, piano
Most Famous For: The coolest of crew-cuts, re-inventing the baritone sax as a front-line instrument, and his innovative 'pianoless' quartet with Chet Baker which elevated both musicians as international poll-winning superstars. Music best described as contrapuntal cool with a dixie twist.
Roots: Commenced arranging for big bands of Gene Krupa, Claude Thornhill, Elliot Lawrence and Stan Kenton while still in his teens, but made biggest impression when supplying the Miles Davis 'Birth Of The Cool' nine-piece (1949–50) with almost half of its chart. Latterly, he regularly fronted his own 15-piece Concert Jazz Band.
Confession: Though his partnership with Baker only lasted nine months, Mulligan saw it as the most creative period of his career. 'Chet was one of the best intuitive musicians I have ever seen and much of the best music I ever made was in his company.' Baker was replaced by Bob Brookmeyer on valve trombone and then Art Farmer (trumpet). Brookmeyer also featured alongside Jon Eardley (trumpet) and Zoot Sims (tenor) when Mulligan expanded the quartet into a sextet.
Best heard on: Pacific Jazz (pianoless quartet) and Verve (sextet and concert jazz band)
Judged By The Company One Keeps: Collaborations included Thelonious Monk, Ben Webster, Johnny Hodges, Stan Getz, Lee Konitz, Paul Desmond, Annie Ross, plus six years partnering Dave Brubeck.

Shorty Rogers

The epitome of the working professional in the jazz world, Shorty Rogers managed to play the triple role of hard-nosed session player, blowin' club gigster and a recording star in his own right

Below: A composite picture of the Stan Kenton Orchestra, which included (second row, l to r) Bud Shank, June Christy, Shorty Rogers and Bob Cooper. Kenton appears twice, bottom row.

'WHEN STAN KENTON disbanded the Innovations Orchestra in L.A. back in '51, it was like the Good Lord had purposely planted us all in this wonderful location out there on the West Coast. I suppose we really were the right people, in the right place at the right time.

And, it wouldn't be too long before we quickly got our toe in the studio door and then it opened wider and wider. All these movie people knew us from the stuff we'd done with Kenton and Woody Herman, so that part was easy.

For the first three years, I stayed at the Lighthouse as part of Howard Rumsey's Lighthouse All Stars. A lot of people don't realise just how important that place was – for a time it was the point of jazz activity in L.A. Though he was never actually a member of the group, I worked a lot with Art Pepper at the Lighthouse. Then, Shelly left Kenton and joined us, then Jimmy Giuffre. Soon we became aware that a lot of movie people would make that one hour drive from Hollywood out to Hermosa Beach just to come and listen to us.

We worked five nights; had Monday and Tuesdays off. But then, we needed to for on Sundays things started up at two in the afternoon and didn't finish until two in the morning. Even before we started playing, people would be sitting around in their bathing suits and they'd be there twelve hours later still in the same clothes!

Howard Rumsey had a fine business talent, which is something quite rare amongst most musicians. Without Rumsey's vision and his business know-how, quite probably we would have all just drifted around.

We saw the before and after. The Los Angeles jazz scene before The Lighthouse was a few Monday night jam sessions – it was very haphazard, nobody got paid. You played just because you were hungry to play.

Things really changed after the success of Rumsey's policy at the club. It became possible to sustain yourself just playing jazz but you

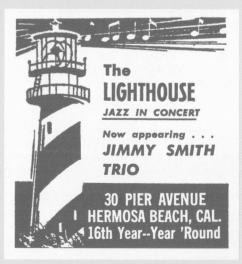

The **LIGHTHOUSE**
JAZZ IN CONCERT

Now appearing . . .
JIMMY SMITH TRIO

**30 PIER AVENUE
HERMOSA BEACH, CAL.
16th Year--Year 'Round**

MODERN JAZZ a la lighthouse

with June Christy and Howard Rumsey's Lighthouse All-Stars

The Lighthouse Cafe
30 Pier Avenue
Hermosa Beach, California
Home of Howard Rumsey's
Lighthouse All-Stars

HOWARD RUMSEY

BOB COOPER   FRANK ROSOLINO   VICTOR FELDMAN   STAN LEVEY

'Lighthouse' line-ups included the regular All-Stars (right) and session variations like the one below with (l to r) Rogers, Milt Bernhardt, Maynard Ferguson, Jimmy Guiffre and Howard Rumsey

wouldn't be toting a lot of money to the bank. However, the money to be made in movies more than compensated. Later, in the '60s, the whole L.A. scene kept slowin' down – a combination of rock and roll, lack of interest and less opportunity to play. All this coincided with us getting more studio work in the movies and television, and as that aspect of our career got bigger our jazz activity became correspondingly less.

Shelly Manne? I first met Shelly in February 1942 when rehearsing for Will Bradley's Band - I was seventeen years old and our friendship lasted 42 years.

Originally, The Giants was a partnership between Shelly and myself until he formed his own group.

We did a few local dates with the Big Band and one big national tour with the quintet on a show featuring Stan Kenton and Art Tatum. The line-up was myself, Jimmy Giuffre, Pete Jolly, Curtis Counce and Shelly.

Sure, we realised there was acceptance for our records – but were unaware just how great that acceptance was.

We'd sometimes sell close to 100,000 LPs when a half million on a pop album was then still considered very big.

But, what we didn't realise until much, much later, was just how well those records did outside of America – particularly in Europe. But by that time we were kept far too busy in the recording studios and didn't have the time to tour Europe, which was a mistake.

A typical day-to-day routine would find either Shelly or myself playing in some club until two in

the morning, going for something to eat and not getting home until four. By ten the next morning I'd start writing music until a nine o'clock gig that evening.

As for Shelly, he might have a studio call at eight-thirty in the morning – which was quite normal before recording a jingle at eleven. Then he'd have a television date the same afternoon before going on to play a jazz engagement in the evening.

We were a product of our musical heritage and Shelly and I grew up listening to Basie and the Kansas City Seven recordings.

All we were doing was just trying to have fun. We were all young guys and full of spirit, that's why I could never understand why people claimed the music was unemotional. We were swingin' we were cookin'. Sure I'd put in a mute, Jimmy would switch to clarinet and it sounded soft — just like those Kansas City Seven sides where Lester was playing clarinet and Sweets Edison was using a mute and that's what we were trying to do.

Just like my use of french horn and tuba with The Giants. I just loved that sound when I heard it on those sides that Miles cut for Capitol at the end of the '40s.

It was inspiring, however, some people tried to make out that the Giants succeeded on record at the expense of Miles' 'Birth Of The Cool' material which failed commercial first time around. But then, that kind of rationale usually came from the East Coast where they attempted to put down the music we were making by cooking up this phoney East verses West rivalry but they never actually came to hear us.

Muted trumpet and clarinet, tuba and french horn? Those were just some of our many flavours. I suppose for a time it looked like Shelly, Bud Shank and myself operated some kind of monopoly out on the Coast, but it was just that people wanted us to record for them. We were reliable and those records did sell. We were all serious about the music we were involved in and overjoyed that we had this much activity. Who wouldn't be?'

thanks again!

Gerry MULLIGAN

Chet Baker

'WHEN I LOOK at all those early photographs taken of me . . . those familiar William Claxton and Bob Willoughby shots of me recording for Pacific Jazz back in the early 50s . . . I did look modern, looked good, should've been a movie star. A handsome guy.

Suppose some people think I blew it . . . drugs and everything. But I was clean in those early days . . . didn't know nothin'. When I was working with Bird – did that tour with him, he was very protective. Like an elder brother, even fatherly. He kept on warning me off drugs, said I shouldn't become like him. If anyone approached me, he'd get real angry. On one occasion he threatened to kill this guy. Later, I heard these rumours that in fact Bird had actually shot and killed two pushers. Now, whether this was all part of people adding to the legend, but it was said, that pay-offs were made by those people who were shielding Bird.

But like I said, I was clean in those days. It was only after Dick's death (Richard Twardick) that I started to have this morbid fascination. See, Twardick's family personally blamed me for their son's death. Insisted that I was responsible. Said, I should've been taking care of him. I didn't think he was that heavy into anything. I was very young myself and going through all these emotions.

I had recently been voted top trumpet player over Dizzy and Miles and everyone else and I didn't deserve it. I knew better than anyone else that I wasn't in their league. But there was nothing that I could do about it other than to try and play better. Back then, everything was happening just too fast for me. In the space of just over a year, I'd toured with Bird and then played on hit records with Gerry Mulligan. I was kinda out there on my own, but then we all were. We didn't have the kind of protective management that the big pop singers of the day enjoyed or earned the same kind of money. Then, when Dick died from an overdose and everyone blamed me – it was a terrible burden. I felt extremely guilty about his death and really didn't have anyone strong to turn to. Soon after, I became obsessed with that whole drug thing . . . built up this morbid fascination and in the end I had to try it for myself. Whether deep down it was all to do with self-destruction or whether in actual fact, I had an addictive personality . . . I guess I'll never really know.

James Dean? Yeah, I remember him hanging around a couple of times – kinda quite . . .always looking at your clothes . . . your shoes. Now when I see some of those pictures of him, guess he'd made a note of what I'd been wearing. But then again, he did that with Marlon Brando. But see, that was pretty much the look of the time.'

Opposite: Chet Baker and Gerry Mulligan in their one and only European appearance together, at a US forces N.C.O. club in Landstuhl, Germany.   Above: Stan Getz at Warsaw's Stodota Club during the city's 1960 Jazz Jamboree.   Below: Dave Brubeck

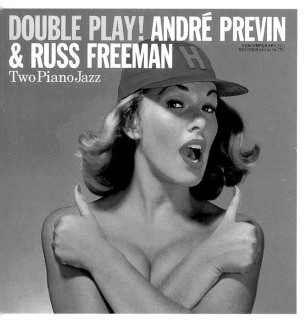

DOUBLE PLAY! ANDRÉ PREVIN & RUSS FREEMAN
Two Piano Jazz
CONTEMPORARY RECORDS C3170

DUANE TATRO'S JAZZ FOR MODERNS
CONTEMPORARY C3514

LENNIE NIEHAUS VOL. 1 'THE QUINTETS' CONTEMPORARY C3518

PACIFIC JAZZ 1224
CHET BAKER & CREW

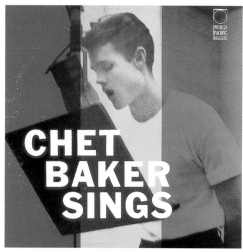

CHET BAKER SINGS
WORLD PACIFIC

WEST COAST JAZZ
WITH STAN GETZ · SHELLY MANNE
LEROY VINNEGAR · CONTE CANDOLI · LOU LEVY

You get more bounce with Curtis Counce
Contemporary C7539

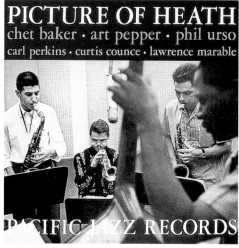

PICTURE OF HEATH
chet baker · art pepper · phil urso
carl perkins · curtis counce · lawrence marable
PACIFIC JAZZ RECORDS

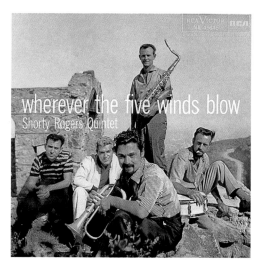

wherever the five winds blow
Shorty Rogers Quintet

JAZZ WEST COAST VOL.3

CHICO HAMILTON
CHET BAKER
GERRY MULLIGAN
BUD SHANK
RUSS FREEMAN
JIM HALL
JOE PEPPE
BILL PERKINS
ZOOT SIMS
BOB BROOKMEYER
SHELLY MANNE

JWC-507

ZOUNDS! THE LENNIE NIEHAUS OCTET!

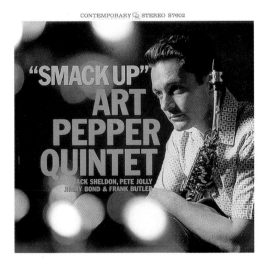

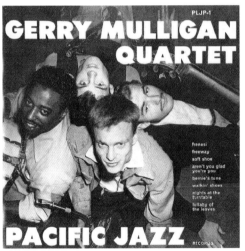

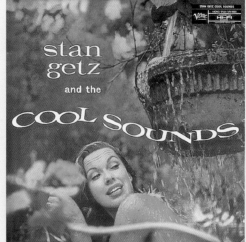

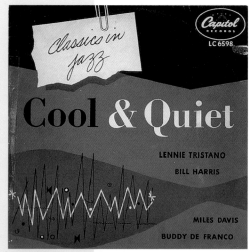

Cool

An influence on the 'cool school' who counted Lee Konitz among his pupils, pianist Lennie Tristano was noted as an experimenter long before avant-garde or free jazz were recognized concepts. Rarely performing in public, he worked in the recording studio with the likes of (below, left) Warne Marsh (tenor), Peter Ind (bass), Al Levitt (drums)

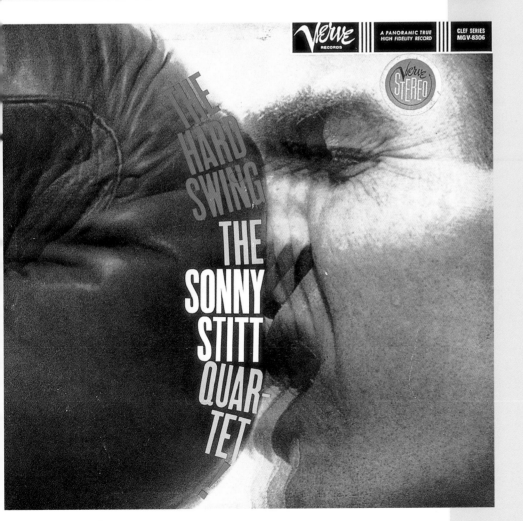

Hard

THE HARD SWING

JAZZ MESSENGERS · CHET BAKER quintet · ELMO HOPE quintet
JACK SHELDON quintet · PEPPER ADAMS quintet

THE HARD SWING THE SONNY STITT QUAR-TET

Out on the coast everything wasn't as cool as you might believe. Years later it was tagged California Hard, in the late-50s a clique of L.A. musicians who blew bop as tough as anything emerging out of Detroit and New York were known locally as Hard Swingers. This wasn't altogether unsurprising, for in the late-40s, Central Avenue L.A. had the biggest count of bopsters outside of the Big Apple.

Hard Swinging altoists Art Pepper, Joe Maini and Herb Geller, trumpeters Jack Sheldon and Gerald Wilson and pianist Hampton Hawes may have already become familiar faces amongst the studio mafia, but most of the other hardliners were journeymen players. Amongst this number were Curtis Amy, James Clay (tenor), Carmell Jones (trumpet), Elmo Hope (piano), Lawrence Marable (drums), shadowy figures such as Frank Morgan (alto) and Dupree Bolton (trumpet) plus, Eric Dolphy who, after a stint with Chico Hamilton, would win his spurs elsewhere.

As the fortunes of California Cool began to fluctuate, three great local hard-edged bands emerged; Max Roach-Clifford Brown Incorporated, Shelly Manne & His Men and the Curtis Counce Quintet. The last great bop band, Roach-Brown Incorporated, included a succession of tenormen commencing with Sonny Stitt, Teddy Edwards and Harold Land before Sonny Rollins took to partner Brownie. If Roach was one of the original architects of bop, Brownie was truly a player of unmatched God-like brilliance: fleet-fingered fluency, full-bodied tone and melodic invention all combining to make him the greatest of all post-Gillespie/Navarro firebrands.

Probably the most recorded of all jazz drummers, Shelly Manne & His Men's ground-breaking five-volume 'Live At The Blackhawk' 1959 sessions affirmed this unit to be a West Coast equivalent of the Jazz Messengers, but with an identity all its own. While Brown-Roach Inc. quit L.A. to tour and prosper and Shelly opened his own Hollywood niterie, The Manne Hole (1960-74), the Curtis Counce Quintet remained behind to struggle and, eventually, disband.

The Harde Come

The West Coast cool breeze was burnt off as Manhattan's maurauding Hard Boppers piled on the pressure and turned up the heat.

SANDWICHED BETWEEN the Bebop revolution of the '40s and the variously titled New Thing, New Wave or Free Music upsets of the '60s is Hard Bop, no revolution but no bland sandwich filler either.

Hard Bop consolidated the harmonic advances of Bebop and introduced a heavier, in-your-face, rhythmic emphasis. One theorist advanced the idea that once Bird died, since no other hornman could approach the rhythmic variety in his playing, that side of things was duplicated by joint effort. Drums moved up into the front line. Others saw Hard Bop as an East Coast reaction against the cool, neat West Coast school of players. The jazz lineage being a less tidy affair than Christian marriage, many players passed through the genre bound for destinations out. Many did not thrive on such a degree of heckling from the tubs. Tension wasn't unilaterally conducive to flights of imagination.

Geography too was an unreliable determinant: California boasted many robust cats like pianist Hampton Hawes and units like the Curtis Counce Quintet with the incomparable drummer Frank Butler. Economic factors usually play a part in determining the shape of the culture, and there's no doubt that the introduction of the long-playing record at the start of the '50s invited the longer, looser blowing sessions framed by brief ensemble themes that typify Hard Bop.

As far as album sleeves were concerned, Hard Bop was anything where the gerund of the title was clipped.

The starting place is usually taken as the quintet led by pianist Horace Silver and drummer Art Blakey which sailed under the name of The Jazz Messengers, and held court at the Café Bohemia during 1955 and 1956. Between them, they redefined accompaniment along the lines of flanking a

SWEDEN GETS THE MESSAGE

Blakey in Stockholm—pic by Bengt Malmqvist

ART BLAKEY SAVES JAZZ

From SVEN WINQUIST

STOCKHOLM, Wednesday.—Art Blakey has broken the jinx which threatened to end jazz concerts in Sweden.

A 90 per cent, full house gave Blakey's Jazz Messengers an ecstatic reception at Stockholm's Concert Hall on Monday—compared with the meagre 40 per cent, drawn by other American stars over the past six months.

It was feared that Sweden's leading jazz promoter, Nils Hellstrom, would have to give up. But he still had some contracts to fulfil and one of them was for the Jazz Messengers.

'Memorable'

The interest in Blakey may save American jazz concerts in Sweden. We hope so, for Sweden has long been considered one of the world's most jazz-minded countries.

Not only did Blakey draw a large audience, but it certainly got its money's worth. The Stockholm dailies called it a really memorable evening."

drunk to the nick. Leaving bassist Doug Watkins the obligation of keeping the pulse, pianist and drummer collaborated on a polyphonic surround for the horns.

Silver's drive to compose – and he wrote 'Doodlin' ', 'Quicksilver' and the massively influential 'The Preacher' during this period – led him to form his own group, leaving Blakey alone to front The Jazz Messengers.

Goading and prodding their hornmen, both leaders ran a species of boot camp for young Bebop marines from which emerged players of the rank of Hank Mobley, Kenny Dorham, Donald Byrd, Lou Donaldson, Clifford Brown, Freddie Hubbard, Lee Morgan, Blue Mitchell, Junior Cook, Benny Golson, Joe Henderson, Jackie McLean, Bill

They

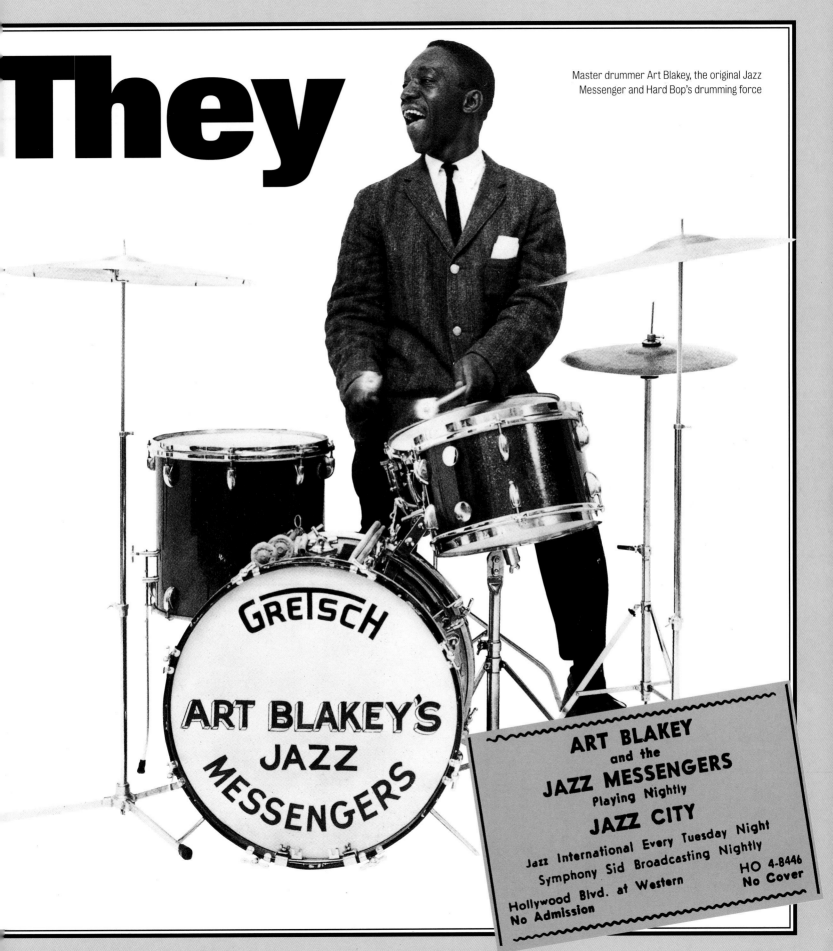

GRETSCH

ART BLAKEY'S JAZZ MESSENGERS

INTERNATIONALLY FAMOUS

ART BLAKEY
& THE JAZZ MESSENGERS
just returned from a triumphal tour of EUROPE (France, Belgium, Germany, Holland, Sweden, Denmark and Switzerland) and a smash success in JAPAN.

JUST RELEASED!

ART BLAKEY & THE JAZZ MESSENGERS A NIGHT IN TUNISIA

A NIGHT IN TUNISIA
With Lee Morgan, Wayne Shorter, Bobby Timmons, Jymie Merritt

ART BLAKEY

A Night In Tunisia, Sincerely Diana, So Tired, Yama, Kozo's Waltz

BLUE NOTE 4049

THE BIG BEAT   BLP 4029*

a night at BLAKEY rd land
CLIFFORD BROWN
LOU DONALDSON
HORACE SILVER, CURLY RUSSELL
ART BLAKEY
BLUE NOTE 1521 VOLUME 1

BIRDLAND   BLP 1521/22

MOANIN'   BLP 4003*

ART BLAKEY AND THE JAZZ MESSENGERS BLUE NOTE 4003

AT "THE JAZZ CORNER OF THE WORLD"   BLP 4015/16*

THE JAZZ MESSENGERS

AT THE CAFE BOHEMIA   BLP 1507/08

P List $4.98—Stereo $5.98   *Also available in Stereo   √ Free Catalog On Request

BLUE NOTE RECORDS INC., • 43 West 61st Street, New York 23, N.Y.

March 30, 1961 • 41

Hardman, Johnny Griffin, Wayne Shorter, Wynton Marsalis, Terence Blanchard, Bobby Watson and a squad of pianomen that ran from Bobby Timmons and McCoy Tyner through to Chick Corea and Keith Jarrett. The late Art Blakey, sometimes known as Buhaina, was a short, squat, muscular man of messianic enthusiasm. No one ever coasted on one of his gigs. He catapulted his soloists on a rumbling tide of drum press rolls and

accents, an intervention of rim shots, whiplash silences broken by the squash of his hi-hat before the entire engine room rose up to engulf the player on the bridge. It is a development from Kenny Clarke's pioneering Bebop approach to drums, and Blakey cut back on the filigree to dig deeper with the directness. It is, in short, a fist. 'Hard Drive', the title of an early Messengers album on Bethlehem, has a rocket ascent on the cover

and the blurb, 'Out of this world . . . And the Next World Too'.

'I'm always kicking them in the ass. It's as much as they can do to keep up with me. When they join, they're scared to death, and most of them grow up or die. When they join The Messengers, the bullshit's over. I'm not running a post-office. This is The Jazz Messengers. You gotta understand, any line-up I get is successful. It's gonna sound like The Jazz Messengers – and why? Because I am there. I am the Messenger.

'I'm the one directing traffic, so it doesn't make no difference who comes or goes, I can always handle it. I don't need no stars, no prima donnas. I make the group the star. I'm not the star, the whole group is the star.'

And, during this conversation over lunch, Blakey reached over and took a handful of chips from my plate. 'You don't want all them French fries.' You would need to be pretty buoyant to ride his relentlessly driving rhythm, and nippy to keep your chips. 'Drums should get to the soul. It's the second instrument. First there's the human voice,

then there's the drum.'

Of all his hornmen, the prototypical Hard Bopper was the Chicago tough tenorman Johnny Griffin. Fast, bristlingly combative with a short fuse that flared into an almost hysterical excitement, he positively throve on Blakey's drumming.

The Little Giant as he became known, served his apprenticeship from 17 with Lionel Hampton's stomping big band circus where he was featured in cutting-contests with fellow tenorman, the veteran Texan honker Arnett Cobb, on 'Flying Home'.

Blakey's accompaniment did not throw him. Instead, idea crowded idea, each one tightening the rackets of tension. Fire called to fire, and Griffin in person is as vehement as his erstwhile leader.

'Art would make one of those rolls and say, "No – you can't stop yourself now!" BLAM! We always had this competition, the front line versus the rhythm section, so it was always war!'

Griffin tells a great story about his day of recuperation at Art Blakey's house one Labor Day. 'He started talking about the drums and I said, "Who needs drums making all that

noise? I play my saxophone, I don't
need no drums." '

They made a fifty dollar bet and
gatecrashed club bandstands
throughout Harlem. 'Art Blakey was
gonna make me spit blood or I was
gonna make him throw away his drum
sticks. Ram Ramirez, he's in this club, got his
nice little programme going – and here come
the maniacs!'

Art's saxophone players seem unanimous
on the Blakey effect. 'Enjoy?' said Benny
Golson. 'Not really. That's an understate-
ment. I'm trying to think of some other
synonyms for fantastic. It was like your folks
might say, "Go on out and play, Johnny, and
here's some money." Art is a character. One
time he announced to the audience, "Our
purpose is to swing. Look, they don't know
it, but if the government were to send us to
Russia, we'd swing them to death." '

Wayne Shorter, long before his stint
with Miles Davis or Weather Report, played
tenor with a coarse-toned, rip-saw edge and
weird asymmetrical logic with The Jazz
Messengers. The swings of mood in his

LEE MORGAN
WITH HANK MOBLEY / KENNY RODGERS / HORACE SILVER
PAUL CHAMBERS / CHARLIE PERSIP   BLUE NOTE 1541

PRESTIGE
FIRST WITH THE GREAT JAZZMEN

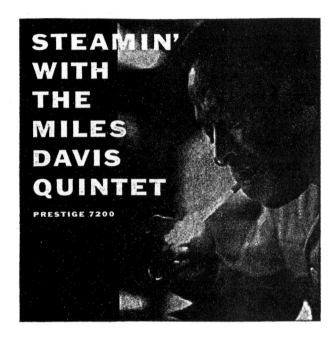
delivery turned on a dime. Listening was like
getting knocked down by a chess player. 'Art
always used to impress upon us that we'd
got three minutes to go out there and upset
everyone while the remainder of the set
would be given over to proving ourselves to
those people. There were no second chances!
We had a lotta fun in those five years. Lee
Morgan was always laughing at Art. "Bash!
We're gonna bash them out tonight, ain't
we, Buhaina?"

'Art was so enthusiastic. He'd want to
be everything. When it was 6am and everybody was tired, he'd say, "Let's go over
Thelonious Monk's house – he should be up
by now" '.

The late trumpet player, Woody Shaw,
worked with both Blakey and Horace Silver.
'When I started playing, Art'd say to me,
"Where you goin', man? Wait. Tell a story."
And when I was tired, he'd say, "Hey – I was
just getting ready to put the fire under ya!"
Horace is different. He's very deep on form
and discipline. That was an experience I
needed in the basic fundamentals of music.'

If the album title, 'The Big Beat', sums
up the approach of Art Blakey and The Jazz
Messengers, then the Horace Silver Quintet
could sit neatly under titles like 'Let's Get To
The Nitty Gritty' and 'Filthy McNasty', the
latter described by the leader as 'a mythical
young man of rather dubious character'.
Away from Silver, Blakey favoured similarly
percussive pianists like Junior Mance and
Bobby Timmons while Silver's chattering
front-line drummers included Louis Hayes
and Roy Brooks.

Goading, prodding, Silver's keyboard
approach utilized rumbling boogie patterns
in the left hand with fractured single-note
fingerings in the right, and locked hands
cadenzas that recalled the call-and-response
rituals of Sanctified Church.

'A cross between Bud Powell and Pete
Johnson,' wrote critic Martin Williams. The
early trios gave an advance warning of the
composer's direction with funky, uncluttered
numbers like 'Opus de Funk', 'Horoscope',
'Ecorah' and 'Quicksilver'. And, as if that
wasn't enough, once he had formed his
quintet, he wrote galvanizing background
riffs in his compositions.

The aptly titled 'Fingerpoppin' ' was
one of his originals; the title 'Filthy McNasty'
came from a WC Fields movie, *The Bank
Dick*; and 'The Preacher' – with chords based
on 'Show Me The Way To Go Home', the
tune that got the whole 'Dat Dere', 'Wade in

September 5, 1959

PROBE INTO BIRDLAND BEATING-UP

From REN GREVATT and BURT KORALL

NEW YORK, Wednesday.—New York Police Commissioner Stephen P. Kennedy is to probe the alleged beating-up of jazz trumpeter Miles Davis by two Broadway cops outside the famed Birdland jazz club.

A battered and bleeding Davis was hauled away in a squad car. Only police reinforcements stopped an angry mob of onlookers from joining in a fracas that jammed the sidewalks and blocked traffic.

The crowd later gathered outside the 54th Street Precinct, where Davis was held. As reported in last week's MELODY MAKER, he was booked for assault and disorderly conduct. Kept in jail overnight, he was released on a $500 bond.

HEADLINES

On Tuesday, the disorderly conduct charge was postponed until September 18. The assault summons will be held in special sessions court at a date to be announced.

The incident brought screaming headlines in the New York newspapers.

Thirty - three - year - old Davis told reporters that he had just finished making a 27-minute recording for the Armed Services to aid a Bond sales drive for free America.

When he went outside Birdland for a few minutes. a policeman approached and

Back Page, Col. 2

Melody Maker

Lyttelton in U.S
See Page 20

September 12, 1959   FOR THE BEST IN JAZZ   Every Friday 6d.

← THIS IS WHAT THEY DID TO MILES DAVIS

THE battered, bleeding figure on the left is trumpeter Miles Davis, one of the great names of modern jazz and the idol of a million disc collectors and fans.

This dramatic picture, flown to the MELODY MAKER from New York, shows Davis, still bleeding from head wounds, being marched into the city's West 54th Street Police Station House by Patrolman Gerald Kilduff.

BEATEN

A few minutes earlier he had been taking a breather between sessions at the world-famous jazz-haunt, Birdland, when he was told to move on by Kilduff.

Miles alleges that the next thing he knew he was being beaten over the head by a detective who came up behind him.

HEARING FIXED

Police Commissioner Stephen Kennedy has ordered a full investigation into the beating.

Local magistrate Morton R. Talleris has fixed September 18 for the hearing of a charge of disorderly conduct against him.

Because of his injuries, Miles was forced to cancel the rest of his week's engagements at Birdland, and at press time was still resting at his New York home.

A member of his group, alto star Julian "Cannonball" Adderley, talks about Miles Davis on page 12.

On the spot picture by "New York Mirror" cameraman.

Obviously, NYPD wasn't overstaffed with jazz fans

'Sonny' Rollins

Checked In: New York City, 7 September 1929

Instrument: tenor saxophone

Famous For: being the best on the block

The Wonder Years:
Played with Miles Davis (1953), Thelonious Monk (1954) and though Miles proclaimed Rollins 'the greatest tenor ever', when the trumpeter formed his first 'classic' quintet, in 1955, Rollins didn't take up the invitation to join, resulting in John Coltrane being hired as second choice! The following year, Rollins joined the Clifford Brown-Max Roach Quintet which like the Davis Quintet and the Jazz Messengers emerged as one of the most venerated of all contemporary jazz combos.

Greta Garbo Syndrome:
At the peak of his career, Rollins withdrew from public life (1959-60), opting for self-exile and inner-peace. The only sight of him was perched high on the Williamsburg Bridge playing to the accompaniment of passing traffic. He again took time out (1968-71) to study in India and Japan.

Beret Me Out On The Lone Prairie
Years later, British post-Hard Bop saxophonist, Courtney Pine took up the tenor sax as a resulting of seeing 'Way Out West' cover for which Rollins posed amongst cacti and sagebrush proudly wearing a Stetson.

Laughing Bones
Blessed with innate sense of humour which has him working out on such unlikely jazz vehicles as 'Sonny Boy', 'If You Were The Only Girl In The World', 'I'm An Old Cowhand' etc, and sporting a Mohican haircut a full decade before either punk or Robert De Niro.

No Home Should Be Without One:
Saxophone Colossus (Prestige/OJC), Newk's Time (Blue Note), A Night At The Village Vanguard (Blue Note), 'Way Out West' (Contemporary/OJC)

Words of (infinite) Wisdom:
'Melody is one thing that endures. Of course, there's room in jazz for all kinds of experimentation but I dig melody. And, don't let anyone fool you. It's difficult to play — great control is needed.
Many players work fast and in doing so overlook detail. This is unfortunate for in the detail of a song lies much of its beauty.'

Right: Americans in Paris included Art Taylor (drums) and Johnny Griffin (tenor sax)

the Water', 'Watermelon Man' soul jazz show on the road – came from the Church.

'It's just the way I felt like playing,' said Silver, a wiry, hunched, diffident man. 'Just one of my many influences seeping into my playing, part of the fact that I've always dug gospel music and I love the blues. It wasn't contrived. I wasn't trying to simplify or over-simplify the music. We can reach back and get that old-time gut-bucket bar room feeling with just a taste of the backbeat.'

He seemed inexhaustibly inventive within the genre. Of 'Home Cookin' ' he said it was 'another one of those nasty-type of numbers. I mean earthy I guess. You know what down home and cookin' signify. Greens and grits and all that kinda stuff.'

Silver's flag-wavers are not necessarily the heart of his music though. Tenorman Junior Cook, who served six years with the quintet, felt that both 'Filthy McNasty' and 'Sister Sadie' became monsters that they had inadvertently created. Silver really preferred the combination of painstakingly created composition with improvisation to marathon blowing sessions. 'Horace used to have a thing about guys staying out there playing long solos. He used to say they'd defeat their own self,' said Cook.

One of the dominant figures in the '50s was Miles Davis. Falling out of the spotlight following his stint with Bird and his own Birth of the Cool band due to drug addiction, the trumpeter came walloping back at the Newport Jazz Festival with a keen version of 'Walkin' '. He and drummer Philly Joe Jones had been reduced to touring, using pick-up bands in the lean years.

'Miles and I had been barnstorming around the country. When we got to a city where we had a gig, I'd get there first and find another horn player and piano player and a bass player. In those days we were really outing the music together. We'd get on the plane and he'd hum the arrangements we'd play,' recalled Philly Joe. Miles often got him to ask the others to lay out, so the band became just trumpet and drums. 'He'd tell me, "I don't like what they play anyhow".'

That relationship was at the heart of Miles' first great quintet formed in 1955. 'I

WHERE & WHEN

NEW YORK

Birdland: Joe Williams, Harry Edison, Toshiko Mariano, to 10/18. Eddie (Lockjaw) Davis-Johnny Griffin, Junior Mance, 10/19-25. Dizzy Gillespie, Olatunji, 10/26-11/8.
Five Spot: Sonny Rollins, Donald Byrd-Pepper Adams, open 10/18, tentative.
Half Note: Al Cohn-Zoot Sims to 1/24. Clark Terry-Bobby Brookmeyer, 1/25-2/8.
Jazz Gallery: Thelonious Monk, Philly Joe Jones, tfn.
Village Vanguard: Modern Jazz Quartet, Bill Evans, to 1/28. Montgomery Bros., Jackie Cain-Roy Kral open 1/30.
White Whale: Sonny Clark, wknds., tentative.

have always felt that great trumpet players need great drummers in order to get their shit off. I know it has always been that way for me,' Miles wrote in his autobiography.

He wasn't concerned that most of the critics didn't approve of Philly Joe's often intrusive volume. (Actually, the jazz writers initially knocked all the Hard Bop drummers). 'Look, I wouldn't care if he came up on the bandstand in his BVDs and with one arm, just so long as he was there. He's got the fire I want. There's nothing more terrible than playing with a dull rhythm section. Jazz has got to have that thing.'

Signing John Coltrane, second choice to Sonny Rollins, proved to be inspired. His multi-note attack was the perfect foil for the economic style of the leader. 'But as great as Trane was sounding, Philly Joe was the fire that was making a lotta shit happen.

'See, he knew everything I was going to do, everything I was going to play, felt what I was thinking.'

Miles, Trane, Red Garland, Paul Chambers, PJJ – in its 18 months together, the quintet laid four great LPs for Prestige before going to Columbia: 'Workin' ','Steamin' ' , 'Cookin' ', 'Relaxin' '. Said the leader, 'It was so bad that

it used to send chills through me at night, and it did the same thing to the audiences too. Man, the shit we were playing in a short time was scary.'

Said Philly Joe: 'That was an uncanny band. All those years, no rehearsals. Miles would say, "Rehearse? I can hear you play at the gig".'

The dominant tenor of the period prior to the rise of Coltrane was Sonny Rollins, who came out in interview once with a very early dating for Hard Bop, finding the symptoms present on Bud Powell's 1949 Blue Note, 'Bouncing With Bud'. Sonny, who cut his

JAZZ 100

Fact File

The trumpet, or so we are given to believe, is a most athletic instrument, and most players, through sheer fatigue, start to go off the rails in their fifties. That's of course, if they are lucky enough to reach such a venerable age. Most appear to violently self-destruct long before that.

Be warned, anyone taking up the instrument isn't going to prove a good insurance risk.

Unrecorded New Orleans legend Buddy Bolden died of madness; Bix Beiderbecke (28), Bunny Berigan (33) and Hot Lips Page (46) drank themselves to death; Ellingtonians Bubby Miley (29) and Al Killian (34) also checked out prematurely – Killian being slaughtered by a previously convicted killer. Woody Herman's solo star Sonny Berman (23) literally blew his heart out.

The hard-boppers also had their share of fatalities.

When, in 1950, a combination of TB and drug abuse felled Fats Navarro (26) it was Clifford Brown who stepped forward to further progress a style created by Diz. Brown – revered for his playing and his non-toxic lifestyle – who co-led a quintet with drummer Max Roach (that also included Sonny Rollins), sadly perished in an auto accident in June 1956. Roach eventually replaced Brown with Booker Little (23) who succumbed to uraemia in 1961.

Shelly Manne sideman, Joe Gordon (35) perished in a house fire. One-time Horace Silver and Jazz Messengers' employee, Woody Shaw (45) fell under a subway train. But it was to be 'Sidewinder' hitmaker, ex-Jazz Messenger and Hard-Bop firebrand Lee Morgan who suffered the most public death, being repeatedly shot outside New York jazz spot Slug's, on a Saturday night by a girlfriend who had originally helped him recovery from severe drug problems. He was just 33.

Jazzman Morgan dead

chops – alongside Clifford Brown – with the great Max Roach Quintet, first hit form with Kenny Dorham, Elmo Hope, Percy Heath and Blakey in 1954 with 'Swingin' for Bumsy' and 'Movin' Out'. One of the most astonishing on-target blowing sessions came about for Blue Note on 'Sonny Rollins Volume 2' when the tenorman met trombonist J.J. Johnson, Silver, Chambers and Blakey, and still produced improvisations that developed formally with no loss of heat. 'Newk's Time' (again on Blue Note) found not only Rollins but also Philly Joe Jones at their best, especially so on 'The Surrey With The Fringe On Top' played as a duet. But blowing sessions – that typical Hard Bop format – were not greatly to his taste. Nor were they to the taste of Thelonious Monk, Hank Mobley or John Coltrane, particularly with the latter two who floundered in the wake of Johnny Griffin on his 'A Blowing Session' (Blue Note).

In no special order, albums by Lee Morgan, Blue Mitchell, Donald Byrd, Jackie McLean, JR Monterose, Freddie Hubbard, and Dexter Gordon – the great veteran Bebopper now updated to take advantage of the economic

Sonny Rollins – the new Sheriff in town

John Coltrane

'**WHEN I FIRST JOINED** Miles in 1955, I had a lot to learn . . . I felt I was lacking in general musicianship. I had all kinds of technical problems – didn't have the right mouthpiece or the necessary harmonic understanding.

I am quite ashamed of those early records I made with Miles Davis. Why he picked me I don't know. Maybe he saw something in my playing that he hoped would grow. I had this desire, which I think we all have, to be as original as I could, and as honest as I could be. But there were so many musical conclusions I hadn't arrived at, that I felt inadequate. All this was naturally frustrating in those early days, and it probably came through in my music.

I've been told my playing is 'angry'. Musicians have many moods – angry, happy, sad, and since those early days perhaps more sides of my musical nature have been revealed on record. I don't really know what a listener feels when he hears music. A musician may feel one way and the listener may get something else entirely from the music.

Some musicians have to speak their anger in their playing. The beauty of jazz is that you're free to do just what you feel. But while their playing might express anger, I wouldn't know whether they are angry people or not. An aggressive frame of mind can create pretty stern music. But this may well be a very rewarding experience for the listener. You can get a feeling of

expectancy and fulfilment in a solo, and an artist of ability may lead you down paths in music where many things can happen. I'd hate to think of an audience missing out on music because they think it's nothing but anger.

Choice of material is entirely individual. I've played some jazz forms so long and so much that I feel the need for other forms, and perhaps, no form. When I started my own group, I'd plan routines like mad, now I don't have to plan so much as I learn to get freer.

Sometimes we start from nothing, no "in" plan, no intro, or solo routine. I just make suggestions as to what I feel and we use this as a starting point.

I know how it's going to end – but sometimes not what might happen in between!

Jazz is a companionable thing, and I like playing in smaller places, so that I can see what people feel. I would like my music to be part of the surroundings, part of the gaiety of a club atmosphere, I realise I'm in the entertainment business, and I'd like to be the sort of guy who can set audiences at ease. If you go about music without a smile, people think you're not happy. I don't make a habit of wishing for what I don't have, but I often wish I had a lighter nature. Dizzy has that beautiful gift – I can't say "People, be happy" – it's something I can't command. You have to be true to your own nature.'

SOULTRANE

JOHN COLTRANE   PRESTIGE 7142

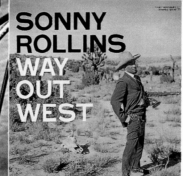

SONNY ROLLINS WAY OUT WEST

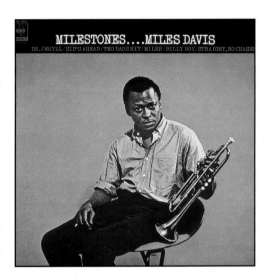

Philly Joe Jones, forever lighting fires under Miles

OOL STRUTTIN'/SONNY CLARK

WITH ART FARMER
JACKIE McLEAN
PAUL CHAMBERS
'PHILLY' JOE JONES
BLUE NOTE 1588

ART BLAKEY'S JAZZ MESSEI
MESSENGERS WITH THELONIO
WITH THELONIOUS MONK
STEREO

monk's music

thelonious monk septet with coleman hawkins, art blakey, gigi gryce

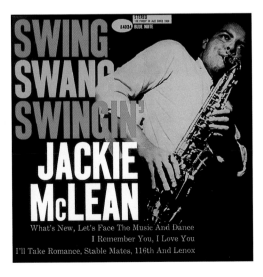

SWING SWANG SWINGIN'
JACKIE McLEAN

What's New, Let's Face The Music And Dance
I Remember You, I Love You
I'll Take Romance, Stable Mates, 116th And Lenox

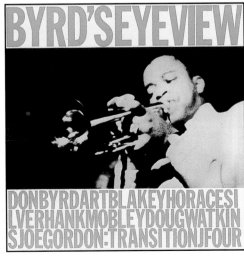

BYRD'SEYEVIEW

DONBYRDARTBLAKEYHORACESI
LVERHANKMOBLEYDOUGWATKIN
SJOEGORDON:TRANSITIONJFOUR

GRIFF & LOCK
EDDIE "LOCKJAW" DAVIS &
JOHNNY GRIFFIN QUINTET

942 JAZZLAND

Jazz trumpet star Clifford Brown killed in car crash

AMERICAN trumpet-star Clifford Brown and pianist Richie Powell were killed in a car crash early on Wednesday morning of this week (cables Nat Hentoff). This tragic accident took place just outside Bedford, Indiana, while the two musicians were travelling to Chicago, for an engagement with the Clifford Brown—Max Roach group of which they were both members.

Powell's wife, whom he married only a month ago, was also killed in the crash.

MIKE BUTCHER writes: The death of Clifford Brown is probably the most lamentable loss to contemporary jazz since Charlie Parker died, last year.

Brownie, a native of Wilmington, Delaware, rose suddenly to fame in

1953 (when he had been playing trumpet only eight years) as a member of the Lionel Hampton Band.

He recorded extensively in Europe that year with contingents from Hamp's group (Vogue, Esquire), and quickly became recognised as one of America's most brilliant jazz trumpeters upon his return to the States. He won the " New Star Trumpet " award in the *Down Beat* critics' poll, 1954.

BUD'S BROTHER

For the past two years, Brownie had been co-leader with Max Roach of the successful Brown-Roach combo, recording exclusively for EmArcy in recent months with the unit, and also as guest star on sessions with Sarah Vaughan, Helen Merrill, etc.

Richie Powell, though overshadowed as a pianist by his famous brother, Bud Powell, was an excellent, swinging musician who can be heard to advantage on records with the Brown-Roach unit (Vogue, EmArcy).

momentum of the Hard Bop movement towards the close of the Fifties – sound as fresh now as they did then.

Pianist Mal Waldron, ex Max Roach and Charlie Mingus, cut two fine albums as 'Mal One' and 'Mal Two' fuelled by drummer Art Taylor. He explained his own repetetive, funky style thus: 'I have an economic approach to my music which has to do with my childhood. We were never rich people and never threw anything away. So when I have a note I make full use of it, milk it in every possible way.'

The main Hard Bop labels were Blue Note and Prestige. The latter was founded in 1948 by Bob Weinstock who started out handling collectors' items in a New York record store, spent his evenings at the Royal Roost, and dreamed of promoting the music. His first long-player in 1951 featured Zoot Sims, after which Weinstock concentrated on the young players circulating around New York.

Miles Davis may have complained that 'they had signed me for peanuts when I was a junkie', but Weinstock did take a chance on him at his lowest ebb. If one title seems to sum up the Prestige policy it is probably 'Young Bloods', a Hard Bop outing for Phil Woods. The great sound recordist, Rudy Van Gelder, was signed up for jazz after Weinstock visited Dr Van Gelder's opticians with an eye problem. Today, those original waxings with their black-and-yellow centres fetch a fortune.

Van Gelder also cut most of the finest recordings released by that Rolls-Royce of labels, Blue Note.

Said Horace Silver: 'Alfred Lion and Francis Wolff were men of integrity and real jazz fans. Blue Note was a great label to record for. They gave a first break to a lot of great artists who are still out there doing it today. They gave me my first break, and they gave a lot of musicians a chance to record when all the other companies weren't interested. And they would stick with an artist even if he wasn't selling.'

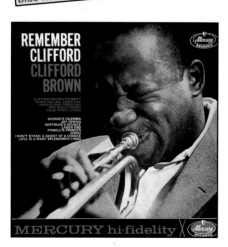

CLIFFORD BROWN memorial album
blue note 1526

AND HIS GRETSCH DRUMS.

Elvin Jones – 'Trane's ultimate time keeper

CD Checklist

ART BLAKEY/JAZZ MESSENGERS
Moanin' (Blue Note)
TINA BROOKS
True Blue (Blue Note)
CLIFFORD BROWN
In Concert (Vogue)
DONALD BYRD
Half Note Vol 1 & 2 (Blue Note)
SONNY CLARK
Cool Struttin'; Leapin' & Lopin'
(all Blue Note)
JOHN COLTRANE
Soultrane (Prestige/OJC)
MILES DAVIS
Cookin'; Relaxin'; Steamin'; Workin' (all
Prestige/OJC)
KENNY DORHAM
Matador/Inta Somethin' (Blue Note)
JOHNNY GRIFFIN
Introducing/Chicago Calling; The
Congregation (all Blue Note)
FREDDIE HUBBARD
Open Sesame (Blue Note)
JACKIE MCLEAN
Lights Out (Prestige/OJC); Swing, Swang,
Swingin'; Bluesnik (all Blue Note)
Hank Mobley: Soul Station (Blue Note)
THELONIOUS MONK
J R Monterose: J.R Monterose (Fresh
Sound)
WES MONTGOMERY
The Incredible Jazz Guitar; Full House (all
Riverside/OJC)
LEE MORGAN
Candy (Blue Note); Take Twelve
(Riverside/OJC)
SONNY ROLLINS
Saxophone Colossus (Prestige/OJC);
Newk's Time; A Night At The Village
Vanguard Vol 1 & 2 (all Blue Note)
HORACE SILVER
Phil Woods: Phil & Quill (Prestige/OJC)

Blue Note encouraged a rotating leadership in the studios, with, say, (star-crossed) tenor player Tina Brooks helming one session and sideman Jackie McLean leading the next. The wonderful Sonny Clark was practically the studio house pianist.

Elder statesmen like tenorman Ike Quebec kept an eye out for new talent, and musicians often recommended each other, remembered townies: Quebec brought Dexter Gordon in out of the cold to cut arguably his best ever albums while Lou Donaldson stood guarantor for the likes of guitarist Grant Green. And, best of all, Lion gave a couple of days rehearsal time. Bob Weinstock at Prestige probably recorded more Hard Bop than any other label – in fact, the trumpeter Donald Byrd played on fifty albums in the first two years of his career – although the proportion of untidy misses is high.

Cover art reached a pinnacle in the period. With such an avalanche of LPs in all fields of music, artists jostled each other to catch the eye. Reid Miles worked for Blue Note and Prestige; Tom Hannan, Don Schlitten, Esmond Evans, Paul Bacon established visual styles as individual as William Claxton's on the West Coast. If the photography was stunning (Francis Wolff, Herman Leonard, Bob Willoughby, Chuck Stewart etc) the graphics were sublime, and the subjects stone hip. Fashionwise, the Fifties jazzman really laid it. Gone was the oldtime swing musician with his hat on indoors; these cats wore their shades indoors instead. It was the era of the three-button, narrow lapel, natural shoulder-line suit, the narrow knitted tie, and the button-down or tab collar. Photographed in the low lighting of the clubs they often resembled undercover FBI agents.

So far Soho
Brit Bop

Largely as a result of the notorious Union ban, jazz in Britain never got the chance to cross-fertilize with its American originators that it enjoyed in France, yet despite this – and some would even argue because of it – home-grown heroes emerged who were definitely world class.

RECEIVED INFORMATION, dispensed by those who wear their music as fashion accessory, would have you believe that pre- the 'Acid Jazz' phenomenon, there was no local British modern jazz scene of any importance save for who was booked into Ronnie Scott's Club and whatever Jamaican-born altoist Joe Harriott was up to.

But Britain experienced first hand American jazz as early as 1919, when the Original Dixieland Jazz Band toured although it wasn't until the late 20s that a real local scene developed. Expansion soon followed highly publicised UK concerts by Louis Armstrong and Duke Ellington in 1933; the former sparking a feisty array of recordings by Satchmo-clone Nat Gonella, while the Duke's arrival prompted some memorable sessions headed by the critic and bass player Spike Hughes.

During the 1930s, Britain sustained probably the most active dance band scene outside of North America – with name bands of the stature of Jack Hylton, Jack Payne, Henry Hall, Ambrose, Lew Stone, Harry Roy, Roy Fox and Ray Noble playing prime-time radio shows on a daily basis from London's smartest Hotels. Like their American counterparts, these star bandleaders enjoyed matinee idol-style acclaim. And even though their repertoire was often slanted to the high-society circuit, each contained an element of hot stylists.

Nevertheless, from 1935 until the mid-1950s, the British jazz scene existed in virtual isolation from the rest of the world.

This was entirely the result of the Draconian policy of the British Musicians' Union, which actively barred American musicians from working in Britain. Formulated as a self-protective ploy, the ban effectively prevented any exchange of musical ideas, the only contact with American music being via a trickle of belated record releases (many US labels didn't have an official UK outlet), and the ability of Teddy Hill (featuring Dizzy Gillespie), Duke Ellington and Benny Goodman to sidestep the issue by appearing as variety acts, often topping bills which featured a motley array of comedians, illusionists, jugglers and high-kicking chorus lines.

THE Fabulous Flamingo CLUB
33 WARDOUR ST.
LONDON. W.1.
GER. 1549
the Jazz Showplace of Europe

"Easter Festival of Modern Jazz"

TONITE FRIDAY 7—11 p.m.
MARCH 27
First appearance in 1959 !
Bix Curtis' sensational
"JAZZ FROM LONDON" UNIT
starring Bob Efford, Keith Christie, Tony Crombie, Tony Kinsey, Bill le Sage, Eddie Blair, Stu Hamer, Stan Tracey, etc.

SAT. ALL-NITE 12.30—7 a.m.
MARCH 28-29
The return of the poll-winners !
"THE JAZZ COURIERS"
with Ronnie Scott and Tubby Hayes
plus !
TONY KINSEY QUARTET
Bill le Sage, Stu Hamer, Ken Napper

EASTER MON. 7—11.30 p.m.
MARCH 30
For the first time in Britain !
America's sensational jazz singer
CARMEN McRAE
accompanied by Don Abney
Also : "The Jazzmakers," Ganley, Ross plus the Eddie Thompson Trio
Pay at the Door ! Come Early !

SATURDAY 7—Midnite
MARCH 28
The slick, swinging sound of
VIC ASH SEXTET
with Johnny Scott, Alan Branscombe
HARRY KLEIN QUINTET
co-starring Red Price on Tenor
OPEN TILL MIDNIGHT !

EASTER SUN. 7—11 p.m.
MARCH 29
Have you heard this great new band ?
Another meeting of
"THE JAZZ COMMITTEE"
with Don Rendell and Bert Courtley
plus new
TONY KINSEY QUARTET

WEDNESDAY 7—11 p.m.
APRIL 1
The fabulous Flamingo proudly presents America's great
CARMEN McRAE
at the piano : Don Abney
Also : Tony Kinsey Quartet
Eddie Thompson Trio with Jack Fallon, Tony Crombie
Come Early ! Tickets at the Door !

Comperes : TONY HALL and BIX CURTIS

Others used different ploys. Benny Carter enjoyed a lengthy British stay in 1936-38 as staff arranger to the BBC Dance Orchestra, Coleman Hawkins toured in 1939 as a demonstrator for the Selmer saxophone company, while pianists Fats Waller and Art Tatum also seemingly circumnavigated the ban and played club dates.

The stationing of Glenn Miller's AAF Band in Britain at Bedford, during World War II, had a profound influence on musicians and fans alike. For the first time in years, there was prolonged and direct access to top flight American musicians, the dance band providing the memorable Swing Shift broadcasts and pianist Mel Powell's Uptown Hall Gang dispensing suitable fare for those who thought in terms of jazz combos.

Additionally, other Uncle Sam military conscripts such as Sam Donohue and Art Pepper, could be found jamming with their British counterparts in London jazz venues.

In austere post-war Britain, a conveyor belt of upbeat US movies, where smooth talking Caesar Romero simultaneously fed knowing ballroom babes a line while keyboard comping for Glenn Miller,

MARQUEE
165 OXFORD STREET, W.1
The London Jazz Centre
Saturday, January 6th
★ JOE HARRIOTT
           QUINTET
featuring SHAKE KEANE
★ TUBBY HAYES
           QUARTET
Sunday, January 7th
★ DANKWORTH
      (See display on this page)
Wednesday, January 10th
★ CHRIS BARBER'S
      JAZZ BAND
with OTTILIE PATTERSON
★ COLIN KINGWELL'S
     JAZZ BANDITS

Above: Towering tenors at Ronnie's, with (l to r) Al Cohn, Tubby Hayes, Zoot Sims and Ronnie Scott

The celebrated Johnny Dankworth Seven with Dankworth (alto), Don Rendell (tenor), and Jimmy Deuchar (trumpet)

made being a musician almost as attractive as being boss of Ford Motors.

Probably this – as much as anything else – motivated a whole new legion of local band leaders such as Ted Heath, Teddy Foster, Ken MacKintosh, Carl Barriteau, Oscar Rabin, Geraldo and Tommy Sampson to follow Stan Kenton's lead – torch the tuxedo and grab at the gaberdine.

This pursuit of the new stretched to arrangements; Tommy Sampson's big band bop charts predated – by at least a year – the scores Tadd Dameron custom-wrote for the Ted Heath band.

Later, Jack Parnell, Basil & Ivor Kirchin, Johnny Dankworth, Vic Lewis and drummer Leon Roy's notorious unrecorded rehearsal band stepped forward to vigorously wave the modern jazz flag.

Meanwhile, contact with the outside (jazz) world was still minimal. One of the most accessible sources of new music was by way of various AFN (American Forces Network) Broadcasts from West Germany. With the exception of the BBC's Radio Rhythm Club (later revamped as Saturday Jazz Club) and Accordion Club broadcasts featuring Tito Burns' brand of boppery, these late night AFN shows ('Bouncin' In Bavaria' and 'Midnight In Munich') were totally unlike anything to be found on straight-laced BBC broadcasts.

With d-js such as Ralph Moffet on an open mike, AFN enthused spontaneous optimism and a playlist of all the latest Stateside platters.

For many, it was through AFN that they first encountered Bird, Diz, Kenton, Herman and left-fielders like Boyd Raeburn, Claude Thornhill and Elliot Lawrence.

IN BRITAIN, the spirit of adventure was alive and, in 1947, inquisitive just-out-of-their-teens saxmen Ronnie Scott and Johnny Dankworth emptied their wallets to visit The Big Apple. Upon their return, they and others immediately took dance band gigs on the refitted transatlantic ocean liner Queen Mary with the sole intention of checking out the New York scene first hand.

As soon as they'd docked and cleared customs, these Englishmen in New York spent the 48-hours turnaround time on 52nd Street checking out Gillespie, Parker, the local record shops and flashy tie racks before guardedly bringing their treasured loot of jazz discs back to London to be deciphered and committed to memory.

As a direct result of these New World visits, the Metropolitan Bopera House opened in early 1948, with a sextet fronted by local-scene founding father, the trumpeter/pianist Denis Rose and featuring Scott, Dankworth, Tommy Pollard (piano, vibes), Lennie Bush (bass) & Tony Crombie (drums).

In this rarefied atmosphere, a milestone event occurred on 11 December 1948, when the truly legendary Club Eleven (at Mac's Rehearsal Rooms in a Soho basement in Windmill Street), was founded by Scott, Dankworth, Rose, Hank Shaw (trumpet) Johnny Rogers, (alto) Pollard, Bernie Fenton (piano), Joe Muddell (bass), Kenny Graham (tenor), Crombie and Laurie Morgan (drums), whose unsuppressible collective enthusiasm often far outstripped their expertise. Occasionally, styles clashed, ideas petered out or sessions sounded more rough than ready, but it was still early days.

Elsewhere, American jazz stars such as Bird, Diz, Miles, Kenton, Herman and Lionel Hampton were undertaking sell-out European tours. But, unless they were booked into a US Forces base, they bypassed the general British public. So desperate were fans to be in the presence of such near-mythical maestros, that charter-planes flew to Paris to see Monk and Mulligan, while in 1953 Vic Lewis organised sailings to Dublin (in high seas), enabling British bopsters to see a Kenton aggregation that included Lee Konitz and Zoot Sims.

Eventually, the British Musicians' Union and its US counterpart agreed to a reciprocal band-for-band, musician-for-musician swop, inaugurated in 1956 when Kenton played seven sell-out dates at London's Royal Albert Hall and Ted Heath embarked on the first of several US tours. As for Ronnie Scott's Sextet, they were reduced to playing one opening number on a touring rock 'n' roll package.

Though most of the local Big Bands secured major recording deals – some even scoring hits – hardcore British boppers still

Leon Roy with Phil Seaman (drums) and Tubby Hayes (far right)

had to rely in the main on independents such as drummer Carlo Krahmer's Esquire label (established Dec 1947) and the even more esoteric Melodisc. Later, Tempo (a Decca off shoot) came on stream.

Despite the brave efforts of local players, instant classics on Prestige and Blue Note by the likes of Miles, Coltrane and Rollins were simultaneously hitting the record shop racks and ultimately attracted the smart money (what there was of it).

IN TIME, PIANISTS George Shearing, Victor Feldman, Stan Tracey, Phil Seaman (drums) and trumpeters Jimmy Deuchar and Dizzy Reece through to saxmen Joe Harriott, Tubby Hayes, Don Rendell, Tommy Whittle, Derek Humble, Harry Klein, Ronnie Ross, Peter King and Ronnie Scott proved that the London jazz scene always abounded with world-class players and countless clubs that included Feldman's, the Flamingo, the Mapleton, Studio 51 and the Marquee.

Soon, The Jazz Couriers – fronted by the tearaway tenors Scott and Hayes – quickly became Britain's major modern jazz attraction followed by drummer Tony Kinsey's Trio with Joe Harriott, and the tenor-playing arranger /composer Kenny Graham's Afro-Cubists. The problem was, day jobs often paid better.

All Night Long, a UK jazz movie take on Othello starring Patrick McGoohan, with cameos by Dankworth, Hayes, Dave Brubeck and Charles Mingus premiered in February 1962, but soon after *Melody Maker* reported that the MU exchange couldn't last much longer on a few 'Big Draws' such as Louis, Basie, Ella, Brubeck, JATP and the MJQ. 'Gone are the days when almost any American group could draw large crowds'.

The exchange was then modified to allow Zoot Sims to play a season at Ronnie Scott's Club as a solo and Tubby Hayes to work and record in New York, but with the advent of Beatlemania the whole game changed.

America's finest were now exchanged for the likes of the Fab Four, The Rolling Stones, Herman's Hermits, The Dave Clark Five and Freddie & The Dreamers, while only concert hall attraction Cleo Laine & John Dankworth, and the ever-popular Tubby Hayes, could still guarantee themselves Stateside gigs.

It would take what seemed like an eternity for things to improve as both the Flamingo and Marquee clubs went over to a Rhythm and Blues policy. Only Ronnie Scott's Club appeared to keep the faith, still showcasing jazz while constantly keeping one jump ahead of its creditors.

And, that's how things remained for years.

Tough times at Tempo

'IF YOU LISTEN TO WHAT The Jazz Couriers were playing, it was quite different to what was being played in the States at the time. Everyone was citing tenor men Sonny Rollins and John Coltrane as an influence, but it didn't really show up in their playing. If anything it was Hank Mobley. I've never quite worked that one out – maybe it was a result of the MU ban – for, with few exceptions, none of the UK players had enjoyed the experience of sitting in 'live' with the best that America had to offer.

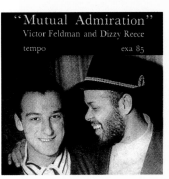

"Mutual Admiration"
Victor Feldman and Dizzy Reece
tempo   exa 85

What I recorded for Tempo was what was happening on the London club scene at the time. Surprisingly, musicians didn't exactly beat my door down begging to record. There seemed to be this strange attitude, them-and-us.

The albums I cut with Jimmy Deuchar, The Jazz Couriers and Victor Feldman were pleasurable – Feldman's Big Band date was nothing short of wild, but more often than not, I had a struggle to get local musicians to record and once I'd got them in the studio, struggle to get some of them in a fit state to actually to do the job at hand. Some lacked concentration finding it difficult to complete a three hour session. They just didn't seem to know how to enjoy themselves in the studio. In

retrospect, some of those sessions could have been infinitely better if the musicians had approached them with a healthier attitude, but if I hadn't been pushing Decca all the time and pushing the musicians, none of them – Dizzy Reece, Bogey Gaynair, Jimmy Deuchar – would have been recorded by any other major label. I've always been convinced that if Jimmy Deuchar had been black and American instead of a Scotsman, he would have been raved about worldwide. As it was, there was little money in recording – musicians getting the MU scale, while I can't ever recall receiving a penny from Decca as a producer.

Swingin' in
Studio Two

with
Jimmy Deuchar
Tubby Hayes
Derek Humble
tempo exa 81

"A VARIATION ON MONK"
DIZZY REECE QUINTET
tempo   EXA 84

Unlike Blue Note, there were no paid rehearsals, Deuchar – usually with Derek Humble and Ken Wray – rehearsed privately and arrived at a session with everything worked out beforehand. Then there was the engineer assigned to me by Decca. He had no real love of modern jazz. I would play him all those Blue Note albums engineered by Rudy Van Gelder and all he would say was, 'what's so special about those?' Meanwhile, there was I trying to get Alfred Lion interested in signing Dizzy Reece to Blue Note. Alfred liked Dizzy's anarchic approach, but pointed out that he was unknown and therefore nobody would buy it in the

States. The only way a Dizzy Reece album would make commercial sense was to involve some big name American players. As luck would have it, Donald Byrd and Art Taylor were in Paris, so we brought them over, gave the doorman at Decca's West Hampstead Studios a fiver to look the other way and spent one Saturday afternoon taping the 'Blues In Trinity' album. In the end, Rudy Van Gelder had to re-master the tapes as Decca's engineer had recorded the bass so badly. Sounds fine now. I think that was the album that prompted Art Blakey to consider Dizzy and Tubbs as a possible front line for

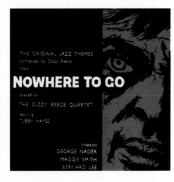

THE ORIGINAL JAZZ THEMES
composed by Dizzy Reece
from
NOWHERE TO GO
starred by
THE DIZZY REECE QUARTET
featuring
TUBBY HAYES
STARRING
GEORGE NADER
MAGGIE SMITH
BERNARD LEE

the Jazz Messengers. The best-sounding album I produced was by The Jazz Five with a tenor and baritone frontline of Vic Ash and Harry Klein. We sold that to Jazzland (a Riverside subsidiary) in the States and surprisingly that date sounded more soulful than most anything else around at that time!   *Tony Hall A&R Director*

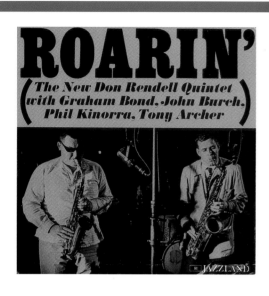

ROARIN'
(The New Don Rendell Quintet
with Graham Bond, John Burch,
Phil Kinorra, Tony Archer)

JAZZLAND

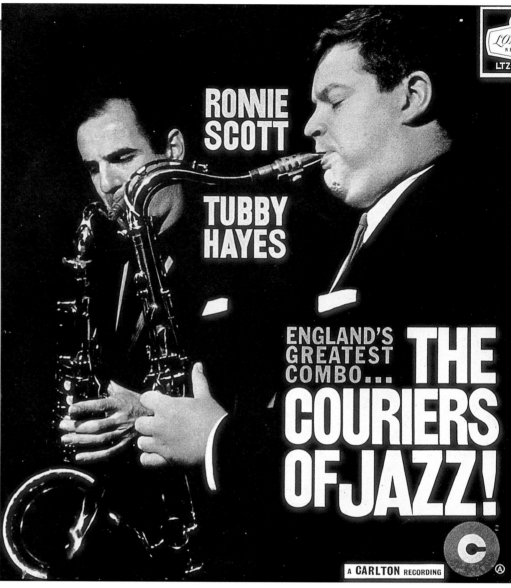

RONNIE SCOTT
TUBBY HAYES

ENGLAND'S GREATEST COMBO... **THE COURIERS OF JAZZ!**

A CARLTON RECORDING

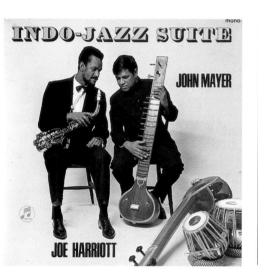

mono
INDO-JAZZ SUITE
JOHN MAYER
JOE HARRIOTT

Esquire

THE RONNIE SCOTT

JAZZ CLUB
VOL. 2.

33⅓ RPM
LONGPLAYING MICROGROOVE

32-002

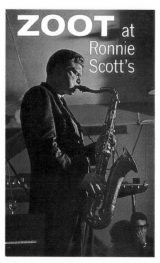

ZOOT at Ronnie Scott's

fontana

Featuring ZOOT SIMS
the RONNIE SCOTT/JIMMY DEUCHAR QUINTET
and the HAROLD McNAIR QUARTET

love for sale
the haunted jazz club
desperation
tangerine
gone with the wind
harry flicks
suddenly last tuesday

Recorded at the RONNIE SCOTT CLUB, London

TRANSATLANTIC ALLIANCE
Victor Feldman with Tubby Hayes,
Dizzy Reece, Jimmy Deuchar
tempo tap 19

PHIL SEAMEN MEETS EDDIE GOMEZ

PAN TONIC STEREO

harold macnair with ornette coleman's sidemen

affectionate fink

DEUCHAR PLAYS DEUCHAR

Featuring
Derek Humble
Ken Wray
Stan Tracey
Lennie Bush
Tony Crombie

tempo

DIZZY BLOWS BIRD

Featuring
Terry Shannon
Lennie Bush
Phil Seamen

TAP 4

SWINGIN' THE BLUES

with
Victor Feldman
Tubby Hayes
Ronnie Scott
Don Rendell
Dizzy Reece
Jimmy Deuchar
Vic Ash

tempo tap 21

A ABSTRACT
THE JOE HARRIOTT QUINTET
revolutionary contemporary jazz
by London's most exciting

Capitol DIMENSIONS IN JAZZ
RECORDED IN ENGLAND

Right: One of the great originals of the British modern jazz
scene of the 50s and 60s, alto giant Joe Harriot

TUBBS in N.Y.
fontana

SLP 12-150   STEREO   SLP 12-150

the joe harriot quintet

swings high

Right: Hot Club de France – Django (2nd right), his brother Joseph (2nd left), and Stephane Grappelli (left)

We'll always have Paris

Like movies and good food, jazz became something of a national institution in France, with American musicians such as Sidney Bechet and Ray Charles even being made honorary citizens.

Left: An advert for Stan Getz and Kenny Clarke at the celebrated Blue Note club, located just off the Champs Elysées

IN 1929, a group of Parisian intellectuals fronted by Jean Cocteau proclaimed that jazz should be recognised as an art form that ranked alongside of cinema and modern painting. Long before Cocteau's perceptive edict, Paris was arguably the first place outside of the United States to widely appreciate Black American jazz. It was the aptly named Jim Europe – leader of the 369th Infantry's Hell Fighters' Orchestra – that first brought these syncopated rhythms to Europe in 1917 to entertain the U.S. troops and in doing so, excited those Parisians exposed to this new music.

Europe, born in Mobile, Alabama, led the Europe's Society Orchestra in pre-war days with Noble Sissle as singer-guitarist. When war broke out, Sissle was promoted to drum major. But Jim Europe had problems with drummers. On returning to the States, he was murdered by one in 1919. After which Sissle became leader.

Persuaded by Cole Porter, Sissle later returned to Europe and led a band of his own at Les Ambassadeurs in the late 20s. His sidemen included Sidney Bechet (soprano sax), Otto Hardwicke (alto sax) and trumpet players Tommy Ladnier and Johnny Dunn – the latter having previously toured Europe in 1923. And it was Memphis-born Dunn who later returned with the all-black revue 'Blackbirds of 1926'.

It was apparent to such visitors that more than anywhere else in the world, blacks weren't subjected to racial intolerance and second class citizen status. Moreover, the Blackbirds Revue proved a sensation with sophisticates, paving the way for Josephine Baker, a Black American

entertainer whose near-naked exotic dancing and comedic flair would transform her into a genuine between-the-wars Superstar.

It was also in Paris, in 1935, that the seminal writer Charles Delauney first published one of the earliest jazz periodicals, *Le Jazz Hot*. A year later, Delauney set himself the task of compiling the prototype jazz record discography. By 1937, he had initiated the Swing label. Two decades later, the MJQ's John Lewis named 'Delauney's Dilemma' in honour of this jazz pioneer. Over the years, a trickle of mainly Black jazz musicians either took up French residency or based themselves, for part of the year, in Paris. The most high-profile import was Sidney Bechet; a frequent visitor since the 20s, it was only when he laid down roots (1951-59) that he enjoyed genuine pop star status with bill-topping seasons at L'Olympia Music Hall, chart singles and starring roles in movies.

However, France's greatest jazz export has to be the Quintette Du Hot Club Du France, a three guitar, bass and violin outfit featuring the unique artistry of Belgian-born gypsy guitarist Django Reinhardt and true-blue Parisian violin virtuoso Stephane Grapelly (Grappelli). Established in 1934, they produced a heavily rhythmic acoustic sound whose uniqueness is still relevant in the 1990s in both popular music and jazz.

In the years that immediately followed World War II, a small coterie of American musicians settled in France forming the nucleus of the French capital's small jazz scene which gravitated around Ben Benjamin's Blue Note Club off the Champs Elysées and in such subterranean Left Bank caverns as Le Chat Qui Peche, Club St. Germain, Les Trois Mailletz and Caveau de l'Huchette.

These US ex-pats included Kenny Clarke (drummer), Lou Bennett (organ), Jimmy Gourley (guitar), Mezz Mezzrow (soprano sax), Albert Nicholas (clarinet), Bill Coleman (trumpet), Benny Waters (alto sax), pianists Art Simmons, Memphis Slim and Bud Powell, tenor stars Don Byas, Johnny Griffin and Lucky Thompson plus Quincy Jones who benefitted from the patronage of Eddie Barclay.

For the most part, modernists were found blowing with such impressive locals as tenormen Barney Wilen and Guy Lafitte or accompanied by Henri Renaud, Martial Solal, Rene Urtreger (piano), Eddie Louiss (organ), Pierre Michelot (bass), Sacha Distel (guitar) and Daniel Humier (drums). Meanwhile traditionalists were centred around Claude Luter's enthusiastic band of jazz purists. This left Bach-obsessed pianist Jacques Loussier, violinist Didier Lockwood and Jean Luc Ponty, plus vocal groups The Blue Stars and The Swingle Singers to do their own highly distinctive things.

While Paris is still an essential stop-over for touring performers, in the last decade the major French jazz voice has been pianist Michel Petrucciani with his breath-taking technique and instantly recognisable signature sound: a player with the lyricism of Bill Evans, the virtuosity of Oscar Peterson and a wry sense of humour very much his own.

Black Rhythm and Blues of the late Forties and early Fifties led directly to Rock'n'Roll, and its subsequent impact on popular music generally.

Good Rockin'

JAZZ OFTEN flourishes best with its back pressed firmly to the wall.

Nonetheless, it has frequently been prone to bouts of paranoia and even conspiracy theories. There may well have been a time when, up until the end of the Second World War, jazz was the popular music of the day, but that time is long gone.

As one trend is rapidly replaced by another and the public's attention span becomes even shorter than its tolerance level, much of what jazz now has on offer will be of scant interest to a large section of young teens.

That's not to say that at a later date, they won't recognise the appeal of jazz in one of its numerous guises as can be seen from the growing popularity of dance-based Acid Jazz.

So while it frequently had to contend with threats to its 'natural' territory being invaded, it doesn't necessarily concur that jazz entirely lost out to rock back in the mid-50s. Gerry Mulligan, Dave Brubeck, Shorty Rogers, George Shearing, Errol Garner, the MJQ and Miles, all flourished as rock gripped the nation. Even Basie was able to revive his big band, being named 'Rock And Roll Band Of 1956' in the process by virtue of his residency on disc-jockey Alan Freed's seminal CBS radio show, *Rock'n'Roll Dance Party*.

Cut to the previous year, and it was to be the hit album 'Count Basie Swings, Joe Williams Sings' that defined the fine line where Rhythm & Blues handed over to rock. The Basie band, minus the Count himself, also

Left: 'Good Rockin' Tonight' man Roy Brown, the song was later part of Elvis Presley's early repertoire

Every Night

masqueraded as The Leiber & Stoller Big Band for 'Yakety Yak', an instrumental album devoted to the songwriting team's seminal rock'n'roll hits.

Because much of popular black music derives its unbridled passion and expression directly from gospel, blues and jazz, artists of the magnitude of James Brown, Aretha Franklin, Marvin Gaye and others exhibit a depth of feeling equally as heartfelt as any of the great jazz hornmen. And, whether it was Bird blowin' the showtunes of the day, Brubeck on a Disney kick or Miles reworking Cyndi Lauper s 'Time After Time', jazz and pop music regularly touch to the mutual advantage of all concerned.

From the late-30s onwards, elements of first boogie woogie, then jump jive, but above all else, various shades of the blues, trickled down into popular black music.

Then, when out of the blues bands leapt the honkin' tenor sax stars chased by barrel-chested big city shouters like Big Joe Turner, Wynonie 'Mr. Blues' Harris, Roy Brown, Bullmouse Jackson and H-Bomb Ferguson in full cry, all delivering the ingredients for a

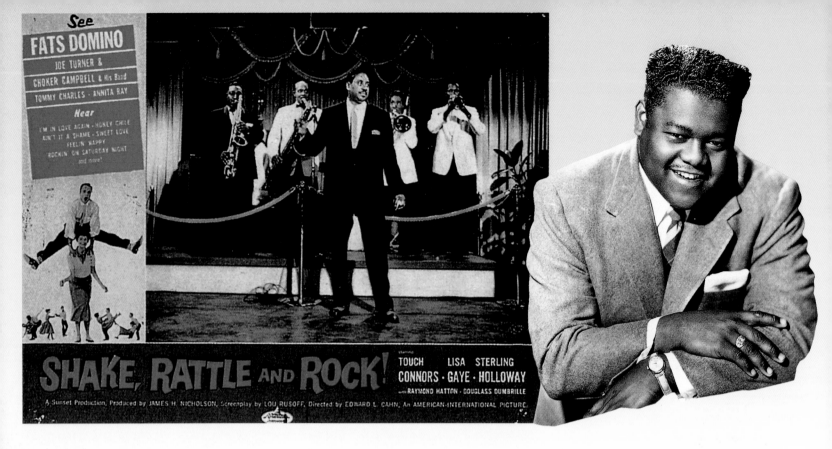

style of a potent new music, nothing could possibly restrain it.

Johnny Otis: 'Rock'n'roll was a direct out-growth of R&B. It took over all the things that made R&B different from big band swing.'

Nobody ever questioned Big Joe Turner's right to be billed as 'Boss Of The Blues'.

A local bartender at the Sunset Club in Kansas City, Joe Turner simultaneously served up shots of liquor and shouted the blues while pianist Pete Johnson frantically rattled the '88s over in the corner. It was the mid-30s and mobster Tom Pendergast was in control of KC's round-the-clock carnality, of which the Sunset was just one of 500 sin-bins under his corrupt administration.

Everyone who caught Joe Turner at full throttle came away from the Sunset mightily impressed. His reputation spread rapidly.

Starting with a show-stopping appearance at John Hammond's 1938 'Spirituals To Swing' Concert at Carnegie Hall, Big Joe would later enjoy the distinction of being the only blues shouter to successfully cross-over into rock-'n'roll when helping to instigate the genre with his hits 'Honey Hush' (1953), 'Shake Rattle And Roll' (1954), 'Flip Flop And Fly' (1955) and 'Corrine Corrina' (1956).

But as with Wynonie Harris, Roy Brown and others, Big Joe's face didn't fit in with this new teen-targeted market; it was left to star-crossed pretty boys Johnny Ace, Jesse Belvin and Sam Cooke to pull that one off.

When Turner was asked to drop 'Shake Rattle And Roll' from his act on a rock'n'roll package show, so as to allow Bill Haley to perform his tepid cover version, the writing was clearly on the wall.

For years, the received information, the official history according to the rock critics, insisted that Bill Haley and Elvis Presley were Godparents at the genesis of rock'n'roll.

In truth, it was a commercially successful white take on an already formulated black style by a couple of artists whose roots were as much in country music as anywhere else.

While not remotely as exciting as the house-rockin' Treniers, whom they initially attempted to emulate, Bill Haley & His Comets may have anticipated rock'n'roll with their 1953 hit 'Crazy, Man, Crazy', but in reality all they had to offer was Louis Jordan re-treads – they even shared the same producer as Louis Jordan, Milt Gabler.

Above, right: The Fat Man himself, with more rhythm and blues hits to his name than anyone, Fats Domino
Below: Promoter Gene Norman with R&B queen Ruth Brown and the 'sepia Sinatra' Billy Eckstine

As rhythm and blues evolved into rock'n' roll, the tenor saxophone was very much the dominant instrument.

A low-slung guitar was often merely a fashion accessory while a tenor sax, on the other hand, was a high velocity weapon, not to be handled unless the user meant serious business. There was no room for flakes.

Fats Domino and Little Richard were but two major artists who fielded a large booting sax team. On occasion, the same one.

Ever since, Illinois Jacquet blasted his way through Lionel Hampton's rough-house hit 'Flying Home' (1942), many tenormen had been making sounds that only dogs could hear, while Jazz At The Philharmonic turned it into a hugely popular spectator sport.

By 1955 the cross-over was complete, and sweat-splashed, bar-walking tough tenors, in over-size jackets shaped like cereal boxes, emerged as the undisputed crowd-pleasing heavyweights of the music circuit.

Among their impressive number were 'Big' Al Sears, Hal 'Cornbread' Singer, Red Prysock, Bullmoose Jackson, Sam 'The Man' Taylor, Maxwell Davis, Arnett Cobb, Big Jay McNeely, Jack McVea, Willis 'Gator' Jackson, Clifford Scott, Wild Bill Moore, Frank Culley, Joe Houston plus turban-totin' Lynn Hope.

Bullmoose Jackson's 'I Can't Go On Without You' may have been 1948's biggest selling R&B hit, but it's for the more salty hits 'Big Ten-Inch Record' and 'I Want A Bow-Legged Woman' that the 'Moose is now most fondly remembered.

Right: One of the most influential voices of Rhythm and Blues, the often-underrated La Vern Baker
Below: A huge (literally) R&B name through the 30s, 40s and 50s, the raunchy-voiced Big Maybelle

Bullmoose was a rare exception in that he also crooned. Fundamentally, what these musical gladiators traded in were juke box-rattling instrumental dance records. More hard-hitting than anything previously heard, it was their propulsive dance beat that was to prove irresistible.

Practically all these tenormen, dubbed by writer Leonard Feather 'extrovert moderns', were first class mainstream jazz players who, in the case of former Ellingtonians 'Big' Al Sears and Hal 'Cornbread' Singer, were just fattening their wallets.

Furthermore, Gene Ammons, Johnny Griffin, Eddie 'Lockjaw' Davis and John Coltrane had all done time as chitlin circuit honkers – the latter in Earl Bostic's hard-swinging, hit-making combo.

Best known for his 1951 million-selling platter 'Flamingo', Earl Bostic blew alto with all the scorched-earth ferocity of a flame-thrower.

In the early 40s, Bostic earned a fast-gun reputation for 'blowing the cats off the band stand' at New York's be-bop incubator Minton's. The fact that these cats often included Bird and Diz says much of the man's prowess.

Much of what was laid down for juke box consumption by these honkin' 'extrovert moderns' was later carried over into the New Thing screams and scrabbles of Albert Ayler, Pharoah Sanders and Archie Shepp, plus the

133

soul stew of King Curtis and Jr. Walker.

Today, records may well carry 'Explicit Lyrics' warning stickers, but in the mid-50s, bible-thumpin' right-wing pressure groups mounted alarmist campaigns urging 'decent' white folk to protect their children from being corrupted by black music. It was much too late.

It wasn't a question of the Devil having the best tunes, but local black radio stations which impressionable young white teenagers tuned into *en masse*. In retaliation, access to white radio was denied to all but the odd 'untainted' black record that became too big to ignore.

To this end, white radio force-fed its young listeners inferior white 'covers' of black R&B jukebox hits.

Bill Haley and His Comets had already taken Joe Turner's 'Shake, Rattle And Roll' out of the bedroom and into the kitchen.

Things got worse – popular mainstream singer Georgia Gibbs sanitized Etta James' lusty 'Roll With Me Henry' by substituting 'Dance' for the raunchier 'Roll'. And even Communism would have been preferable to the spectre of Pat Boone, in his white bucks, ritually slaughtering dozens of black hits from 'I Almost Lost My Mind' (Ivory Joe Hunter) to 'Ain't That A Shame' (Fats Domino). Elsewhere, the male of the species busily attempted to curl an Elvis lip.

Women were another problem.

Whereas it was customary for young white female singers to adopt a more submissive role, a select few were allowed to gently smoulder. In stark contrast, there is a lineage from Bessie Smith and Julia Lee right through to Aretha Franklin and Tina Turner, of sexually-knowing, stuff-struttin' black Divas.

Above: A souvenir programme from Bill Haley's British tour in February 1957, the first by a US rock'n'roll band

Below: An early publicity shot of Chuck Berry

Right: The Treniers in *Don't Knock The Rock*

They appeared invincible, and throughout the 50s the irrepressible Dinah Washington, LaVern Baker, Ruth Brown, Etta James, Big Maybelle and Esther Phillips took immense pride in their assertiveness, dominating both the charts and major touring package shows.

In retrospect it has always been about attitude, be it Bird taking on all-comers at 52nd Street hangouts, Garner attempting to attention-grab by merely placing his ass on the Manhattan telephone directory before commencing to play, Wynonie causing would-be censors apoplexy with an array of lyrics copied from the toilet wall, or Tina Turner rising from an ever-battered wife situation to stomp stages in ultimate triumph -- in your face and in your heart.

But none more so than when, in 1956, a 30-year old black R&B singer-guitarist named Chuck Berry articulated, better than anyone else has ever done, about what it was like to be young and white and sweet little sixteen.

Above: Elvis Presley in *King Creole*

Left: Little Richard and band in *Don't Knock The Rock*

Right: R&B giant Ike Turner with vocalist/ wife Tina

135

The New Thing

Free form, new wave, avant garde, the new thing;
these were some of the more polite names for the
biggest revolution in jazz since the birth of be-bop.

BY THE MIDDLE of the 1950s, jazz was reaching another crossroads in a history that had already seen plenty of divergence. As bebop gave way to hard bop, the music seemed ready to implode. After the breathtaking innovations of Charlie Parker, there were few avenues left open to musicians exploring the familiar route of preset chord patterns and standard tunes. Horn and rhythm players could pile through the chord changes as they wished, but that still didn't change the chords. As the 50s progressed, some of the more adventurous players were chafing at bar lines and harmonic sequences. Perhaps the leading conservative dissident was saxophonist John Coltrane, whose 'sheets of sound' technique led him to try slamming through all the permutations of a single chord during an improvisation before moving on to the next one – and that sometimes meant shifting the entire harmonic base from beat to beat.

THE ORNETTE COLEMAN TRIO

There had to be another way out – and it was heralded properly in the work of two musicians in particular. There had been a few experiments in freedom before, most notably in a little-known 1949 recording by a Lennie Tristano group called 'Intuition'. In these the musicians simply played without recourse to a thematic path. That, however, was just a one-off experiment. It was in the work of Cecil Taylor and altoman Ornette Coleman that jazz became really and truly free. But this was for perhaps the first and last time.

An Ornette Coleman box set and (above) a programme from a 60s UK tour

Ornette Coleman

Checked in: 9 March, 1930, Forth Worth, Texas.

Instruments: alto sax, trumpet, violin

Famous for: Putting the avant garde cat amongst the bebop pigeons and throwing away all the rule books. In cahoots with trumpet player Don Cherry, Charlie Haden (bass) and either Billy Higgins or Ed Blackwell on (drums), he reinvented a whole area of jazz: a wild terrain where chord sequences were abandoned in favour of a melodic, yet confrontational, rhythmic pulse (harmolodics).

Evidence for the defence: His self explanatory Atlantic albums 'Tomorrow Is The Question', 'The Shape Of Jazz To Come', 'This Is Our Music' and 'Change Of The Century' were aptly titled examples of Coleman's take on things.
   Ornette, Hero or Heel: Just when his devotees became used to his untutored trumpet and violin gymnastics, then the formation of his all electric Prime Time Band (comprising twin guitars, bass and drums) caused a deep divide amongst his followers similiar to that experienced by Miles when he decided to attach a plug to everything.

Famous for saying: 'It was when I noticed that I was making mistakes that I realised that I was on the right track or something.'

Dues-Paying: Initially, fellow musicians regarded Ornette as plain crazy. As a result, he was regularly frozen out of jam sessions or paid not to play! In the face of such opposition, he worked as elevator operator in Los Angeles.

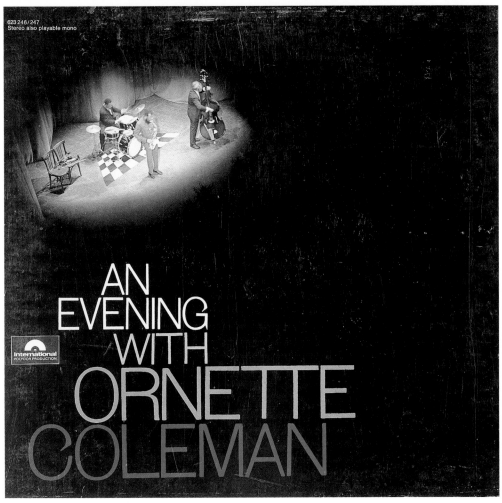

Coleman's music has become much more celebrated, but it was Taylor who first broached the idea of a new, free music within a jazz vocabulary. A New Yorker who had begun by playing piano in rhythm and blues bands, Taylor had studied the acknowledged masters of 20th Century composition as well as the jazz writing legacy, and somehow came up with a synthesis that was strikingly different to anything that had gone before – yet still kept a toehold in jazz tradition.

He admired Dave Brubeck and Horace Silver, and their influence can be felt in Taylor's earliest recordings, specifically the amazing 'Jazz Advance' album of 1956, which also featured soprano saxophonist Steve Lacy and stood out as the boldest kind of manifesto. Taylor worked regularly at New York's Five Spot club and was lionised by a small but dedicated coterie. His unique piano manner – pushing out of chordal and bar structures, using the piano as a percussion as well as a harmonic/melodic instrument, and basing themes around contrasting blocks of sound – was a shocking development away from accepted jazz terms. With his favourite players – alto saxophonist Jimmy Lyons and drummer Andrew Cyrille – he worked when he could and recorded occasionally during the next 20 years. His resolve toughened and his grasp stretched. By the end of the 1970's his contribution had grown magisterial enough to be both recognised and celebrated. Now in his sixties, his particular vision uncompromised by any kind of fusion or sellout, Taylor is a grandmaster by anyone's standards.

Still, back then, his work didn't have the impact of Ornette Coleman's first recordings. Coleman (born in 1930, the same year as Taylor) was originally from Texas – the signature wail of the Lone Star State resides in his saxophone sound to this day – and, like Taylor, he served his apprenticeship in various R&B bands. But he always seemed to hear differently to everybody else. In Los Angeles, he appeared as a sideman at various clubs, often working with a trumpeter and kindred

The leading new piano name to come out of the free jazz movement, Cecil Taylor

WHEN THE CHARLES MINGUS Sextet arrived in Europe in April 1964, it immediately became clear that the outcome of each concert was dependent on whatever mood took the leader. At the best of times a difficult person to deal with, the Big Man's usual kick-ass-take-no-prisoners demeanour became amplified due to the fact that he was enduring the agonies of a 'crash diet' – claiming to have shed 90-pounds of body weight in 90 days – with the aid of numerous prescribed drugs held in a briefcase which never left his side.

From day one there were problems from the side effects of the medication, in escalating confrontations with bureaucracy, tour operators, hotel staff, police, fans and, especially, the press.

It was no surprise that his musicians, except Eric Dolphy, kept to themselves. Dolphy, by nature gentle, was never intimidated by Mingus but nonetheless was wise enough to restrict his on-going dialogue with his mood-changing mentor strictly to a musical level. Without doubt, their on-stage exchanges were the high point of every performance, as can be gleaned from the many official and unofficial tapes, now released on CD, of the European concerts.

Then there was The Beatles. Mingus, as ever very conscious of finance, found it difficult to come to terms with the success enjoyed by 'those four guys from England with the funny haircuts'. Reluctantly, he had to admit to liking some of Lennon and McCartney's melody lines, once saying – albeit tongue in cheek (or was it?) – that if a fifth members was needed, then he was more than ready for the job. Indeed, there were those close to Mingus who believed he secretly felt his services would be called upon. The phone never rang.

Prior to his European onslaught, and, as part of his personal 'program of respectability', Mingus insisted that in future people should address him as 'Charles' rather than 'Charlie' by which he had been universally known since early in his career.

Resplendent in three-piece suits, bowler hat and spats, and carrying a walking cane, he was totally unaware of the comic effect his new 'respectable' image had on disbelieving European audiences.

At every border, his travelling pharmacy came under scrutiny, and on one occasion the discovery of a switch-blade knife almost resulted in his incarceration.

To European audiences the Mingus Sextet was either like a breath of fresh air or the hot breath of the beast, improvisation at its most basic performed with a frenetic energy that demanded total concentration, a purist dream or nightmare, depending upon the purist.

spirit named Don Cherry, and although he spent long hours working at musical theory, he managed to fashion a style of improvising that bypassed the harmonic obstacle course of bebop altogether. Instead, his music was as open and free as folk-song with melodies drenched in blues tonality but absent from those chordal restrictions of the conventional AABA song form. It called for a particularly special kind of inspiration, but he and Cherry – and, subsequently, the bassist Charlie Haden and drummers Billy Higgins and Charles Moffett – all created an intuitive interplay that dispensed entirely with bebop's stringent rulebook.

His first recordings didn't come until 1958, when the West Coast label Contemporary commissioned two albums, 'Something Else!!' and 'Tomorrow Is The Question!'.

Under the patronage of the MJQ's John Lewis, it was, though, his subsequent move to New York, and a contract with Atlantic Records, which brought him the attention and notoriety that ushered in a new wave in jazz. Albums like 'The Shape Of Jazz To Come' and 'This Is Our Music' rocked musicians and listeners alike, and Coleman's work for the label reached a sort of climax with 'Free Jazz', a 37-minute collective improvisation by a double quintet featuring Eric Dolphy and Freddie Hubbard, an augmented band which essentially paved the way for everything that the avant garde would produce.

What held back chaos was the lovely, lyrical sound of this music. Coleman was as interested in beauty as much as he was in chance, and there was something inevitable and poetic about his music, as

Mingus

IMPRESSARIAAT PAUL ACKET — DEN HAAG
Theresiastraat 11—13 Telefoon: (070) 722546
in samenwerking met
N.V. NEDERLANDS THEATERBUREAU — DEN HAAG

VRIJDAG 10 APRIL 1964
CONCERTGEBOUW — AMSTERDAM

CHARLES MINGUS
sextet
met

ERIC DOLPHY
altsax — basclarinet — fluit

CLIFFORD JORDAN
tenorsax

JOHNNY COLES
trompet

JAKI BYARD
piano

DANNY RICHMOND
drums

Naar Nederland gebracht in samenwerking met
FESTIVAL PRODUCTIONS INC. (George Wein, president)

Na de presentatie van concerten in dit seizoen 1963-64
met

JOHN COLTRANE QUARTET
ROLAND KIRK QUARTET
MAX ROACH QUARTET
THELONIOUS MONK QUARTET
en het
CHARLES MINGUS SEXTET

op vrijdagavond 24 april, 8.00 uur in het
Concertgebouw:

NORMAN GRANZ presenteert

ELLA FITZGERALD
OSCAR PETERSON TRIO
met Ray Brown en Ed Thigpen

ROY ELDRIDGE QUARTET
met Tommy Flanagan, Gus Johnson en Bill Yancey

Prijzen der plaatsen: ƒ 6,50, ƒ 8,—, ƒ 10,50 en ƒ 13,—.
INclusief plaatsbespreking en vestiaire. Kaartverkoop en
plaatsbespreking aan het Concertgebouw vanaf woensdag
15 april, dagelijks 10-3 uur (behalve op 18-19 april).

Wilt u d.m.v. berichtkaarten op de hoogte blijven van de
door ons te organiseren jazz-concerten: geef uw naam
en adres dan schriftelijk per briefkaart op aan Impressariaat Paul Acket, Theresiastraat 11, Den Haag.

CHARLIE MINGUS

The sheer physical demands of the tour took their toll with trumpeter Johnny Coles collapsing on stage in Paris, while trying for a high note – a result of an unsuccessful ulcer operation in the States. Eric Dolphy, who decided to stay on in Europe, unexpectedly succumbed to a diabetic death, on June 29,1964, in a Berlin hospital. He was 36. Mingus, plagued by demons and money problems, gave up engagements for almost the remainder of the decade.

Above: Pages from a Dutch souvenir of a 1964 appearance by Mingus, signed by all the band.
Right: Mingus samples from his case of pills, note the switch-blade!

The Art Ensemble of Chicago (l-r) Joseph Jarman, Malachi Favors, Lester Bowie, Don Moye and Roscoe Mitchell. Opposite, the great Eric Dolphy

free as it purported to be. He remains a maverick, unguessable man, having moved through his own kind of fusion in the 70s and 80s and setting himself up in the 90s as the founder of Harmolodic, originally a free concept, now also a record label.

When Coleman temporarily retired from the scene in 1962, there were other players ready to take up the torch. Eric Dolphy was in fact primarily a bebop man, but he was intrigued by the potential that Coleman's music offered, and in such pieces as his extraordinary alto sax solo 'Love Me' or much of the music on the celebrated 'Out To Lunch' album for Blue Note, he pushes against the barriers of form with a rare intensity.

John Coltrane, who hired Dolphy for one of his bands, attempted to follow Coleman's lead into areas that were becoming increasingly dense, crowded and furious: his own collective record called 'Ascension', is like a steam bath next to the cooler atmosphere of Ornette's music. Still obsessed with form and release, Coltrane toiled on tirelessly until his death in 1967.

Younger players were inspired in the same way that a previous generation had been by bebop. But they were fewer in number, and found recording opportunities hard to come by. One of the most significant was the Cleveland-born saxophonist Albert Ayler. He went to Europe while in the army in 1959, and stayed there to play with Cecil Taylor in Copenhagen. So, when he made his major recordings in New York, for the ESP independent label, he was already immersed in the stuff of the avant garde.

Still, nobody could have been prepared for the astounding 'Spiritual Unity', a trio session with bassist Gary Peacock and the drummer Sunny Murray, that features the fiercest and most uncompromising sax playing on record. Ayler, like Coleman, used simple themes and motifs, yet transformed them into various cathartic hymns and strange, impassioned squalls of sound. He blazed a

unique and enigmatic path through the rest of the 60s and his mysterious death in 1970 was like an epitaph for the music of the era.

As jazz did its best to fight off the assault of The Beatles and its commercial appeal died, the music's free movement seemed a little lost in space. Coleman and Taylor worked on throughout the 60s but were reduced to a hard-core of admirers. The New York Art Quartet, with saxophonists Archie Shepp and John Tchicai and the trombonist Roswell Rudd, had some impact, as did the work of players such as Marion Brown, Bobby Bradford and Sonny Simmons; but, while they had their following, and while their art mirrored some of the volatility of their times, it was the music that seemed exclusionist rather than inspiring to most. The players were scattered and isolated within their own musicial communities.

Except in one city: Chicago, which had largely missed out on much of the excitement of bop and hard bop. In 1965, the pianist Muhal Richard Abrams founded a collective called the Association for the Advancement of Creative Musicians which was to prove crucial in focusing the work of many of the key players of the 70s and 80s.

Getting to work with organising concerts, workshops and master-classes, the AACM helped to midwife the arrival of a number of performing bands, the most important of them being the Art Ensemble Of Chicago, originally a quartet of Lester Bowie, Roscoe Mitchell, Malachi Favors and Joseph Jarman, who were subsequently joined by drummer Don Moye.

This team of multi-instrumentalists played music that brimmed with exuberant virtuosity, touching on every part of the jazz tradition while exploring all the freedoms which the avant garde had made available, and they weren't afraid to introduce satire or theatre or whatever they felt would work within their own idiom. In the 90s, they continue to perform, though some of their visionary flash has dimmed somewhat over the years.

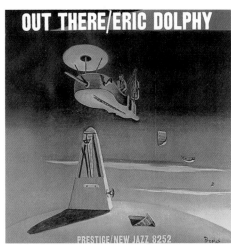

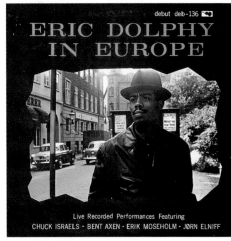

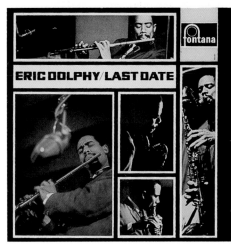

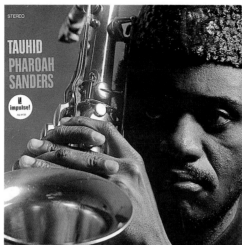

TAUHID
PHAROAH
SANDERS

TALES OF
CAPTAIN
BLACK

pharoah sanders quintet

GRACHAN MONCUR III
LEE MORGAN
JACKIE MC LEAN
BOBBY HUTCHERSON
BOB CRANSHAW
ANTHONY WILLIAMS
EVOLUTION

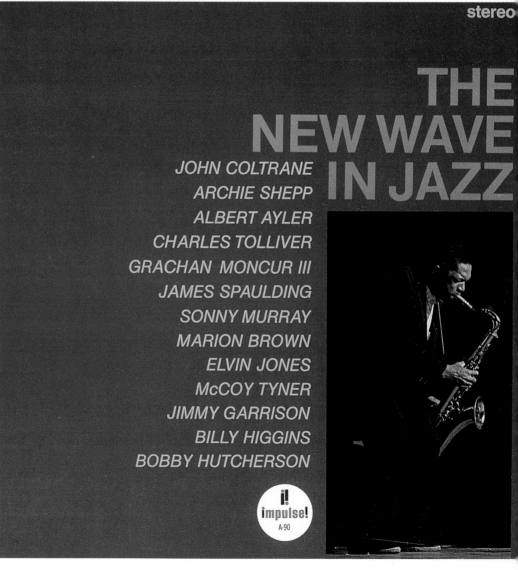

stereo

THE
NEW WAVE
IN JAZZ

JOHN COLTRANE
ARCHIE SHEPP
ALBERT AYLER
CHARLES TOLLIVER
GRACHAN MONCUR III
JAMES SPAULDING
SONNY MURRAY
MARION BROWN
ELVIN JONES
McCOY TYNER
JIMMY GARRISON
BILLY HIGGINS
BOBBY HUTCHERSON

impulse!
A-90

A Love Supreme/John Coltrane

MOONDOG

Theme
Stamping Ground
Symphonique #3
Symphonique #6
Mini-Sym #1
I-Allegro
II-Andante adagio
III-Vivace

Chicago also produced other major personalities in the new music, such as Anthony Braxton, the saxman/composer whose works for many orchestras are mildly infamous and whose vast range has been better documented on record than any other figure in the avant garde; and Henry Threadgill, another saxophonist/writer, whose groups Air, the Sextet (with seven players) and Very Very Circus have cut a colourful path through jazz's subsequent progress. If the city's wider influence on modern music has waned at all in the past ten years, it still remains a remarkable centre of ideas.

One figure who remained completely avant garde until his death, yet who didn't really fit properly into any school or system, was the bandleader Sun Ra. Originally Sonny Blount, he was an arranger for Fletcher Henderson. Ra tried to convince the jazz world that he was actually from Saturn, and that along with his Solar Arkestra he had come to help mankind out of the darkness.

If he never really did this, he still made a lot of enlightening and joyful music along the way. From his beginnings in the 50s until his death in 1993, Ra made hundreds of albums, for his own Saturn label as well as for many other companies. These albums document a compositional output that rivals that of Ellington or Monk. He also inspired an incredible loyalty among many of his key players: men such as John Gilmore, Marshall Allen and Pat Patrick stayed with Ra for literally decades. With his jostling, cacophonous and explosive music, Sun Ra borrowed and bartered his way though the jazz vocabulary while remaining *sui generis* to the end of his life.

If the avant garde was seen as jazz's furthest outpost in the 60s, it was a little displaced by the advent of jazz-rock in the 70s. If that genre turned out to be somewhat musically conservative, it still seemed a lot more glamorous and exciting to a new audience than the one-time new thing. While Europe sustained fresh flights of development, America could boast only the most modest advances. Braxton and Threadgill were being extensively documented, but other scenes had to settle for a small span of attention. In the 80s, it didn't help that the new interest in jazz was centred around the arrival of the neotraditionalists such as the Marsalis family. But there was also a new underground which was starting up in New York, Texas and California.

Above: Moondog (Louis Hardin), a blind musician who lived on the New York streets, was a familiar sight in Viking helmet and robes. He made many records, some with home-made instruments, others with large orchestrations

CD CHECKLIST
ORNETTE COLEMAN The Shape of Jazz to Come (Atlantic), Change of the Century (Atlantic), This Is Our Music (Atlantic), Free Jazz (Atlantic)
CHARLES MINGUS Mingus Dynasty (Columbia), Mingus Oh Yeah (Atlantic)
JOHN COLTRANE Olé Coltrane (Atlantic), My Favourite Things (Atlantic), A Love Supreme (Impulse), Ascension (Impulse)
ERIC DOLPHY Out To Lunch (Blue Note)
ARCHIE SHEPP New Thing At Newport (Impulse)
PHAROAH SANDERS Tauhid (Impulse)
ART ENSEMBLE OF CHICAGO Fanfare For The Warriors (Atlantic)
MARION BROWN Three For Shepp (Impulse)
DON CHERRY Symphony For Improvisers (Blue Note)

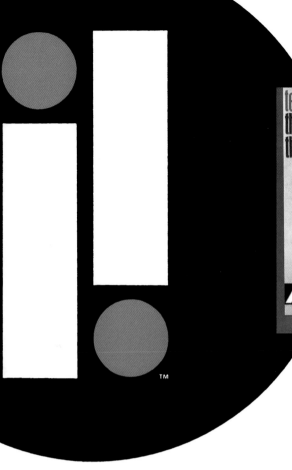

Left: The logo for the highly influential Impulse label, at the sharp end of the jazz avant garde

New York's live jazz was buoyed up in the mid-70s by a number of musician-run lofts that hosted regular sessions, including Sam Rivers's Studio Rivbea. New voices such as Julius Hemphill, David Murray and Oliver Lake were as firmly in the jazz tradition as Wynton Marsalis, but their take on it also encompassed what Ayler and his contemporaries had achieved.

The city also spawned a school that came to be thought of as the Lower East Side set. It numbered player/organisers such as saxman John Zorn, whose fractured aesthetic, bred a new kind of avant garde 'hardcore', and also a host of musicians whose backgrounds owed as much to rock as any strict jazz lineage: Bill Frisell, Tim Berne, Wayne Horvitz and dozens of others. The Knitting Factory, a small club in the city, became world-famous as the unofficial headquaters for this kind of music.

California had its own little outcropping of performers. In the wake of Bobby Bradford and John Carter in the 60s, there was a small coterie led by musicians such as the reed specialist Vinny Golia. In Texas, Dennis Gonzalez carried on the initiatives inspired by Coleman many years before.

Most of these players have had to struggle to get any kind of attention for their work. Though seniors such as Coleman and Taylor have been in the game long enough to have been honoured and at least relatively rewarded for their efforts, today's avant gardists have scarcely come in from the cold. What has changed is the teeming environment they work in. Compared to the 'pure' direction of Coleman's day, there are numberless situations which such players could find themselves in. This perhaps illustrates how jazz itself now travels, in many, many directions.

100

Fact File

SUN RA'S real name was Herman and he came to Earth somewhere in Alabama, circa 1914. As Sonny Blunt he made a modest name for himself in swing circles, but it wasn't until 1948 that he deigned to inform the universe that he was, in fact, Le Sony'r Ra (later shortened to Sun Ra) a Cosmic Communicator whose role in life was to bring The Creator's message to Planet Earth. His vehicle was the Arkestra, a garishly-robed ever-mutating big band, mainly fashioned around tenor saxman John Gilmore. What emerged was Space Jazz, weird but often wonderful, with the colourful Ra dispensing free-flowing stomps from Saturn, and music myths from Mars. Though his (often self-financed/limited edition) album releases caused computer failure – around 120 of them were known to exist last time IBM was put to the test – in some ways they often didn't contain as many tunes from the asteroid belt as might have been expected. Eventually, in 1993, his sonic fun run came to an end and he headed for some distant Pyramid in the sky in best ET mode.

Soul To Soul

With gospel chords and call-and-response arrangements, soul jazz was a back-to-the-roots movement that recalled the sound of sacred Black American church music as much as the secular heritage of the blues.

HORACE SILVER, ART BLAKEY and Cannonball Adderley were the first to admit that all those classic small band sides Ray Charles cut for Atlantic Records, featuring soul-drenched saxmen David 'Fathead' Newman and Hank Crawford, determined the sanctified stance of their own ground-breaking quintets.

In 1959, Ray Charles' 'What'd I Say' may well have been banned by many radio stations for what was considered as sexually explicit references, but that didn't impede it's progress to No.6 on the US charts or its lasting influence upon jazz and pop groups alike.

As early as the mid-50s, the terms 'funk' and 'soul' (both being later applied to pop music) were widely employed amongst the hard-boppers to describe gospel-informed, down-home, call-and-response blues.

Horace Silver: 'When I was a boy, I used to catch negro religious programmes on the radio and they really swung. Blues and gospel music was what really turned me on. I also used to play boogie-woogie piano. So all this crept into my work along with swing and bebop and it all meshed together.'

Because jazz has frequently got its back to the wall, it needs every opportunity it can grab. Soul served such a purpose. Soul was just a natural outpouring of Hard Bop and, for the most part popularized by many of the genre's stellar soloists – Ex-Blakey sidemen Horace Silver, Lee Morgan, Lou Donaldson, Bobby Timmons, Hank Mobley, Donald Byrd plus Grant Green, Gene Ammons, Stanley Turrentine, Willis 'Gator' Jackson, The Jazz Crusaders, The Three Sounds, pianists Ramsey Lewis, Herbie Hancock, Les McCann, Junior Mance, Ray Bryant and a whole legion of soon-to-be-popular Hammond organists.

It quickly became evident that it was Silver's highly percussive two-fisted piano punching that shaped Hard Bop into gospel-drenched backbeat soul jazz as he continually knocked out such jukebox jazz hits as 'The Preacher', 'Opus De Funk', 'Doodlin'', 'Senor Blues', 'Sister Sadie' and more, as rapidly as that other heavyweight Muhammad Ali dispatched successive opponents.

Left: Creator of soul standards like 'The Preacher', 'Doodlin' ' and 'Opus De Funk', Horace Silver
Opposite: Alto soul server 'Cannonball' Adderley

ON THE SPOT with **Horace Silver**

BLUE NOTE PRESENTS HORACE SILVER IN HIS FIRST-ON-THE-SPOT RECORDING.

In these rousing performances of four new exciting compositions, Horace proves his ability to communicate deeply and directly to his audience. The applause that greets the finish of Filthy Mc-Nasty is not made by any "jive" audience. These people are genuinely knocked out and they let the group know it.

When it comes to "doin' the thing", Horace Silver and the Quintet really know how to do it.

doin' the thing the horace silver quintet at the village gate

with Blue Mitchell, Junior Cook, Gene Taylor, Roy Brooks.
Filthy McNasty — Doin' The Thing — Kiss Me Right — The Gringo — The Theme.
BLUE NOTE 4076

FINGER POPPIN'
BLP 4008*

THE STYLINGS OF SILVER
BLP 1562

SIX PIECES OF SILVER
BLP 1539

BLOWIN' THE BLUES AWAY
BLP 4017*

HORACE SILVER AND THE JAZZ MESSENGERS
BLP 1518

HORACE-SCOPE
BLP 4042*

*Also available in Stereo

For Complete Catalog Write To
BLUE NOTE
Records Inc.
43 West 61st Street, New York 23

Above: Dubbed 'the Genius' and the 'High Priest of Soul', Ray Charles
Right: Charles with his full touring Orchestra plus The Raelettes

Below: A huge draw on the American jazz club circuit, mainstream chart success eventually came to Les McCann in the early 70s with the million-selling single 'Compared To What'

Les McCann

WORLD PACIFIC RECORDS | Pacific Jazz

Horace Silver: 'The whole thing happened almost by accident. I was playing a lot of dance dates around New York, and at the end of the night, to show the people that the dance was over we used to play "Show Me The Way To Go Home." The chord changes were so simple to play on and it felt so good, that I decided to sit down and compose an original melody line based on those chords. The result was "The Preacher".'

If Silver devised this instantly appealing formula, it was Cannonball Adderley's articulation that took it to the people. The emergence of Julian 'Cannonball' Adderley coincided with the death of Charlie Parker in March 1955, leading to the young altoist from Florida being unnecessarily hailed by some grieving commentators as 'The New Bird'. Fortunately, Adderley was able to distance himself from such hysteria, first, being bookended by Miles Davis and John Coltrane, in the trumpeter's sextet (1957-59) and then by leading popular small combos with his cornet-blowing brother Nat. In time, Cannonball would become acknowledged as the most influential post-Bird sharp-shooter.

While jazz frequently informs pop, there's no denying it's pop that regularly instructs jazz in the art of selling its wares. Cannonball Adderley was acutely aware of this, back in 1967, when he saw his recording of 'Mercy, Mercy, Mercy' effortlessly scale the pop charts. Cannonball: 'We have a generation of kids who were raised on a diet of music; they all buy records and have transistor radios and a radio in the car, but they don't get to hear jazz on them. For the mass public today, the jazz scene includes Ramsey Lewis, Wes Montgomery, Stan Getz, Jimmy Smith, Charlie Byrd . . . our group, luckily, and maybe a couple more. What used to be a jazz audience, the young crowd, has turned to other forms of music.'

Soul was an attempt to win them back, and to a degree it succeeded. Soul was but one of a number of jazz strains that ran concurrent with America's turbulent Civil Rights Movement and the rise of Black Power. The gloved clenched-fist scrabbles and screams of the avant garde were another, but it was safe-sounding soul that sold in pop proportions.

Cannonball Adderley: 'We were pressured quite heavily by Riverside records when they discovered there was a word called 'soul'. We became, from an image point of view, soul jazz artists. They kept promoting us that way and I kept deliberately fighting it, to the extent that it became a game.'

Soul as roots music may well have been blues-based, but it didn't conjure up the kind of negativity commonly associated with the bad-luck-and-trouble variety. Spurred on by a Baptist back-beat, soul was seen as the newest state-of-grace which, in many instances, still carried many of the same values inherent in R&B - most notably raucous trace elements of saxmen Earl Bostic and Louis Jordan and uncompromising rhythm sections. It was very much a black thing. In time, the much-used phrase 'blue-eyed soul' would surface to denote white performers seemingly touched by the hand of God!

Originally known as the Night Hawks in the 50s, they were called the Jazz Crusaders in the 60s, evolving through soul jazz into soul music *per se*, and in the 1970s explored jazz-rock, by then simply known as The Crusaders

Below: The original (Jazz) Crusaders featuring (l to r) Stix Hooper (percussion), Joe Sample (keyboards), Wilton Felder on tenor sax and Wayne Henderson on trombone

While Main Street retail outlets were the primary source for weekly sales figures, many jazz records achieved impressive sales without ever gracing the charts. Art Blakey's 'The Preacher' sold well in excess of 100,000 copies as did numerous singles on the Blue Note, Riverside, Prestige, Chess, and Pacific Jazz labels by Horace Silver, Bobby Timmons, Gene Ammons, Brother Jack McDuff, Les McCann, Stanley Turrentine and others.

The Ramsey Lewis Trio may have become chart regulars with their clap-a-long covers of Dobie Grey ('The "In" Crowd'/1965) – a top five smash, The McCoys ('Hang On Sloopy'/1965), The Beatles ('A Hard Day's Night'/1966), but it was the pianoman's Top 20 entry 'Wade In The Water'(1966) that dripped genuine soul grease.

With unashamed haste, Young-Holt Unlimited (Lewis' former bass player Eldee Young and drummer 'Red' Holt) promptly cloned the formula for hit singles 'Wack Wack'/1966 (No.40) and 'Soulful Strut' /1968 (No.3) while organmeister ('The Incredible') Jimmy Smith notched up one dozen Hot 100 entries between 1962 and 1968.

As with rock, the big reputation-building money was in album sales. Lee Morgan may well have nudged into the lower reaches of the singles charts, in 1964, with 'The Sidewinder' but it was the album of the same name that yielded the thickest bankroll by reaching number 25. Recorded 'live', the combined sales of Cannonball Adderley's 'Jazz Workshop Revisted' (No.11) and 'Mercy, Mercy, Mercy!' (No. 13) ran to hundreds of thousands, four Ramsey Lewis albums made the Top 10 with 'The "In" Crowd' peaking at Number 2 in November 1965, while no less than ten Jimmy Smith LPs spent a total of 107 weeks on the Top 40.

Even before signing to Pacific Jazz where he cut a string of phenomenally successful albums including 'Les McCann Plays The Truth' and 'The Shout', the L.A,-based pianoman was already a local celebrity. On the recommendation of Miles Davis, Cannonball offered him the piano chair in his quintet, but he decided to stick with his own trio to pursue what became a full-blown career.

Soon, McCann became almost as big a box office attraction as Silver and Cannonball. Cross-over chart honours evaded McCann until 1970, when, with tenorman Eddie Harris in tow, his impromptu made-in-Montreux 'Swiss Movement' album and attendant single 'Compared To What', attracted over a million buyers. In 1995, 'Compared To What' would form an integral part of the acclaimed Martin Scorsese movie *Casino*.

In double quick time, soul jazz assembled a much-covered repertoire which, aside from Silver's originals was supplemented by 'Sack O'Woe' (Cannonball Adderley); 'Work Song' (Nat Adderley); 'Moanin'', 'This Here' (aka 'Dis Here'), 'Dat Dere' (Bobby Timmons) and 'Wade In The Water'.

Despite the popularity of such tunes, the big soul-jazz single was 'Mercy, Mercy, Mercy' by Cannonball Adderley. Written by pianist Joe Zawinul, 'Mercy, Mercy, Mercy' peaked at Number 11, (and went on to eventually sell one million copies) during the last week in February 1967 on a pop chart dominated by The Rolling Stones ('Ruby Tuesday') and that also included The Supremes, The Monkees, Buffalo Springfield, Sonny & Cher and the Electric Prunes. The on-going strength of Cannonball Adderley's popularity resulted in his appearance at the Monterey Jazz Festival being incorporated in Clint Eastwood's 1971 thriller *Play Misty For Me*.

Sadly Cannonball died in 1975, age 47, leaving Lou Donaldson as the strongest link in a chain of alto-blowin' popularisers that ranged from Earl Bostic and Tab Smith through to Maceo Parker and David Sanborn. Donaldson's expertise was in refining Bird's word for mass-market appreciation without ever falling foul of passing trends.

Soul was as evident in the the majestic work of Charles Mingus on 'Blues And Roots' (1959), 'Mingus Ah Um' (1959) and 'Oh, Yeah' (1961) as it was in the music of Ray Charles and Horace Silver.

Even the emerging avant gardists weren't oblivious to the quasi-political implications of soul. While the more militant factions of the jazz fraternity used their music for expressing anger, frustration and rage, others regarded soul as an alternative means of self-definition, as a way of taking a more positive stance in celebrating their blackness.

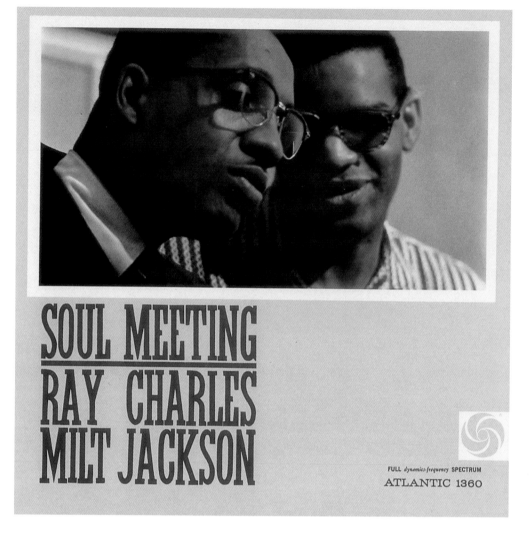

'All music is related. A gospel music background is important to a jazz musician, for it draws out feeling. The important thing in jazz is to feel your music, really feel it and believe it.'   Ray Charles

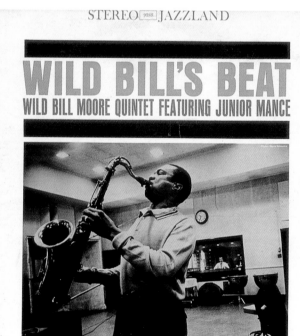

CD CHECKLIST
CANNONBALL ADDERLEY
Mercy, Mercy, Mercy (Capitol), Live At The Lighthouse (Riverside/OJC)
DONALD BYRD
The Best Of Donald Byrd (Blue Note)
LEE MORGAN
The Sidewinder (Blue Note)
HORACE SILVER
The Best Of Horace Silver (Blue Note)
BOBBY TIMMONS
This Here Is Bobby Timmons (Riverside/OJC)

FULL *dynamics frequency* SPECTRUM

ATLANTIC 1259

THE GREAT RAY CHARLES

STEREO ARGO LPS 704 STEREO

SOUL COOKIN'
THORNEL SCHWARTZ WITH BILL LESLIE

STEREO ATLANTIC SD 1455

HANK CRAWFORD / AFTER HOURS

'I hate to see people making contrived synthesised funk. There is a pure kind of soul music, you can't deliberately play funky jazz just for the sake of being funky.' Horace Silver

PRESTIGE

Soul Food Bobby Timmons

les mccann
joe pass
paul chambers
paul humphrey

SHINY SILK STOCKINGS · SERMONETTE
LI'L DARLIN' · BACK AT THE CHICKEN SHACK
SACK O' WOE · SISTER SADIE · BAG'S GROOVE
WORK SONG · GROOVE YARD · SONNYMOON FOR TWO

pacific jazz records

the **JAZZ CRUSADERS**

RECORDED LIVE AT THE NEWPORT AND PACIFIC JAZZ FESTIVALS · 1966

THE NEWPORT FESTIVALS

THE CANNONBALL ADDERLEY QUINTET AT THE LIGHTHOUSE

RECORDED "LIVE" AT THE LIGHTHOUSE, HERMOSA BEACH, CALIFORNIA
FEATURING NAT ADDERLEY

RIVERSIDE

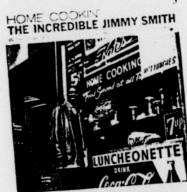

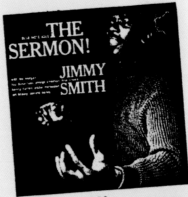

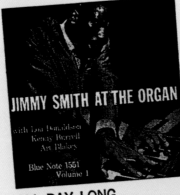
The Organ

The vibrato-heavy Hammond with its trademark reverberating bass debuted in 1935, but with the soul movement it became a genre in its own right.

'I WAS A PIANO PLAYER, you know that? Some of the clubs you play in, they're too cheap to tune the piano. Art Tatum told me he'd play pianos where all the ivory was off the keys, scruff your nails, scruff your fingers, pianos where some keys weren't there at all.

He's a blind man, right? He'd run his hands over the keys one time, and when he comes to do his performance, you wouldn't hear none of the bad keys. He's memorised them! That's what we call hop-over-the-bridge. I switched to muthafuckin' organ because the pianos were out of tune. I can sound bad on my own self. I don't need the help!

Now wait a minute! Count Basie was not an organ player. He just liked to tinkle with it. Sun Ra couldn't play shit, I should've shot him. Billy Preston is a church organ player. I never heard him play anything. Most guys just play with two hands, man, but you got all those pedals down there. Why don't the rock players play those pedals? Because they're too fuckin' lazy to learn them. So they make more money than we do. I'm an expert at it and I don't make no fuckin' money. Who do I like? Fats Waller. I went and played on the same damn organ he'd played in Amsterdam Cathedral. Believe me, he must have practised at least fifteen days before he recorded. There's a lotta work to it. You got dampers, you got the pedals – it's like having intercourse with about five midgets down there. "No, no no – not your turn – git me off – git away!" So much shit to do, man. I like all my pupils – Don Patterson, Jack McDuff, Groove Holmes, Shirley Scott, Larry Young, George Fame. Everybody's playing Jimmy Smith, believe me. Freddie Roach is a Jimmy Smith copy but he tries to cover up the clichés. John Patton, he's a fair organ player, average, not dynamite. They're my understudies.

When I teach, I'm down there on the floor putting their feet on the pedals. When I taught Shirley Scott . . . Shirley's wearing this short

154

A Century Of **JAZZ**

trio with John McLaughlin. I liked them, but no one goes beyond what I play because they don't practise, they don't listen, they don't adventure.

I bought my first organ and I left it in the warehouse. My father had just plastered the warehouse owner's house so I asked if I could practise there. I stayed in there for six months. I had a little room in back and I took my lunch just like a guy who was working in the warehouse. I put up a big chart of the pedals so I wouldn't have to look down. That's how I taught myself to pedal. I could look up and see where C was, D was, D-flat. When I came outta that fuckin' warehouse I was just like a wild stallion! I'd locked up on the sound I get on the records – that's just three flutes to a percussion – and everybody's trying to find that sound! I'd paid for

my truck, and I was ready! I hit a club called Spider Kelly in 1954. Everybody started runnin'! See, I'd asked Wild Bill Davis how long it'd take me to learn organ. He told me it'd take fifteen years alone to learn the pedals. Fifteen years! I'd have a fuckin' beard! I was playing opposite him in the same club four months after that!

He felt bad, bad, bad baaaad. "Git this young muthafucker away from me!" I was playing with that Oklahoma funk that I got from Charlie Christian. That POW! That POP! That PUNCH! Charlie played all down notes and it gives that impact like a horn. I'm not a keyboardist – I'm a horn player, I'm a voice.'

dress. I say, "Shirley – close the gates. I can't teach with the gates open." After that, she played in a long dress. Larry Young, he had a 15 shoe. His one foot would cover four pedals. I had to teach him to side-toe. He was about six foot six. He died when Anthony Williams had that Lifetime

Jimmy Smith

OUTSIDE OF THE CHURCH, the organ seldom earned good press. For years, it's public image had it pitched somewhere between a rinky-dink ice rink and a wheezing monstrosity with acute catarrhal problems. As a front line jazz instrument, the organ appeared to have no real future despite brief flirtations involving the likes of Fats Waller, Count Basie and Milt Buckner. It was about as mobile as a cumbersome Sherman tank and cursed with a deeply depressing tone that immediately conjured up images of musty funeral parlours and Ol' Rugged Cross radio evangelism.

But things were very different across the tracks. In those familiar neighbourhood store-front churches, the gospel passionately preached wasn't the guilt-ridden fire-and-brimstone variety, but one genuinely aimed at uplifting souls and offering salvation to the disenfranchised. In that context, the organ took on a joyous central role accompanied by much feverish hand-clappin', rattling tambourines and later, additional support from piano, guitar and drums. Even bar-walkin' tenor saxes weren't discouraged. It was a sound that rocked hallowed walls, filled congregations with optimism and served notice on Satan that he didn't have all the best tunes.

It was here that talents as diverse as Sam Cooke, Aretha Franklin, Billy Preston, Ray Charles, James Brown and John Coltrane drew life-affirming inspiration. And seeing as so many black musicians initially came from a church background, it seemed only natural that such righteous influences would eventually surface.

Although up to the mid-50s black American inspirational music was still dominated by some dramatically flamboyant piano stylings, the electric organ as built by Hammond and Wurlitzer almost simultaneously contemporised its role in both church and jazz. In the latter, it was basically a question of economics.

The termination of World War Two meant a tightening of belts. As the war machine ground to a halt, fast money was harder to come by and disposable income dollars were staying in the wallet. Suddenly organ, guitar and drums and, more frequently, sax, became the ideal club combo, capable of kicking up as much dust as a big band and at a fraction of the cost.

Former Louis Jordan keyboard star Wild Bill Davis and then the popular duo of tenorman Eddie 'Lockjaw' Davis and grand-slam organist Shirley Scott were among the first to reveal the commercial possibilities of this once neglected instrument. Soon organ-led combos would briefly supersede two horns, piano, bass and drums as the archetypal jazz line-up. For years, the electric organ had suffered the same kind of persona non grata position within jazz, that the saxophone had previously held a few decades earlier. While it took Coleman Hawkins to elevate the tenor sax

as a bona fide jazz instrument, in later years Philly-born Jimmy Smith almost singlehandedly created a new role in jazz for the hitherto much-vilified electric organ.

Jimmy Smith revolutionized the organ's place as a legitimate jazz instrument through a series of Blue Note albums that began with his upfront versions of 'The Preacher' and 'The Champ' on 'A New Star – A New Sound'. Whereas tenor totin' Young Guns are always looking to make their reputation at the expense of someone else's, organists wisely avoided being drawn into some kind of one-sided 'High Noon' confrontation with Jimmy Smith whose total supremacy has never been challenged. He wasn't nicknamed 'The Incredible' without good reason. Such a dominance over one instrument has guaranteed Jimmy Smith a place in the virtuoso category occupied by Bird, Diz, Pres and Miles.

Jimmy McGriff, a self-confessed fan of Smith and a chart star via his instrumental remake of Ray Charles' 'I Got A Woman', sidestepped the question, insisting 'What I play isn't really jazz . . . it's sort of in between. Just old time swing with a jazz effect on it.'

And all this action wasn't just restricted to jazz, the electric organ played an integral part in the development of R&B and soul music and, later, mainstream pop. From the myriad budget organ combos of the early-50s, by way of such million-plus selling milestones as 'Honky Tonk' (Bill Doggett), 'Green Onions' (Booker T & The MGs), 'Billy's Bag' (Billy Preston), 'You Can't Sit Down' (Phil Upchurch), 'I Got A Woman' (Jimmy McGriff), the organ ran second only to the electric guitar as pop's main sound.

MOST OF THE FIRST WAVE of organ pumpers such as Larry Young, Freddie Roach, Baby Face Willette and Big John Patton came from R&B road bands, including those of Lloyd Price, Big Jay McNeely and Johnny Otis. As with Baby Face Willette, Kansas City-slicker Big John Patton was another Lou Donaldson discovery. Patton's rhythm partners were Grant Green on guitar and Ben Dixon (drums); together they evolved into Blue Note's 'electric' house band.

Furthermore, it was Patton's 'Along Came John' album which, three thousand miles due East of Rudy Van Gelder's New Jersey studio, promptly influenced the Hammond 'n' Horn bands of Georgie Fame and Zoot Money, then resident at London's famed Flamingo Club.

Screamin' Brother Jack McDuff was also a prime mover in the instrument's popularity. A mainstay of the Prestige operation (over two dozen albums in six years), Brother Jack fended off all-comers to retain his coveted position as chitlin' circuit top gun. This McDuff achieved, sharing the frontline with tough tenors that

included Willis 'Gator' Jackson, Gene Ammons, Sonny Stitt, Harold Vick and Red Holloway. En route, the Hammond hero also gave initial breaks to guitarist George Benson and a guitar protege of Lou Donaldson, Grant Green.

Larry Young was one of the few organists who tried a new approach to the instrument, with Coltrane rather than Smith as reference. Initially an R&B sideman, Young arrived at Blue Note in 1964 to join drummer Elvin Jones on a Grant Green trio date 'Talkin' About'. But it was his 'Into Somethin'' debut with Sam Rivers on tenor that remains his finest achievement. More sessions followed before he joined John McLaughlin and Jack Bruce as a member of Tony Williams' jazz-rock Lifetime as well as contributing to a number of Jimi Hendrix sessions.

It was about this time that the Hammond fell out of favour. Commencing with the Fender Rhodes electric piano, the phasing in of a whole arsenal of electronic hardware and synthesizers more or less corresponded with the instrument being sidelined. Other than on reissues, little was heard of the instrument for almost a decade.

Renewed interest came with the revival of the Blue Note catalogue. In Britain, pop groups like The Charlatans added a Hammond to their line-up, after which it dominated the 70s soundtrack-obsessed stylings of Acid Jazz jockeys, the James Taylor Quartet. Elsewhere, the presence of Barbara Dennerlein, Joey Francesco, Larry Golding, John Medeski at the two tier keyboard may have further reactivated its role, but a 60s-type renaissance of the sound doesn't really appear in the runes.

STEREO

LET 'EM ROLL BIG JOHN PATTON

GRANT GREEN
BOBBY HUTCHERSO
OTIS "CANDY" FINC

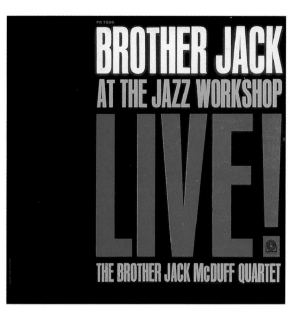

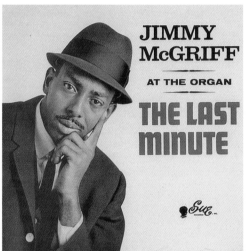

As well as Jimmy Smith and Johnny Smith (both page 155), Hammond heavies included 'Brother' Jack McDuff, Big John Patton, 'Baby Face' Willette, Jimmy McGriff and (right) Wild Bill Davis

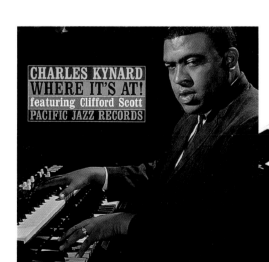

That **Latin** tinge

The tango, rumba and samba were popular dance
crazes from South America, but it was via jazz
that the world felt the real heat of the Latin beat.

DIZZY **GILLESPIE** was not only one of the prime architects of
be-bop, but also a major player in the development of Afro-Cuban
jazz. From the early days of Jelly Roll Morton and Duke
Ellington, exotic rhythmic textures ('latin tinges') have
been a featured element in jazz, while, as early as the 1930s, a
Cuban rumba craze swept the States. But it wasn't until the
mid-40s that the music transcended novelty status.

The catalyst was trumpet playing Cuban émigré,
Mario Bauza. Prior to joining Cab Calloway, Dizzy
Gillespie briefly worked around Manhattan in
the band of Cuban flautist Albert Socarras
who, in 1938, hired this gifted young firebrand because he wanted his band to sound
American. Socarras may have got what he
paid for, but, evidentially, Dizzy gained
much more from the transaction.

When Dizzy eventually joined Calloway,
he found himself rooming with Mario
Bauza, whom he had first met when
the Cuban was making a reputation

Maracas man
Machito, Latin
superstar whose
recordings also
appeared on the
V-Disc label

No. 528B
ALMENDRA
Valdes
TRA LA LA
Morales
Machito and his Afro-Cubans
Vocals by Machito
VP 1410
Latin Music
"V" RELEASE

Produced by the Music Branch,
Special Services Division,
Army Service Forces

ARMY — NAVY — MARINE CORPS — COAST GUARD

OUTSIDE START 78 RPM

AFRO-CUBANO

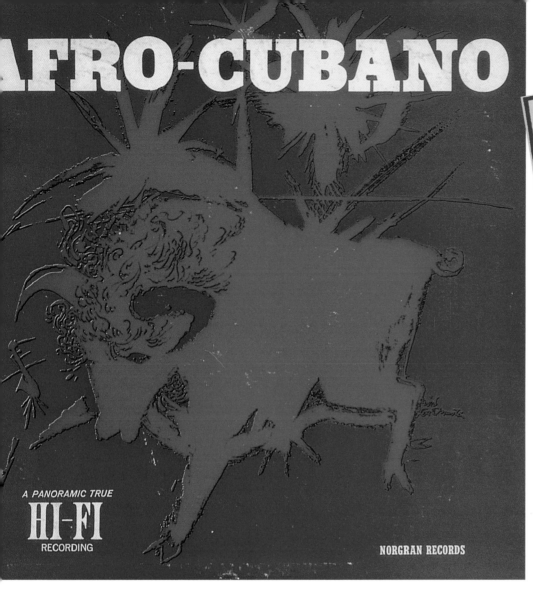

A PANORAMIC TRUE

HI-FI
RECORDING

NORGRAN RECORDS

for himself with Chick Webb. Dizzy Gillespie: 'Mario was the first to impress me with the importance of Afro-Cuban music.' It was Bauza who also composed 'Tanga' for Machito (Frank Grillo) back in May 1943, a hit in New York widely recognised as the first authentic Afro Cuban jazz record. In time, Bauza became both Machito's brother-in-law and the band's musical director.

However, 1947 was to be the watershed year for both Machito and Afro-Cuban music when he clicked big with 'Killer Joe'.

A triumphant appearance at New York's Town Hall on 24 January, supporting Stan Kenton, greatly upped his profile, especially when Stan the Man promptly recorded a single 'Machito' in honour of the Cuban maestro. It was also the same year that Kenton his cut most popular recording, 'The Peanut Vendor'. Then, at Bauza's behest, the great Cuban conguero Chano Pozo joined Dizzy Gillespie's Orchestra to perform Chico O'Farrill's 'Afro-Cuban Suite' during a roof-raising appearance at Carnegie Hall on 29 September. It was the first instance of a conga drummer working with a jazz group.

Later, over Christmas, Dizzy and Chano made another rapturously received showing together, at New York's Town Hall, in between two RCA Victor sessions that produced Afro-Cuban jazz classics 'Algo Bueno' ('Woody 'N' You'), George Russell's two-part 'Cubana Be, Cubana Bop' and the most famous of all Afro-Cuban compositions, 'Manteca' (Grease).

Tragically, this fruitful alliance proved to be short-lived. Pozo was a well-known hoodlum back in Havana, and even carried a gruesome souvenir of his wayward lifestyle in the form of a bullet permanently lodged closed to his spine. Furthermore, Chano Pozo spoke hardly any English and couldn't read music. Yet, assisted by Dizzy Gillespie ('I just contributed the 16-bar bridge') and the inspired arranger Gil Fuller, Pozo was to come up with the all-time classic 'Manteca'.

While not discounting the real historical importance of 'Tanga', both Socarras and Bauza credited 'Manteca' as being the genre's original blue-print and is still Cubop's main reference point.

One year later, on 2nd December 1948, Pozo (32) was shot dead by a drug dealer.

A few weeks prior to Pozo's murder, bop star Howard McGhee fronted the Machito Orchestra for a Roost label date that produced 'Cubop City Parts 1 & 2'.

Norman Granz was the next to get on the Cubop case when, over Christmas 1948, he hired arranger and occasional bandleader Chico O'Farrill to oversee a studio production involving Machito and guest artists Charlie Parker ('Mango Mangue' and 'Okiedoke') and Flip Phillips ('Tanga').

One year later (21 Dec) Bird, Flip and drummer Buddy Rich again teamed up with Machito for a recording of Chico O'Farrill's extended 'Afro Cuban Jazz Suite.'

The bandwagon began to roll with Kenton cutting a succession of Latin jazz dates that included his spectacular concept album 'Cuban Fire', Woody Herman taped a studio date with Tito Puente, while Tito Rodriguez regularly used big-name jazz soloists on some of his most popular releases.

Even Perez Prado, whose 1949 hit 'Mambo No. 5' had instigated both a worldwide dance craze and a cross-over precedent, would be trading ideas with West-Coast jazz supremo Shorty Rogers. Incidentally, it was Rogers who had penned the 'Viva Prado' tribute while still with Stan Kenton.

Sensing a fast buck, the owners of Birdland (who also distributed most of the Manhattan-based Latin labels) promptly booked Machito, Puente and Rodriguez to broadcast frequently from the famed 'Jazz Corner Of The World'.

Soon, it appeared as if hand drumming was the fastest-expanding career option in jazz with Jack Costanzo, Candido, Ray Barretto,

Above: Chico O'Farrill with saxmen Ed Wasserman and Hal McKusick

Below: Latin-rock guitar supremo Carlos Santana

Potato Valdes, Sabu Martinez and Big Black all elevated to first call status.

George Shearing further personalised his quintet's already highly commercial soft-bop signature sound with the addition of Amando Peraza while, in 1954, his vibes player and one-time Brubeck drummer Cal Tjader quit to hook up with Puente percussionists Willie Bobo and Mongo Santamaria in a move that considerably increased the future popularity of all three. It was Cal Tjader, as much as any other musician, who helped popularise the Latin Jazz kick.

By now, such was the attraction of Afro-Cuban jazz that, throughout the 50s, the general public proved instantly receptive to first the Mambo and then the Cha Cha Cha, just two of many dance crazes that were to dominate the juke boxes and move records as fast as any rock'n'roll act.

And it was this era, with a plot centred around a Cuban trumpet player and his vocalist brother on the make in Manhattan, that was vividly depicted in the 1992 movie *The Mambo Kings*.

Later, the process would be repeated with the mass cross-over acceptance of the Bossa Nova, the Boogaloo and Salsa.

But then, New York City has always been ahead of any other metropolis in the way it reflects its street-level action through the music of its multi-cultural inhabitants. In the 40s, it was the innovative jarring of bebop

that infiltrated the corner lounge bars and dance halls of Harlem, replacing swing, and finally moving down to midtown Manhatten around 52nd Street and Broadway.

Later it would be adenoid doo-wop, folk-rock protests, Uptown R&B and the Civil Rights demands of ghetto soul children. Along with boom box hip hop, be it 'Salsa' (sauce), 'La Neuva Ola' (the new wave) or whatever sales-tag is currently pinned to the latest variant, one sound that has dominated Manhattan (and Miami) has been the raucous, life-affirming chilli-hot rattle of Latin music played at excessive volume.

Outrageously brassy and blatantly sexual, it can be as brutally funky and soulful as the hard-hands impact of callused palms slapping congas and the hickory-rattle of cowbells and copper timbales.

It now bears very little resemblance to the supper-club sophistication of the pre-Elvis 50s, when society bandleaders Xavier Cugat and Desi Arnez portrayed the stereotype hand-kissing Latin lounge lizard, slumming beneath plastic palm trees in padded white tuxedos smelling of hair oil and cologne as they waited for the begine to begin!

Up until the Castro regime – apart from a few jazz-favoured Latin bands – the mainstay of popular mainstream Latin music was 'tipico', romantic ballads softly crooned over syrupy strings, acoustic guitars and a clipped rumba or cha cha rhythm.

Then, with the influx of immigrants that descended upon New York (and Florida) from Cuba, Puerto Rico, Dominica, Argentina, Brazil, and a dozen other Latin-American countries, this tropical sophistication soon began to be replaced by an urban hardness. As, in the 50s, acapella doo-wop groups rehearsed in the natural echo of tenement stairwells, almost two decades later Latinos took to jamming on neighbourhood rooftops.

The new bands that sprang up averaged about ten musicians evenly divided between a burnished brass section and an assortment of percussionists that excluded a standard drum kit. With both Latin and black ghettos in such close proximity to one another, it was inevitable that a volatile musical wedlock would manifest itself.

Soul borrowed the punchy eroticism of the Afro-Cuban rhythm section in much the same way as, in the early 70s, Salsa absorbed the emotion and rich texture that packed Harlem's Apollo Theatre.

New trends in Top 40 pop may have overshadowed just how deep Salsa penetrated the international market but it didn't alter the fact that performers such as Tito Puente, Johnny Pacheco, Larry Harlow, Charlie & Eddie Palmieri, Hector Lavoe, Orchestra Broadway, the Fania All-Stars and the Cuban diva Celia Cruz were box office attractions of the very first order.

Below: Vibraphone ace Cal Tjader

Bossa stars Stan Getz and Astrud Gilberto in the movie *Get Yourself A College Girl*

Bossa Nova boys from brazil

BACK IN 1953, the drummer Roy Harte and Harry Babasin (bass) and Bud Shank (alto sax/flute) coaxed Brazilian guitarist and Kenton sideman Laurindo Almeida into a recording studio to see if perhaps they could get the classically-trained Brazilian 'to swing a little.'

Things turned out much better than anticipated and very soon their seductive mix of cool bop and 'baia' was pressed up onto a ten-inch album by Pacific Jazz and labelled the Laurindo Almeida Quartet featuring Bud Shank.

On a return visit to Rio de Janeiro, Almeida distributed a few copies of the disc among local musicians who assumed it to be the latest in US jazz, and promptly copied it.

Nine years later, in 1962, Stan Getz was recording with local guitarist Charlie Byrd. Recently returned from a U.S. State Department Tour of South America, Byrd urged the saxman to record some Brazilian songs he'd brought back as souvenirs.

Recorded in just one night, the result was 'Jazz Samba', which rapidly became both one of the all-time best selling jazz albums plus one of the most widely influential.

Along the way, 'Jazz Samba' spawned the 1962 Grammy Award winner 'Desafinado' (Slightly Out Of Tune) and 'Samba De Una Nota So' (One Note Samba). A follow-up, 'Jazz Samba Encore' proved to be a more concerted effort at assimilating the genre, teaming Getz with two of Brazil's most revered recording stars, guitarist Luiz Bonfa and pianist Antonio Carlos Jobim, who had earlier composed the haunting samba soundtrack for the art house Brazilian movie *Black Orpheus* (Orfeu Negro). Suddenly, bossa was big. Even Elvis joined in with the frantic 'Bossa Nova Baby', but it was left to Eydie Gorme to reach an artistic nadir when bemoaning 'Blame It On The Bossa Nova'.

Whereas most 'pop' trends are dead in the water within a year of peaking, bossa nova thrived as everyone from Coleman Hawkins, Zoot Sims, Ike Quebec, Herbie Mann Cannonball Adderley, and Dave Brubeck offered their versions. However, the smart money was again on Getz when, in March 1963, he recorded with Jobim and the guitarist Joao Gilberto.

Of the small handful of sun-kissed sambas recorded, 'The Girl From Ipanema' proved to be the material from which everlasting standards are struck.

A luxurious mix of Getz's sax and the intimate burr of Gilberto's voice seemed to be the ideal formula until the realisation that Joao could only sing in Portuguese. However, Gilberto's young Bahia-born wife Astrud was one of a small group of onlookers. She spoke English and had a breathless voice of sorts. Though more suited to just singing in the shower, she was persuaded to softly croon Norman Gimbel's English lyric as well as 'Corcovado'.

At the time, her vocal was viewed as no big thing and she went uncredited on initial copies of the LP 'Stan Getz /Joao Gilberto.'

As soon as the album was shipped, radio programmers and juke box operators immediately responded and demanded a single version of 'The Girl From Ipanema'.

The version they received was drastically cut to the point where Joao Gilberto's vocal was completely edited out, leaving just Getz and Astrud to gain a US Top 5 hit during the summer of '64, plus a Grammy for the year's best single. Likewise, the Best Instrumental Jazz Performance and Album Of The Year awards completed a trio of Grammy honours. The bossa nova remained hot commercial property right up until the mid 60s, but by then Stan Getz had moved on to other things, leaving Astrud Gilberto to be forever tagged as the tall and tanned and young-and-lovely 'Girl

Some would claim that while a transient hard rock band could make headlines from appearing before a crowd of 20,000 fans, Salsa stars such as Panamanian-born Ruben Blades easily attracted three times that number.

A protégé of Willie Colon, percussionist Ruben Blades went on to further enhance his stature as a result of his proven ability as an actor in a dozen or more Hollywood movies.

While not originally perceived as a jazz artist, the big commercial breakthrough for contemporary Latin music occurred at the very end of the 60s in San Francisco when Tijuana-born acid-blues guitarist Carlos Santana put together an all-electric rock band and proceeded to buffer it violently against an authentic Latin percussion team.

It was the realisation that Santana chose to rework, amongst other things, Tito Puente's 'Oye Como Va' and 'Para Los Rumberos' that caught the ear of those not normally tuned into Top 40 formats. In the wake of past Latin crazes, the possibilities of even more logical

collaborations were fast becoming apparent.

So, whereas, Ray Barretto ('El Watusi',1963), Mongo Santamaria ('Watermelon Man',1963), Cal Tjader ('Soul Sauce-Guacha Guaro',1965), Joe Cuba ('Bang Bang',1966), Sergio Mendes & Brasil '66 ('Mas Que Nada',1966), Joe Bataan ('Subway Joe',1968) had peddled Latin music of varying degrees of authenticity into the US Hot 100, the success of Santana's high energy musical commitment was instant.

The incessant clatter of Latin-American percussion has long become as much an everyday urban pulse as a fatback rock beat or white-hot blast of bop.

Like all innovations, the absorption of Latin music into the mainstream soundtrack was a natural and inevitable process. What were once decorative 'latin tinges' have now reached a level of acceptance where, next to Hard Bop, they constitute the most widely-played and most popular strain of contemporary jazz.

It's an accepted fact that Latin percussion has now become an integral part of any major rhythm section. Some players like Mongo Santamaria, Pancho Sanchez and the highly extrovert Brazilian Airto Moreira remain hot tickets attractions in their own right. As with all parallel strains of popular music, Latin music constantly reinvents itself and, each time, gleefully draws even more from whatever other music is in close proximity.

In some areas, the music manages to remain relatively unaffected. In particular Irekere (founded in 1973, and led by pianist Chico Valdez), continues to represent the contemporary in Havana-based Afro-Cuban jazz. And even the asylum-seekers, trumpeter Arturo Sandavol (1980) and alto saxist Paquito D'Riviera (1981), haven't damaged the popularity of these talented Cuban government-sponsored Cuboppers.

With New York City continuing to serve as both a melting-pot and obstacle course, a new generation of young Latin musicians that includes pianists Hilton Ruiz, Gonzalo Rubalcaba and Danilo Perez, tenorman David Sanchez and Jerry Gonzalez's Fort Apache Band have taken it upon themselves to be regarded as individual voices rather than just off-kilter imitations.

As ever, these are exciting times.

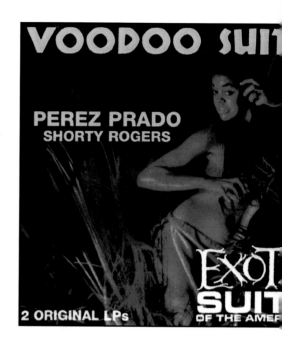

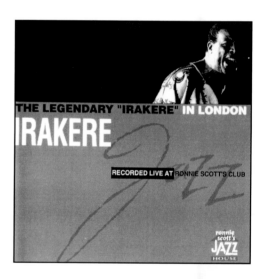

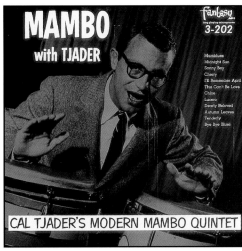

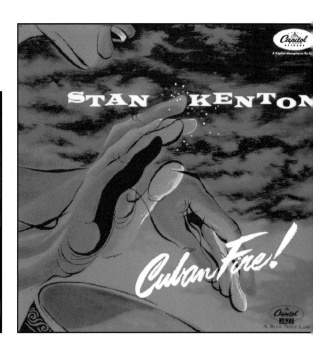

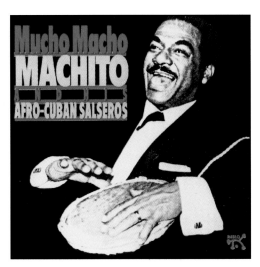

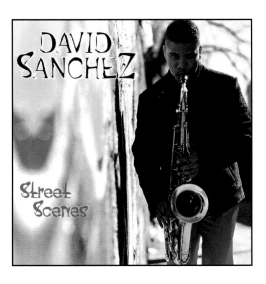

Opposite: Panamanian star Ruben Blades at the Montreaux Jazz Festival
Right: The great Chano Pozo

Jazz on the Juke Box

'Jazz is king, jazz is the thing the folks dig most' duetted Satch and Bing in High Society.

JAZZ HAS NEVER BEEN a stranger to America's best selling record listings. Throughout the 1930s and into the early 1940s, jazz was as popular as any music could be, taking over control of the teenage (before the term was coined) dance hall and jukebox market. It would remain so until the featured crooners moved out of the big band scene to establish themselves as solo stars. In turn, all but the most resilient would eventually find themselves sidelined by rock'n'roll.

The superficial affluence that was the trademark of the post-war '50s, accompanied the expansion of network television and, along with other gadgetry, the phasing out of 78 rpm shellac singles and the advent of unbreakable 45 rpm microgroove seven-inch singles, long-playing record albums and high-fidelity technology.

In total, it represented a quantum leap in home entertainment not experienced since the widespread introduction of both the domestic gramophone and radio earlier in the century.

As to be expected, jazz was never far away from both the fast action and the easy money; The Count Basie Orchestra was voted the top rock'n'roll band (!) of 1956 by *Cashbox* magazine by virtue of their weekly presence on the *Camel Rock & Roll Dance Party* (CBS) hosted by celebrity disc jockey Alan Freed.

Shorty Rogers & The Giants moonlighted as Boots Brown & His Blockbusters, ('Cerveza') while it seemed that everyone from Earl Palmer and Barney Kessel through to Plas Johnson and the Ellington sidemen at one time fattened their wallets reworking 12-bar sequences on innumerable record dates.

Swing no longer being the thing, vested interests used the media to stage-manage hostilities been traditionalists and modernists – 'mouldy figs versus hipsters' – and each was to have their day.

In Britain, what started out as a student-based cult erupted into a full-blown craze when, between 1960-62, a commercialised brand of 'Trad' jazz infiltrated an otherwise lacklustre pop scene. The 'trad fad' pivoted around bands fronted by Kenny Ball, Chris Barber and Acker Bilk; between them, this triumvirate quickly logged up no less than twenty domestic Top 40 hits including 'Midnight In Moscow' (Ball), 'Petite Fleur' (Barber) and 'Stranger On The Shore'(Bilk). However, in the ensuing clamour created by those who recognise a bandwagon when it rolls by, things quickly descended into grotesque vaudevillian parody complete with silly hats and fancy dress costumes.

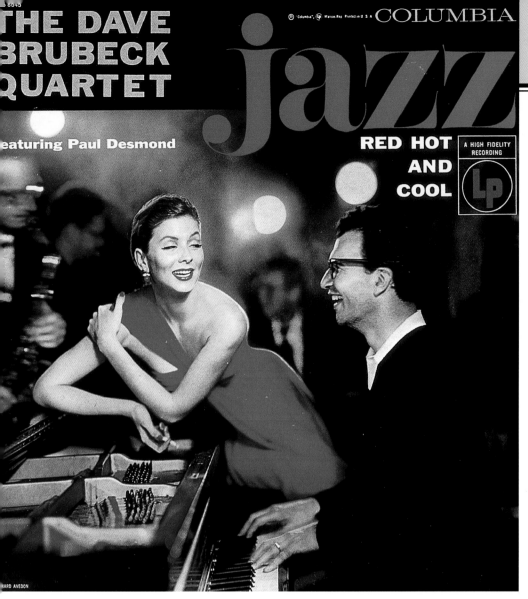

THE DAVE BRUBECK QUARTET

featuring Paul Desmond

COLUMBIA

jazz

RED HOT AND COOL

A HIGH FIDELITY RECORDING
LP

herbie mann at the village gate

STEREO

1380

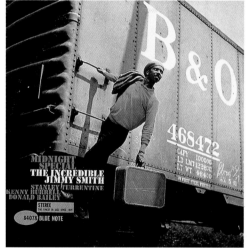

MIDNIGHT SPECIAL
THE INCREDIBLE JIMMY SMITH
STANLEY TURRENTINE
KENNY BURRELL
DONALD BAILEY

STEREO
84078 BLUE NOTE

Immediately prior to the advent of Beatlemania, the last genuine worldwide musical phenomenon was the sensual sound of Stan Getz (and Charlie Byrd) personalising a seductive hybrid that blended Brazilian samba rhythms with lyrical cool bop and known as the *bossa nova* (Portugese for 'new disturbance').

Getz quickly achieved long-term pop-star status by virtue of his recordings of 'Desafinado', 'One Note Samba' and 'The Girl From Ipanema' (featuring Astrud Gilberto) without ever being accused of compromising his position as a major jazz artists. If anything, his chart success enhanced his reputation.

Unlike most trends, bossa nova never posted a sell-by date and, along with other contemporary forms of Brazilian music, has become absorbed into the musical mainstream.

The arrival of the British Beat Boom onto the international stage didn't just shake-up pop music in general, but also put jazz on notice – a not uncommon occurrence.

Yet, despite everything else happening around town, straight-ahead modern jazz singles still slipped under the wire to scamper up the charts. Similarly, over on the Hot 100 albums listings, jazz sales still flourished no matter which Devil spawn was branded as the latest threat to America's dollar-waving youth!

The common denominator was the same as for pop – a mindworm of a tune welded to an irresistible dance beat.

Across the board, labels from Blue Note to Verve regularly lifted the most tuneful track from an album and either spread it over two sides

Opposite: Herbie Mann with flute and assorted percussion. Below: Jonah Jones, who had three chart LPs in the late 50s

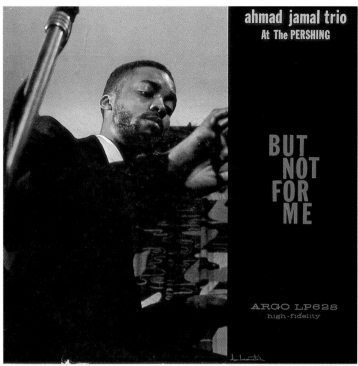

ahmad jamal trio
At The PERSHING

BUT
NOT
FOR
ME

ARGO LP628
high-fidelity

CANNONBALL ADDERLEY
SEXTET
JAZZ WORKSHOP REVISITED
featuring Nat Adderley and Yusef Lateef
Recorded 'live' in San Francisco

RIVERSIDE

contains
the hit single
JIVE
SAMBA

THE SIDEWINDER

JOE HENDERSON   BARRY HARRIS   BOB CRENSHAW   BILLY HIGGINS
LEE MORGAN

of a juke box seven-inch single or ruthlessly edited the tapes in an effort to attract precious radio airtime.

All this heavy chart action was due to the fact that it was an era when it was essential – as well as coming up with 'catchy' numbers from time to time – that the overall sound of a group had to be distinctive: Dave Brubeck, Gerry Mulligan, George Shearing, Jimmy Smith, Chico Hamilton, the Modern Jazz Quartet, Shorty Rogers & His Giants.

Each and everyone of these groups may have contained many of the leading soloists of the day, but it was the signature sound of the context in which they excelled that attracted attention and generated the kind of sales previously undreamt of.

Shorty Rogers, who was certainly no stranger to 100,000-plus album sales, didn't buck the system: 'I did a couple of jazz versions of big hit musicals, albums such as "Gigi" along with the music from the successful TV Private Eye series *Peter Gunn*, Dave Brubeck did a collection of Disney tunes and Shelly Manne did phenomenally well with his "My Fair Lady" collection. For a time, it was supposed to be the biggest-selling album ever, probably still is. But it was albums like these that brought a lot of people to jazz who otherwise might have passed the music by.' While musicians as diverse as Eddie Harris (tenor sax), Jimmy Smith (organ), Ahmad Jamal (piano), Jonah Jones (trumpet) and, most notably, Dave Brubeck – whose quartet hit pop star status among the campus set via 'Take Five', 'It's A Raggy Waltz', 'Blue Rondo A La Turk' – regularly witnessed their albums crashing into the nation's Top 10 best-sellers, a number of other jazz albums have quite probably outsold many rock chart albums issued at the same time to eventually attain gold and platinum sales. Though he was forever pushing back the musical barriers, Miles Davis always remained extremely proud of the music that he recorded for Prestige, but by the mid-50s he was aware that the bottom line was how many units an artist moved at retail. 'The real money was in getting to the mainstream of America,' and Miles realised that nobody served this market better than Columbia. 'Prestige didn't,' insisted the trumpet star, 'it was making great records, but outside the mainstream.' At the time of their release, Miles Davis' 'Kind Of Blue' and 'Sketches of Spain' may not have effected major crossover action, but then Columbia never allowed these back catalogue cornerstones to lapse into the deletion twilight zone.

Likewise, it was a similar story with Coltrane's 'A Love Supreme' (Impulse) and Horace Silver's 'Song For My Father' (Blue Note).

These and other key albums by the Modern Jazz Quartet, Oscar Peterson, Cannonball Adderley, Mose Allison, Chico Hamilton, Charlie Parker, Thelonious Monk, Charles Mingus, Red Norvo, Cal Tjader, Bill Evans, The Jazz Messengers and Chet Baker have also become perennial best sellers, established as the core of any respectable collection.

There are a number of less obvious reasons why, back in the 1950s and 1960s some jazz albums never figured in the national charts despite stacking up impressive sales far in excess of 100,000. Often such figures were achieved by virtue of long-term consistency, rather than a four week instant peak followed by an even more rapid burn-out.

And it wasn't uncommon for many jazz and R&B record labels to do their own distribution – selling direct to convenience store outlets and working class neighbourhood one-stops that dealt strictly in cash and didn't file chart returns.

On a more sinister level, there was the failure of some independent labels to honestly account for over-the-counter public response, even though in many instances, artists either received a one-off payment or derisory royalty break. However, there were those artists – with good lawyers – who earned and collected their rightful dues.

Trumpeter Freddie Hubbard was once quoted as saying 'Coltrane's music was on the radio. He made big money. Miles makes big money. All the jazz cats I know who are making it are making big money or trying. You have to put limits on it, though, as far as going for the money. It's still basically up to the artists.'

Contrary to received wisdom now, it was cool to dig jazz in the mid-60s: pop stars regularly name-checked Cannonball, Miles, Getz, Tjader, while the very latest Jimmy Smith album was deemed an essential fashion accessory and a means of publicly stating that the owner was totally aware.

But reaching a much wider audience outside of jazz can also be something of an albatross. Audiences expected the Dave Brubeck Quartet to enact a note-for-note re-run of 'Take Five' while, after years of introducing 'Desafinado' as 'the record that put my son through college', Stan Getz finally refused to include it in his repertoire.

167

Also, it became commonplace to find the likes of Miles Davis, Charles Lloyd (tenor sax), Herbie Mann (flute), Hugh Masekela (trumpet) playing alongside of Jimi Hendrix, Jefferson Airplane, The Byrds and The Grateful Dead at rock temples such as the prestigious Fillmore auditoriums in New York and San Francisco. Some even made it to the large outdoor festivals.

Masekela and Lloyd went one better. The former recording with Eric Burdon ('San Franciscan Night') and The Byrds ('So You Want To Be A Rock'N'Roll Star') while the latter became part of The Beach Boys entourage.

Later, with the advent of first jazz-rock and then the more funkier variety as choreographed by Creed Taylor (who quit Verve to organise his hitmaking CTI and Kudu labels) with Freddie Hubbard's 'Red Clay', George Benson's 'White Rabbit' and Grover Washington's 'Inner City Blues', straight ahead post-Hard Bop acoustic jazz began to make its presence felt less and less in the everyday urban soundtrack.

However, a contemporized mix of jazz was still a constant: be it themes for prime-time TV sitcoms, commercials or AOR hits, the most emulated sound has its roots in the emotional blues-wail of altoist David Sanborn.

Too intense for some, elsewhere jazz has been marketed as some kind of sex opiate with the more bevel-edged. smoothed-down 'lite' variety as purveyed by soft-focus multi-million selling Kenny G, Najee, George Howard or Dave Grusin finding mass-market favour.

On a less sensual note, Kentucky Fried Chicken picked-up on US3's million-plus selling 'Cantaloop' to help draw attention to the good Colonel's bucketed blow-outs!

Below: With no less than three entries in the American album charts, Stan Kenton looks suitably triumphant

The Chart

From Louis Armstrong to Stan Kenton, through the 50s and 60s, and into the 70s, jazz continued to make its mark on the American album charts.

TOP 40 US ALBUMS

Cannonball Adderley: Jazz Workshop Revisited (Riverside) 1963 (11)
Cannonball Adderley: Mercy, Mercy, Mercy (Capitol) 1967 (13)
Laurindo Almeida: Viva Bossa Nova (Capitol) 1962 (9)
Louis Armstrong: Satch Plays Fats (Columbia) 1955 (10)
Louis Armstrong/Ella Fitzgerald: Ella And Louis (Verve) 1956 (12)
Louis Armstrong: Hello Dolly (Kapp) 1964 (1)
Count Basie: This Time By Basie (Reprise) 1963 (19)
Count Basie: Sinatra-Basie (Reprise) 1963 (5)
Count Basie/Frank Sinatra: It Might As Well Be Swing (Reprise) 1964 (13)
Les Brown: Concert At The Palladium (Coral) 1955 (15)
Dave Brubeck: At Storyville 1954 (Columbia) 1955 (8)
Dave Brubeck: Brubeck Time (Columbia) 1955 (5)
Dave Brubeck: Jazz: Red Hot And Cool (Columbia) 1955 (7)
Dave Brubeck: Jazz Impressions Of The USA (Columbia) 1957 (18)
Dave Brubeck: Jazz Goes To Junior College (Columbia) 1957 (24)
Dave Brubeck: Time Out (Columbia) 1960 (2)
Dave Brubeck: Bernstein Plays Brubeck, Brubeck Plays Bernstein (Columbia) 1960 (13)
Dave Brubeck: Time Further Out (Columbia) 1962 (8)
Dave Brubeck: Countdown – Time In Outer Space (Columbia) 1962 (24)
Dave Brubeck: Bossa Nova USA (Columbia) 1963 (10)

Dave Brubeck: The Dave Brubeck Quartet At Carnegie Hall (Columbia) 1963 (37)
Eddie Cano: Eddie Cano At PJ's (Reprise) 1962 (31)
Ray Charles: The Genius of Ray Charles (Atlantic) 1960 (17)
Ray Charles: Genius + Soul = Jazz (Impulse) 1961 (4)
June Christy: The Misty Miss Christy (Capitol) 1956 (14)
June Christy: June – Fair And Warmer (Capitol) 1957 (16)
Nat Cole: After Midnight (Capitol) 1957 (13)
Nat Cole: St Louis Blues (Capitol) 1958 (18)
Nat Cole Sings/George Shearing Plays (Capitol) 1962 (27)
Miles Davis: Bitches Brew (Columbia) 1970 (35)
Duke Ellington: Ellington At Newport (Columbia) 1957 (14)
Ella Fitzgerald: Songs From Pete Kelly's Blues (Decca) 1955 (7)
Ella Fitzgerald: Sings The Cole Porter Songbook (Verve) 1956 (15)
Ella Fitzgerald: Sings Rodgers And Hart (Verve) 1957 (11)

Ella Fitzgerald: Mack the Knife/Ella In Berlin (Verve) 1960 (11)

Ella Fitzgerald: Ella In Hollywood (Verve) 1962 (35)

Erroll Garner: Other Voices (Columbia) 1957 (16)

Erroll Garner: Concert By The Sea (Columbia) 1958 (12)

Erroll Garner: Dreamstreet (Columbia) 1961 (35)

Stan Getz: Jazz Samba (Verve) 1962 (1)

Stan Getz: Big Band Bossa Nova (Verve) 1963 (13)

Stan Getz: Getz/Gilberto (Verve) 1964 (2)

Stan Getz: Getz Au Go-Go (Verve) 1965 (24)

Benny Goodman: B.G. In Hi-Fi (Capitol) 1955 (7)

Benny Goodman: The Benny Goodman Story (Decca) 1956 (4)

Glen Gray: Casa Loma In Hi-Fi (Capitol) 1957 (18)

Glen Gray: Sounds Of The Big Bands (Capitol) 1959 (28)

Vince Guaraldi: Jazz Impressions Of Black Orpheus (Fantasy) 1963 (24)

Eddie Harris: Exodus To Jazz (Vee-Jay) 1961 (2)

Eddie Harris: The Electrifying Eddie Harris (Atlantic) 1968 (36)

Eddie Harris/Les McCann: Swiss Movement (Atlantic) 1970 (29)

Ted Heath: Big Band Percussion (London) 1961 (28)

Ted Heath: Big Band Bash (London) 1962 (36)

Woody Herman: The 3 Herds (Columbia) 1955 (11)

Eddie Heywood: Canadian Sunset (RCA) 1959 (16)

Ahmad Jamal: But Not For Me '58 (3)

Ahmad Jamal: Ahmad Jamal Vol.IV (Argo) 1958 (11)

Ahmad Jamal: At The Penthouse (Argo) 1960 (32)

Harry James: In Hi-Fi (Capitol) 1955 (10)

Jonah Jones: Muted Jazz (Capitol) 1958 (7)

Jonah Jones: Swingin' On Broadway (Capitol) 1958 (7)

Jonah Jones: Jumpin' With Jonah (Capitol) 1958 (14)

Stan Kenton: In Hi-Fi (Capitol) 1956 (13)

Stan Kenton: Cuban Fire (Capitol) 1956 (17)

Stan Kenton: Kenton's West Side Story (Capitol) 1961 (16)

Ramsey Lewis: The 'In' Crowd (Chess) 1965 (2)

Ramsey Lewis: Hang On Ramsey (Chess) 1966 (15)

Ramsey Lewis: Wade In The Water (Chess) 1966 (16)

Gloria Lynne: At The Las Vegas Thunderbird (Everest) 1963 (39)

Gloria Lynne: Gloria, Marty & Strings (Everest) 1964 (27)

Herbie Mann: At The Village Gate (Atlantic) 1962 (30)

Herbie Mann: Memphis Underground (Atlantic) 1969 (20)

Hugh Masekela: The Promise Of A Future (Uni) 1968 (17)

Jimmy McGriff: I've Got A Woman (Sue) 1962 (22)

Wes Montgomery: A Day In The Life (A&M) 1967 (13)

Wes Montgomery: Down Here On The Ground (A&M) 1968 (38)

Lee Morgan: The Sidewinder (Blue Note) 1964 (25)

Gerry Mulligan: I Want To Live (United Artists) 1959 (39)

Andre Previn: Secret Songs For Young Lovers (MGM) 1959 (16)

Andre Previn: Like Love (Columbia) 1960 (25)

Lalo Schifrin: Bossa Nova – New Brazilian Jazz (Audio Fidelity) 1962 (35)

George Shearing : Velvet Carpet (Capitol)

1956 (20)

George Shearing: Black Satin (Capitol) 1957 (13)

George Shearing: Burnished Brass (Capitol) 1958 (17)

George Shearing: White Satin (Capitol) 1960 (11)

Donald Shirley: Tonal Expressions (Cadence) 1955 (14)

Nina Simone: Nina At Newport (Colpix) 1961 (23)

Jimmy Smith: Midnight Special (Blue Note) 1962 (28)

Jimmy Smith: Bashin' (Verve) 1962 (10)

Jimmy Smith: Back At The Chicken Shack (Blue Note) 1963 (14)

Jimmy Smith: Hobo Flats (Verve) 1963 (11)

Jimmy Smith: Any Number Can Win (Verve) 1963 (25)

Jimmy Smith: Who's Afraid Of Virginia Woolf? (Verve) 1964 (16)

Jimmy Smith: The Cat (Verve) 1964 (12)

Jimmy Smith: Monster (Verve) 1965 (35)

Jimmy Smith: Organ Grinder Swing (Verve) 1965 (15)

Jimmy Smith: Got My Mojo Workin' (Verve) 1966 (28)

Sarah Vaughan: Linger Awhile (Columbia) 1956 (20)

Sarah Vaughan: Sassy (EmArcy) 1956 (31)

Sarah Vaughan: Great Songs From The Hit Shows (Mercury) 1957 (14)

Sarah Vaughan: Sings George Gershwin (Mercury) 1957 (14)

Dinah Washington: What A Diff'rence A Day Makes (Mercury) 1960 (34)

Dinah Washington: Unforgettable (Mercury) 1961 (10)

Dinah Washington: Dinah '62 (Roulette) 1962 (33)

Jack Webb/Matty Matlock: Pete Kelly's Blues (Columbia) 1955 (2)

Paul Whiteman: 50th Anniversary (Grand Award) 1957 (20)

Nancy Wilson: Nancy Wilson/Cannonball Adderley (Capitol) 1962 (30)

Young-Holt Unlimited: Soulful Strut (Brunswick) 1969 (9)

Soundtrack: Man With The Golden Arm (Decca) 1956 (2)

Various: I Like Jazz (Columbia) 1955 (5)

TOP 50 SINGLES

Cannonball Adderley : African Waltz '61 (41)

Cannonball Adderley: The Jive Samba '63 (46)

Cannonball Adderley: Mercy, Mercy, Mercy '67 (11)

Kenny Ball: Midnight In Moscow '62 (2)

Chris Barber: Petite Fleur '59 (5)

Count Basie: April In Paris '56 (28)

Elmer Bernstein: Main Title Theme / Man With The Golden Arm '56 (16)

Acker Bilk: Stranger On The Shore '62 (1)

Blue Stars: Lullaby Of Birdland '55 (16)

Dave Brubeck: Take Five '61 (25)

Ray Bryant: The Madison '60 (30)

Ray Charles: One Mint Julep '61 (8)

Cozy Cole: Topsy II '58 (3)

Stan Getz: Desafinado '62 (15)

Stan Getz/Astrud Gilberto: The Girl From Ipanema '64 (5)

Vince Guaraldi: Cast Your Fate To The Wind '62 (22)

Eddie Harris: Exodus '61 (36)

Moe Koffman: Swingin' Shepherd Blues '58 (23)

Ramsey Lewis: The In Crowd '65 (5)

Ramsey Lewis: Hang On Sloopy '65 (11)

Ramsey Lewis: Wade In The Water '66 (19)

Herbie Mann: Memphis Underground '69 (44)

Wes Montgomery: Windy '67 (44)

Mongo Santamaria: Watermelon Man '63 (10)

Don Shirley: Water Boy '61 (40)

Jimmy Smith: Walk On The Wild Side '62 (21)

Kai Winding: More '63 (8)

Young-Holt Trio: Wack Wack '66 (40)

The Blues Brothers

The blues boom of the early Sixties occurred thousands of miles away from its US source, in Europe and particularly Britain, where it revolutionised popular music.

BOTH BLUES AND JAZZ experienced innovation in the immediate postwar years but each in a different way. In jazz it was a revolution in style, as big bands became too expensive to maintain for all but the major names, and even they struggled. Smaller groups perforce relied upon technique and virtuosity, and an aggressive new style termed bebop emerged.

A simultaneous upheaval took place in blues, but its advent was heralded by the musicians' use of developing technology. One of the first to use an amplified guitar on mid-30s blues sessions was the teenage George Barnes, closely followed by Big Bill Broonzy, and its use was then perpetuated postwar by Tampa Red and Willie Lacey. Arthur 'Big Boy' Crudup also used an amplified acoustic guitar when recording 'That's All Right (Mama)' a cover of which launched Elvis Presley's recording career.

Both technology and technique had moved on by the end of the decade. In Chicago, Muddy Waters revived bottleneck blues, an eerie, emotive sound enhanced by crude but effective amplification which coarsened and distorted the guitar's sound. Though Muddy hailed from Mississippi, he earned the title of King Of Chicago Blues by masterminding the small band sound.

John Lee Hooker went even further to achieve a sound that complemented the sheer drama of his compositions by retaining the turbulent rhythms of his Mississippi origins, and refining them in Detroit's urban jungle.

Left: Backstage during one of his first of many visits to the British Isles, a blues legend who enjoyed yet another revival in the 90s, the great John Lee Hooker

PARKWAY ARENA
SAGINAW, MICHIGAN
SATURDAY, MAY 31, 1958
12:00 A. M. TO 4:00 A. M. - ADMISSION $2.00

PRESENTING
MEMPHIS SLIM
AND HIS HOUSE ROCKERS

PLUS AN EXTRA
ADDED ATTRACTION

SONNY BOY WILLIAMSON

RHYTHM & BLUES AGENCY   CHICAGO, ILL.

Above: Memphis Slim introducing a bowler-hatted Sonny Boy Williamson during a television recording *I Hear The Blues* made in Manchester, England, in 1963. Bass player Willie Dixon can be seen in the background

Meanwhile, down in Texas, Sam Lightnin' Hopkins made a more subtle but nonetheless dynamic use of electric guitar.

The most innovatory sound in postwar blues was the guitar playing of West Coast-based Aaron 'T-Bone' Walker, heard on the records he made for Black & White and Capitol using small groups of jazz-oriented session men. By the end of the 40s, his lead had been followed by the likes of fellow Los Angelinos Lowell Fulson, Pee Wee Crayton

and, most significantly, B.B. King who had transferred from Memphis to the Coast. As the music business thrived on postwar affluence, these musicians resumed the use of large orchestras. Small bands still set the pace in Chicago, where Muddy Waters and

Howling Wolf dominated the club scene, while Little Walter, Walter Horton and Snooky Pryor were kings of the amplified harmonica.

In the second half of the 50s, a younger generation of Chicago blues musicians adapted the declamatory style perfected by B.B. King, although their repertoire still reflected existing blues standards. Buddy Guy, Magic Sam and Freddie King also had an eye on the hit parade, unlike contemporary Otis Rush, who managed to straddle the widening gap between the old and the new. Meanwhile, young black audiences were deserting blues

CLUB PARADISE
645 E. GEORGIA AVE. - MEMPHIS, TENN.
SAT. OCT. 24
8:00 P. M. UNTIL
ADVANCE ADMISSION $3.50 - AT DOOR $4.00
FOR RESERVATIONS CALL 774-4871
BATTLE OF THE BLUES

THE
HOWLING WOLF
"TAKE IT FOR ME"
"SPOONFUL" * "EVILS"
"I SHOULD OF QUIT YOU A LONG TIME AGO"

VS

MUDDY WATERS
"I GOT MY MOJO WORKING"
"THE SAME THING"
"HOOTCHIE COOTCHIE MAN"

2 - BIG BANDS - 2

Left: Howling Wolf in a British record company publicity hand-out
Right: A young-looking shot of Muddy Waters used by his European agency

MUDDY WATERS   EUROPEAN REPRESENTATION
HAROLD DAVISON LTD.
EROS HOUSE
29-31 REGENT STREET
LONDON, S.W.1

Above: Alexis Korner's seminal Blues Incorporated with (l-r) Korner, tenor player Dick Heckstall-Smith, harp maestro Cyril Davies and tenor man Art Themen

(and it's connotations) for the more positive stance soul music represented, and the 'young turks' (as Buddy and Magic were termed) struggled to follow the trend.

As a new decade began, and just when it seemed that the blues was entering an unstoppable decline, help arrived from an unexpected quarter. Fired by their interest in the records of Chuck Berry, Jimmy Reed and Bo Diddley, a number of English groups led first by Alexis Korner and Cyril Davies, and then the Rolling Stones and the Yardbirds, were fostering an increasing interest in what they termed 'rhythm and blues'.

The seminal Alexis Korner band Blues Incorporated was a major catalyst in a British-based blues boom which was to impact on the

Below: The Graham Bond Organisation, with (clockwise from left) Ginger Baker, Dick Heckstall-Smith, Jack Bruce and alto sax/organist leader Graham Bond

oncoming rock revolution that would sweep the world. Mick Jagger was part-time vocalist in an early line-up, along with drummer Charlie Watts with whom he was forming his own group the Rolling Stones; and rock idols-to-be in Cream, bassist Jack Bruce and Ginger Baker (drums), also passed through its ranks.

Beginning in 1962, an annual American Folk Blues Festival, combining rediscovered veterans with their younger counterparts, toured Europe. Acoustic and electric blues and an array of regional styles jostled for attention, all receiving universal acclaim.

Likewise, individual blues artists toured with young British groups as backing bands – Sonny Boy Williamson with the Yardbirds, John Lee Hooker with the Groundhogs and so

on – on a burgeoning circuit of UK club venues that included the Marquee in London, Liverpool's Cavern Club and in Manchester the Twisted Wheel.

Interest in the originators of the music reached its peak in the middle of the decade and declined thereafter. However, those young white musicians on both sides of the Atlantic – like Eric Clapton who graduated from John Mayall's Bluesbreakers to become

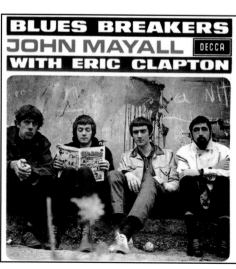

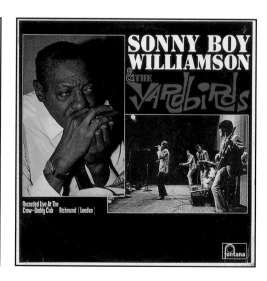

Above: An early line-up of Blues Incorporated shot at London's Marquee Club with Jack Bruce on bass, Mick Jagger on vocals and (hidden) drummer Charlie Watts
Right: A button badge featuring the early Rolling Stones

the lynchpin of the power trio Cream, and Paul Butterfield, Mike Bloomfield and the Grateful Dead in America – used blues as a springboard for progressive or 'psychedelic' rock. At the same time, Taj Mahal was a blues player who found fame as part of the rock scene. But none attained the state of grace exclusive to Jimi Hendrix, who was to blues what Bird and Trane were to jazz

Blues artists such as Albert and B.B. King, Muddy and Wolf benefitted from the increased attention, regularly appearing on shows with their young admirers. But for lesser lights the wave soon passed, leaving them in much the same circumstances as they'd endured before its arrival.

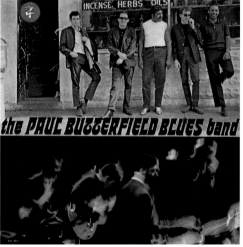

Caribbean cool

Jamaican music will forever be associated with its most successful exports of Blue Beat, Ska and Reggae, but a potentially vibrant jazz scene never quite happened, its big names making it elsewhere.

JAMAICA IS POSSIBLY jazz's most neglected geographical area, and not due to any lack of talent. Remember, the island has never had a population larger than London, but has produced a staggering number of first class players: alto players Joe Harriott and Harold 'Little Jesus' McNair, trumpeter Alphonso 'Dizzy' Reece, tenorman Wilton 'Bogey' Gaynair, pianists Monty Alexander and Wynton Kelly, and guitarist Ernest Ranglin can all claim Jamaican nationality. There was no absence of appreciation for the music either: New Orleans and Miami radio stations came through loud and clear in Jamaica, anything that could swing could always find a home in the island's numerous dancehalls, and such big names as Louis Armstrong, Errol Garner and Nat King Cole were frequently on the bill at downtown Kingston theatres like The Carib or The Ward. As for a tradition, as far back as the 30s, both Jamaican trumpeter Leslie 'Jiver' Hutchinson and alto saxist Bertie King were making noise in British jazz circles. But to succeed in jazz, Jamaican musicians had to present themselves as pretty much anything but Jamaican.

Go back to the 40s and 50s, when jazz was the hippest music world-wide, and Jamaica was no exception to the rule. At that time it was practically impossible to leave your yard in Kingston without your tripping over a jazzman looking for somewhere to jam. One important catalyst was The Alpha Boys Catholic School, a semi-reform boarding school where teaching music was the top of the nuns' list. The lessons were formal, classical, comprehensively theoretical, and the only way to get out of doing chores was to join the pupil's orchestra.

Alpha seemed to specialise in hornsmen, and among its alumni were, as well as Harriott, Reece, Gaynair and McNair, trombonists Rico Rodriguez and Don Drummond and saxmen Tommy McCook, Roland Alphonso and Val Bennett. Meanwhile the National Volunteers,

a government-sponsored scheme to set up bands and music lessons for Jamaica's youth, meant that you didn't need to be living in Kingston to learn to play properly. The sax player Dean Frazier is a product of this operation.

Jitterbugging and jive were so popular that there were over two dozen dance orchestras operating in Jamaica in the post-War years.

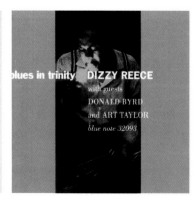

Right: Leslie 'Jiver' Hutchinson
Opposite: From the collection of photographer Val Wilmer, an archive picture of the Alpha Cottage School Band, Kingston Jamaica

as the island's dance music of choice. Jamaica's jazzers were left with two choices: to change their (musical) ways, or go abroad.

While the likes of Ernest Ranglin, Tommy McCook, Don Drummond and Lester Sterling stuck around and, by the end of the 1950s, had osmosed R&B into ska, so many players went 'a foreign'. And of those who did, many of them left an indelible yard-style handprint on jazz around the world. Initially a hard-bopper, Joe Harriott became a key figure on the British jazz scene via his success with the Indo-Jazz Fusion project and his excursions into Free Jazz; Dizzy Reece had the distinction of cutting three fine albums for the Blue Note label; Monty Alexander went to the States; Harold McNair relocated in Paris, where he worked with Quincy Jones and Ornette Coleman before becoming a member of folk-rock singer Donovan's road band; Wilton 'Bogey' Gaynair cut a classic album for London-based Tempo before decamping to Germany; Rico Rodriguez settled in London as did bassist Coleridge Goode, and Wynton Kelly ended up playing with Miles Davis.

On the upside, nearly 40 years later now that Jamaican music and its music industry is established worldwide, Jamaican jazzmen are coming back to their roots. Island Records have released albums by Ranglin, Alexander and Frazier performing jazz interpretations of Jamaican standards, while London-born saxman Courtney Pine occasionally fronts a reggae based band for road work. But, for the best surviving example of what Jamaican jazz might have sounded like had it developed naturally, absorbing such influences as Rastafari and reggae, Count Ossie's all-time classic triple album 'Grounation' holds the evidence – enough to make the listener almost as frustrated as the JA musicians themselves, that this scene was never allowed to blossom.

Big band swing outfits fronted by Eric Dean, Roy White and Val Bennett who modelled themselves on Basie, Ellington and Cab Calloway played the tourist hotels along the island's North Coast or Kingston's more salubrious clubs like the Silver Slipper, Union Hall and The Glass Bucket.

But while there was no shortage of work, this was hardly the ideal environment for innovation. The tourists wanted to hear either what they were already familiar with – cover versions of American dance hits – or a very sanitised version of

Caribbean music, which involved a basis of jazz with Cuban rhythms and mento (the Jamaican approach to calypso) phrasings stirred in. And in the capital's nightclubs, although the locals wanted it played hotter, they only wanted to hear American hits, so the bands most in demand were the ones that could sound like their U.S. counterparts.

Even the local radio wouldn't support home-grown jazz. Radio Jamaica Rediffusion's weekly *Jazz Hour*, a popular, influential and comparatively leftfield programme in the 50s, refused to acknowledge

the enormous pool of local talent, devoting itself exclusively to Miles, Monk, Milt Jackson and Art Blakey.

The problem lay with the post-slavery colonial attitudes that were so ingrained in the island's people that homegrown culture tended to be scorned, treated as second rate compared to anything imported from America or Britain.

There was no Jamaican record industry at the time, so discs being bought for private consumption or for use by the embryonic sound system scene were all American. So at the time when jazz was at its biggest on the island, in order to make a living from it a musician needed to deliberately avoid native Jamaican characteristics. In other words, any way forward was likely to be second hand at best.

Frustrating is probably not strong enough a word. Then, in addition to such a sense of discouragement, the end of the big band era meant R&B (once again imported from the USA in the form of Louis Jordan, Bill Doggett, Wynonie Harris, Earl Bostic and Lynn Hope) taking over

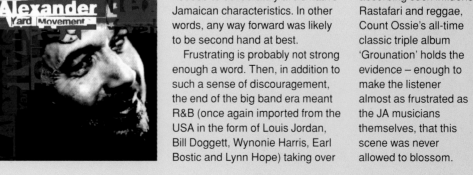

Jazz plugs in

Rock was the main musical force in the late Sixties but jazz, as in the past, touched the popular music of the day.

Left: Guitar man Hiram Bullock with saxophone supremo David Sanborn

AS PSYCHEDELIA'S strobes flickered over the end of the 60s, a new hybrid blinked into the stabbing light. Until then, it had been a universal truth that jazz and rock didn't mix. The two were diametrically opposed; both were created in the mind perhaps, but jazz stayed home while rock music journeyed south to warmer parts. When the new blend manifested itself, there was confusion over its title. Some called it 'fusion', others called it 'crossover'. But the phrase on disciples' and doubters' lips alike was 'jazz-rock'. For the doubters, the new jazz-rock was the runt of a forbidding litter, an Ebola virus destroying itself from lack of victims. But, like the scenario of a Michael Crichton bestseller, the rest of the litter had already colonised the popular undergrowth.

Even those who discounted jazz-rock's toxicity were cautious in their enthusiasm. 'Jazz-rock does exist,' vibester Gary Burton asserted in March 1969, 'though we don't play it, and I don't think it's as important as it might seem. I don't really see an evergrowing fusion between jazz and pop – just a social overlap, really.' Despite his demurral, Burton's group became a training ground for fusion

Left: Dreams, with (l-r) Billy Cobham, John Abercrombie, Eddie Vernon, Mike Brecker (centre back) Doug Lubahn, Jeff Kent, Randy Brecker and (seated) Barry Rogers

guitarists Jerry Hahn, Larry Coryell and Pat Metheny. For some time, musicians on both sides of the musical divide had cast flirtatious eyes at one another. Herbie Hancock's 'Watermelon Man', a 1963 hit for Mongo Santamaria, had become a standard for young rock and blues bands intent on flourishing their 'chops'. Joe Zawinul's 'Mercy, Mercy, Mercy', written on and featuring his electric piano, became a No. 2 R&B hit for Cannonball Adderley in 1967.

Blues-based power trios like Cream and the Jimi Hendrix Experience and, the much larger band of Paul Butterfield indulged in extended improvisation on stage and record, while Burton and flautist Jeremy Steig (whose band, the Satyrs, opened for the Mothers of Invention at New York's Garrick Theater in June 1967) encouraged their band members to adopt amplified instruments.

On the album front, Charles Lloyd's 'Dream Weaver' (1966), Burton's 'Lofty Fake Anagram' (1968), Don Ellis' 'Electric Bath', 'Shock Treatment' and 'Autumn' (all cut in 1968), Eddie Harris' 'Plug Me In' (1968) and Herbie Mann's 'Memphis Underground' (1969) saw the jazz mainstream flirting with rock rhythms.

On the other side of the street, Electric Flag, Blood, Sweat And Tears and Chicago Transit Authority used blues and R&B as a looking-glass through which to step into the time-signatures and disciplines of jazz, while brothers Michael and Randy Brecker, John Abercrombie and Billy Cobham formed Dreams.

Reactions were mixed. West Coast stalwart Bud Shank said Blood, Sweat And Tears had 'opened up a great big door for jazz musicians'. Miles Davis didn't agree: 'Blood, Sweat And Tears is embarrassing to me,' he told *Rolling Stone* in 1969. 'They try to be so hip, I could put together the greatest rock and roll band you ever heard,' he boasted. 'But I don't like the word 'rock' and all that shit. Jazz is an Uncle Tom word. It's a white folks' word.' It was also a smokescreen. Miles had noted the popularity of Charles Lloyd's band, largely due to pianist Keith Jarrett and drummer Jack DeJohnette, when their two bands played at New York's Village Gate.

Lloyd wasn't highly regarded by contemporaries but his post-Coltrane melodies driven by rock-oriented rhythms made him acceptable to the flower power fraternity and a Fillmore regular. His drummer, Spencer Dryden left to join Jefferson Airplane. Miles had also been listening to Sly Stone and Jimi Hendrix, having previously developed a taste for James Brown, Smokey Robinson & The Miracles, Muddy Waters and B.B. King. Like them, Miles had the arrogance of stardom and was tired of playing to small audiences in smaller clubs. He wanted to play in stadiums as the other stars did.

He may not have liked the labels others habitually attached to music, but Miles was to be the conduit through which jazz-rock passed. The catalyst for change that inspired a generation of younger musicians who also sensed the need for new direction.

A novelist, and singer with a huge cult following, the highly literary Gil Scott-Heron

Below: Keyboards man Brian Auger and singer Julie Driscoll made early UK moves into jazz-rock before the term was coined; they are seen here with soul queen Aretha Franklin

He'd been experimenting in the studio with sound textures using amplified pianos, guitars and bass guitars, augmenting his regular band with musicians like George Benson (guitar), Joe Zawinul (keyboards) and newly-recruited English bassist, Dave Holland. Selected tracks found their way onto 'Miles In The Sky' and 'Filles de Kilimanjaro' but much of what was recorded remained unissued until the early 80s.

His new album, 'In A Silent Way', like 'Filles' before it, bore the legend 'Directions In Music by Miles Davis'. With this innovatory compilation of minimal but galvanising events performed by a septet that included Herbie Hancock, Chick Corea (keyboards), Wayne Shorter (tenor & soprano saxes) and Tony Williams (drums), Miles made a decisive move towards a more rock-oriented perspective. Like other landmarks in his career, it was a combination of calculation and chance. Guitarist John McLaughlin was enlisted the night before the February 18 1969 session; Joe Zawinul responded to an early morning summons from Miles with the injunction to 'bring some music'. He arrived with 'In A Silent Way'.

Miles liked Zawinul's music (he'd recorded 'Ascent' and 'Directions' the previous November) but he was not a respecter of composers' wishes. 'When we recorded I just threw out the chord sheets and told everyone to play just the melody,' Miles noted. His own compositions, 'Shhh/Peaceful' and 'It's About That Time', were even more formless and repetitive, rhythmically driven rather than chord based. Minimal percussion and chattering keyboards created a shimmering backdrop for soloists. He'd tried something similar in

December 1967 with 'Circle In The Round' but the nerve and resources of his musicians had let him down.

Before In 'A Silent Way' hit the streets, Miles spent three days in August 1969 laying down the 'fusion' template for what followed in his next album's wake. Producer Teo Macero was enjoined to keep the tapes running at all times. With the exception of the terse 'John McLaughlin', all the double album's titles churned and meandered their way through anything from ten to 27 minutes. Catching the mood of the time, 'Bitches Brew' was a monumental achievement in sonic organisation, using a small army of musicians some of whom would soon form the nuclei of Weather Report (Shorter and Zawinul) and Return To Forever (Chick Corea and Lenny White). Also present, Larry Young and John McLaughlin were part of Tony Williams' Lifetime, an explosive trio that, with temporary recruit Jack Bruce, went further into the realms of rock rhythms and amplified distortio.

A Miles Davis session could be daunting. Musicians would rehearse the day before, only to discover entirely new material was to be recorded the following day. Tunes could be recorded in sections with the musicians sometimes unaware that the tapes were rolling. 'We did a number of sessions just like that,' said Dave Holland, 'where he had a number of things to do, pieces, and we recorded them one by one. A lot of the records were pieced together later.'

'With Miles we delved into very nebulous musical areas as far as our own understanding was concerned,' Herbie Hancock noted. 'Suggestions would come up where you couldn't pinpoint your own responses. I remember John McLaughlin walking out of one session, scratching his head. I felt that way myself, more than once.' Chick Corea analyzed the situation: 'Miles structured the music mostly by predicting the way interrelationships between musicians develop. He would write out little or nothing, but he would put the musicians together and nudge them with comments in such a way that he would in effect be structuring the music.'

John McLaughlin thought Miles 'makes you creative. He puts your creativity on the line. He'll make you do something that's YOU, but also in tune with what he wants. 'McLaughlin, along with Herbie Hancock, Michael Henderson and Billy Cobham, played a crucial role in 'Jack Johnson' (1971), Miles' most overt 'jazz-rock' excursion. Ostensibly the soundtrack for a documentary about the legendary black boxer, the record consisted of two improvisations, 'Right Off' and 'Yesternow', into which sundry other material was edited.

According to Macero, Miles had little to do with the compilation: 'Miles says, "Lookit, I'm going to California. I've got $3,000. I'll give you $1,500. You put together some music from the vault." He left for California and I went to the vault, found some music. I pasted it together, edited it together, and we turned it all around.' 'Live/Evil' (1971) adopted the same format, with brief studio events framing an appearance at Washington's Cellar Door club – a band featuring Gary Bartz, Keith Jarrett, McLaughlin, Henderson and Jack DeJohnette.

The degree to which Miles had manipulated his musicians became evident in the musical diaspora that grew out of those 1970/1 sessions. He was still playing what he termed 'the same old blues shit' but for his backgrounds he adopted a more linear, modal approach, dispensing with form in order to enhance content. But Zawinul and Shorter's Weather Report (with Miroslav Vitous, for gold status, became a chanting Nichiren Shoshu Buddhist; John McLaughlin became a disciple of guru Sri Chinmoy and recruited (Devadip) Carlos Santana and (Narada) Michael Walden along the way; while Chick Corea and his bass player Stanley Clarke were processed into Scientology.

The message seeped into Britain and groups like Colosseum, Gentle Giant, Osibisa and the Keef Hartley Band adopted the mantle of jazz-rock while pursuing broader and less complex musical schemes. One group to announce itself as a jazz-rock band was Dick Morrissey's If; when the band's first self-titled album was issued in 1969, cynics posed the question, 'Why?' Other bands, like Soft Machine, Isotope and Back Door steered clear of being labelled. While European audiences appeared receptive, the movement never really caught on with the Britain's fashion-conscious audiences, although If continued to make albums throughout the early 70s.

As jazz-rock gained in popularity Stateside, individual musicians negotiated their own solo contracts. The same faces turned up at studios no matter whose name was at the top of the session sheet, each peddling their particular expertise. Contractual obligations sometimes necessitated pseudonyms but the disguises were usually transparent. The music they made often seemed to have had more to do with egocentric display than cooperative improvisation, and the results very quickly became bland and predictable.

Despite emulating their rock contemporaries and coveting their star status – right down to patched denim flares, stacked-soled shoes and embarrassing headware – few jazz-rockers crossed the cultural divide. Three exceptions were Jan Hammer, Billy Cobham and Stanley Clarke. Hammer began a prolific solo career in 1973 when the Mahavishnu Orchestra dissolved after three albums. Developing a synthesizer style that deliberately emulated guitar techniques, he became the ubiquitous session man, recording with John Abercrombie, Stanley Clarke, Steve Grossman, Horace Arnold, David Lee Johnson and numerous others.

Mahavishnu drummer Billy Cobham joined Atlantic and his first solo effort, 'Spectrum' (1973), was another milestone in jazz-rock's progress. On it, he assembled a band that included Joe Farrell (tenor sax), Jan Hammer, Ron Carter (bass) and ex-Zephyr guitarist Tommy Bolin. Then in rock band, the James Gang and soon to join Deep Purple, Bolin was a volatile and gifted musician whose playing on Cobham's album and Alphonse Mouzon's 'Mind Transplant' (1975) encouraged rock guitarists like Jeff Beck to seek broader horizons. Beck recorded with Stanley Clarke and Hammer and toured with the latter's group.

Clarke's self-titled debut album (1974) and 'Journey To Love' (1975) rounded up the usual suspects, including Hammer, Corea, McLaughlin, plus drummers Lenny White and Tony Williams. No longer content with his usual role in jazz ensembles, Clarke's later albums became simplistic vehicles for his increasingly bravura technique. The sartorial elegance he affected on his record sleeves reflected the rock chic to which he and his cohorts pretended. Like Alphonso Johnson, who joined Weather Report in 1974, his profile seemed more that of a guitarist than a bass player.

For a time, guitarists were jazz-rock's defining image. John McLaughlin and Al DiMeola were the Butch and Sundance of their ilk, pursued by a posse that included John Abercrombie, Joe Beck, Larry Coryell, Pat Metheny, Lee Ritenour, John Scofield and Ralph Towner. Joe Zawinul was asked in 1973 why Weather Report hadn't recruited one. 'There's a certain chemistry in the band which would be destroyed by adding another melodic instrument,' he averred. 'Actually, I just haven't found a guitar player that I'd like to have in

Above: Patrice Rushen on keyboards, in a one-off all-star group at the Montreux festival that included (in the background) Carlos Santana

Alphonse Mouzon and Airto Moreira), John McLaughlin's Mahavishnu Orchestra (with Jan Hammer, Jerry Goodman and Rick Laird) and Chick Corea's Return To Forever (with Bill Connors, Stanley Clarke and Lenny White) became obsessed with both to produce widely varying results.

While Miles kept his feet in the street, calling his album 'Bitches Brew', his alumni turned their heads inward and upward with 'I Sing The Body Electric' (1972), 'The Inner Mounting Flame' (1972) and 'Hymn Of The Seventh Galaxy' (1973). Rhythmically complex ensemble themes and a virtuoso level of improvisation were realised using every resource studios offered. 'I don't think we've left Miles behind,' said Zawinul. 'We are just somewhere else, man. Another entity that grew out of him. He's the father and we are the sons.'

With prodigal habits, it seemed. Along with their new younger audiences, some Davis progeny explored non-chemical means of enhancing their 'creativity'. Herbie Hancock, who virtually invented jazz-funk with 'Head Hunters' (1973), a Top Ten album that qualified my group.' Three years later, he was to recruit Jaco Pastorius, a prodigiously gifted musician who'd never played acoustic bass and wielded his fretless bass guitar like a latterday Hendrix.

1976 was something of a watershed. While Weather Report entered their most popular period, Return To Forever disbanded, and the increasingly grandiose Mahavishnu Orchestra pulled the plug when John McLaughlin formed Shakti, an acoustic Indo-jazz fusion band with violinist L. Shankar and two percussionists. Herbie Hancock had continued to plough a funk groove with 'Thrust' (1974) and 'Manchild' (1975) but, like Chick Corea and Keith Jarrett, he too returned to playing acoustic piano. Until the mid-80s, he combined tours with V.S.O.P., a re-formed Miles Davis Quintet with Freddie Hubbard in the trumpet chair, and some technologically profligate albums aimed, primarily, at the expanding Japanese market.

Previously associated with hard-boppers Cannonball Adderley and Dexter Gordon, the ebullient George Duke was working with violinist Jean-Luc Ponty in 1969 when Ponty made 'King Kong' (1969), an album of Frank Zappa tunes produced by the composer. Both became members of the Mothers of Invention in 1970/1, but Duke returned for a second stint between 1973/5. Through Zappa, he embraced new technology and made a series of jazz-funk albums, including 'Feel' (1974), 'The Aura Will Prevail' (1975) and Liberated Fantasies' (1976).

In 1976, he formed a band with Billy Cobham, Alphonso Johnson and John Scofield and toured Europe with Shakti and Weather Report. Duke then joined Epic and recorded 'Reach For It' (1977) and had a No.2 R&B hit with the title song.

As the decade ended, the 'rock' and 'funk' varieties of jazz died back into the undergrowth. Weather Report continued to make an album a year, losing Pastorius after 'Weather Report' (1982) and calling it a day with 'This Is This' (1986). Stanley Clarke and George Duke joined forces for the Clarke/Duke Project, a profitable enterprise pursued on and off through the 80s. Herbie Hancock continued on his bifurcated way, with a series of conventional jazz and overtly commercial albums, the latter including 'Sunlight' (1978), with its single hit, 'I Thought It Was You', 'Feets Don't Fail Me Now' (1979), 'Mr Hands' (1980), 'Magic Windows' (1981) and 'Future Shock' (1983), from which the frenetic 'Rockit' was a hit.

After Big Fun (1974), Miles Davis made two albums – 'Agharta' and 'Pangaea' both recorded live in February 1975 in Japan, the band included Sonny Fortune (alto sax), Reggie Lucas, Pete Cosey (guitars) and Al Foster (drums), before disappearing into unhealthy seclusion to add to his Prince Of Darkness aura.

Davis re-emerged six years later with 'The Man With The Horn' (1981). Successive albums, 'Star People' (1983), 'Decoy' and 'You're Under Arrest' (1985), found him veering directly into popular music and support slots with Diana Ross.

By then no-one was talking about jazz-rock anymore. Arguably no-one was playing it either. Back in 1969, Gary Burton had said 'Jazz-rock may turn out to be pretty unimportant in the future of music. The creation of meaningful music takes alot more than intention. Rock music offers more psychological appeal and the music is less complex, easier to grasp. The emphasis is on charisma, not content.'

Jazz-rock's epitaph had been written at birth.

Left: Ex-Miles tenor giant
and jazz-rock pioneer
Wayne Shorter
Opposite: With a
collection of their albums,
Shorter and Zawinul's group
Weather Report
Overleaf: George Duke &
Stanley Clarke

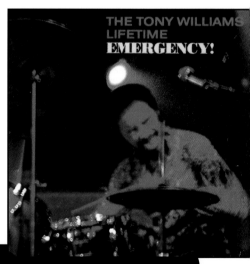

CD CHECKLIST
MILES DAVIS Bitches Brew (Columbia), Water Babies (Columbia)
WEATHER REPORT I Sing The Body Electric (Columbia)
MAHAVISHNU ORCHESTRA Inner Mounting Flame (Columbia)
DON ELLIS Electric Bath (Columbia)
STANLEY CLARKE/GEORGE DUKE Clarke/Duke Project (Epic)
HERBIE HANCOCK Head Hunters (Columbia)
TONY WILLIAMS LIFETIME Emergency! (Polydor)
DREAMS Dreams (Columbia)

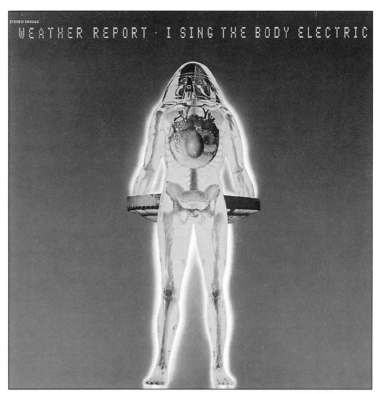

Jazz Funks (

F TECHNOLOGY CHANGES
society, it also changes music; and if
jazz is to act as a reflection of the
times, it too must undergo a drastic
overhaul at crucial points in its
development.

By the same token, if musicians are to
sustain a career, they must be
prepared (yet again) to dance to a different drummer.

That time had arrived once more.

From the mid-60s onwards, jazz appeared
to absorb almost anything that hovered into
view, the most high profile being that of
'Mod' culture which had been instigated by
way of post-Beatles pop, black dance music
and the cross-over faction represented by
Herbie Mann, Charles Lloyd, Ramsey Lewis,
Eddie Harris, Cannonball Adderley, etc.

To emphasise this point, electric bass players took their cue from Sly & The Family
Stone's Larry Graham – throwing away their
picks to vigorously slap, chop and pop the fret
board or, as 'Dance To The Music' so noisily
affirmed, kicked down hard on the fuzz-box
effects pedal.

While jazz rock was getting more complex, a self-conscious 'musician's music', jazz funk brought fusion back to the streets of the ghetto with dance-oriented million-sellers in the charts, and a no-nonsense attitude on stage which echoed James Brown's 'Say It Out Loud, I'm Black and I'm Proud'.

In between the assassinations of Malcolm X in 1965 and Martin Luther King three years later, Merritt College students Bobby Seale and Huey P. Newton launched the Black Panther Party in Oakland in 1966, prompting the emergent avant garde to supply an often cacophonous soundtrack as ghettos from Watts to New Jersey burned.

Closer inspection may have determined that even the most abstract squawking of saxophones weren't all that far removed from headstrong honking R&B bar-walkers. But, ultimately, such outpourings only succeeded in alienating much of their potential audience.

Even more confusing, the appeal of the front-runners Albert Ayler, Roscoe Mitchell, Archie Shepp and Ornette Coleman seemed to find majority support in both the States and Europe amongst young white campus radicals as opposed to young blacks.

In fact, disenfranchised young black ex-GIs returning home from a tour of duty in Vietnam had become more politicised than ever and demanded music that was more instantly accessible if it was to both attract attention and justify their growing 'Black Power' stance.

This, they discovered on records such as James Brown's 'Say It Loud – I'm Black And I'm Proud' (1968); Edwin Starr's 'War' (1970); The Temptations' 'Ball Of Confusion' (1970); Donny Hathaway's 'The Ghetto' (1970); Gil Scott-Heron & Brian Jackson's 'The Revolution Will Not Be Televised' (1970) and 'The Bottle' (1974); Marvin Gaye's 'What's Goin' On' (1971); Sly Stone's epochal chart-topping album, 'There's A Riot Goin' On' (1971); War 'Slippin' Into Darkness' (1972); The Staples Singers' 'Respect Yourself' (1972); The Ohio Players' 'Skin Tight' and 'Fire' (1974), plus any number of songs from soul laureate Curtis Mayfield, first as lead singer with The Impressions and later, with albums under his own name such as the damning 'There's No Place Like America Today' (1975).

More provocative was the apocalyptic rhetoric espoused by New York's black Muslim street commentators – The Last Poets on their self-titled 1970 debut album.

Despite selling in excess of 350,000 copies to reach as high as number 29 on *Billboard* magazine's weekly albums listing, the great vehemence expressed later excluded it from most 70s nostalgia playlists. Instead, it acted as a handbook to any number of rap acts from NWA to Public Enemy.

Silk-suited vocal groups who executed their routines with choreographed military precision had long been the mainstay of black pop, but now their once unassailable position was about to be successfully challenged by groups who simultaneously sang and played instruments like white rock bands.

Earth Wind & Fire, The Ohio Players, Sly & The Family Stone, War, Mandrill, Charles Wright & his Watts 103rd Street Rhythm Band, The Fatback Band, The Bar-Kays, The Tower Of Power and Kool & The Gang (who had first started out in '64 as The Jazziacs) set the running, leaving The Isley Brothers to make great capital out of the fact that Jimi Hendrix had at one time been amongst their illustrious number.

Furthermore, while it was commonplace to flash Black Power salutes, the seven strong Sly & The Family Stone were both racially mixed and included females whose role was much more than decorative – sister Rose Stone played keyboards leaving, Cynthia Robinson on trumpet. Yet Sly was never subjected to the kind of pressures Hendrix endured from black activists for carrying an all-white rhythm section.

Over the years, James Brown may have proclaimed himself to be the Godfather of practically every good-foot innovation that has come along but the term 'funk' was common terminology in modern jazz when referring to the soul-drenched East Coast hard bop of Horace Silver, Art Blakey and Cannonball Adderley.

Still, there's no question about it that James Brown was to funk what Ray Charles had been to R&B – a font of all knowledge and an on-going inspiration to successive generations of musicians.

Even it the 90s, a crowd of courtiers that included George Duke, Stanley Clark, Joshua Redmen, Quincy Jones, Pat Metheny, Eddie Harris and Joe Sample all stood in line backstage, at the Montreux Jazz Festival, wildly applauding JB as he majestically strolled from

Opposite: From jazz-rock to jazz-funk, Herbie Hancock, and (below) his guitar support Melvin 'Wah Wah' Watson

they were being created right there on the studio floor amongst the empty beer bottles and cigarette stubs. But that's precisely what was happening, as JB skilfully directed the traffic, handing out precise instructions to Maceo and Jabo.

Sensing the occasion, the rhythm section dug deeper than anyone had ever attempted before, as the brass riffed incessantly and guitarist Jimmy Nolen chops away. Like a major league coach, Brown urged Maceo on – 'can I get a little?'– before telling the band what to do next.

There were few jazz groups around who could cook up such natural excitement and everyone from Miles Davis to his former cohort Herbie Hancock weren't slow on the new groove uptake.

Neither were Blue Note Records' sanctified mainstays Donald Byrd, Lou Donaldson, Horace Silver and hordes of organists who had no problems adapting – thickening up the textures and intensifying the back beat or, as James Brown testified on 'Cold Sweat' 'give the drummer some'.

By 1970, Brown was exclaiming in the loudest possible terms 'Get Up, I Feel Like Being A Sex Machine'. Furthermore, his backing musicians were no longer stiffly billed as the James Brown Orchestra but the more snappier JBs.

For the time being, section leaders Fred Wesley (trombone), Maceo Parker, Pee Wee Ellis and Clyde Stubblefield were replaced by a new out-of-leftfield rhythm squad built around an axis involving the Collins brothers Catfish (guitar) and Bootsy (bass), plus Jabo Starks (drums) and Bobby Byrd (organ).

his dressing room towards the stage and a capacity audience.

Though the same age as Brown, Quincy Jones was adamant, insisting that 'JB is our Elvis . . . our Beatles.'

It was in May 1967 that James Brown made one of his most important career moves when he recorded 'Cold Sweat' a track seemingly created there, on-the-spot with tenorman Pee Wee Ellis.

'Cold Sweat' proved to be a showcase as much for altoist Maceo Parker as legendary 'Funky Drummer' Clyde Stubblefield.

Atlantic Records' producer Jerry Wexler later confessed that 'Cold Sweat' was a record that deeply affected everyone who heard it, especially the likes of Aretha Franklin and other major soul stars: 'For a time, no one could get a handle on what to do next.'

John 'Jabo' Starks, who took over from Stubblefield to further push the new groove, on the follow-up 'Get It Together' admitted: 'You couldn't write that feel.'

'Cold Sweat' and 'Get It Together' and 'Funky Drummer' (the latter much-sampled by hip-hoppers) all gave the impression that

Below, left to right: Earth Wind and Fire, Funkadelic and the Isley Brothers

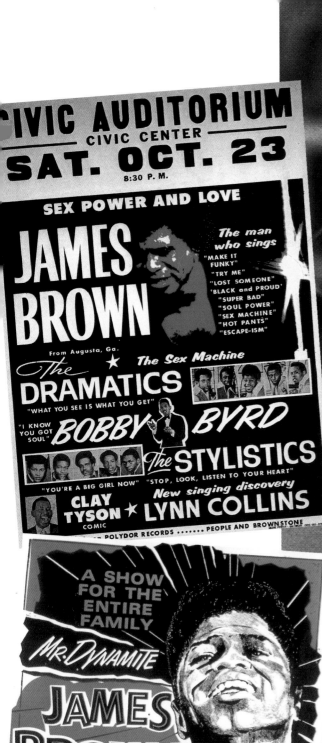

CIVIC AUDITORIUM
CIVIC CENTER
SAT. OCT. 23
8:30 P. M.

SEX POWER AND LOVE

JAMES BROWN

The man who sings
"MAKE IT FUNKY"
"TRY ME"
"LOST SOMEONE"
"BLACK and PROUD"
"SUPER BAD"
"SOUL POWER"
"SEX MACHINE"
"HOT PANTS"
"ESCAPE-ISM"

From Augusta, Ga.

The Sex Machine
The **DRAMATICS**
"WHAT YOU SEE IS WHAT YOU GET"

"I KNOW YOU GOT SOUL" **BOBBY BYRD**

The **STYLISTICS**
"YOU'RE A BIG GIRL NOW" "STOP, LOOK, LISTEN TO YOUR HEART"

New singing discovery
CLAY TYSON COMIC ★ **LYNN COLLINS**

POLYDOR RECORDS .... PEOPLE AND BROWNSTONE

A SHOW FOR THE ENTIRE FAMILY

Mr. Dynamite

JAMES BROWN

N.Y. APOLLO
Theatre

THUR. JULY 28 8:00 P.M.
GUARANTEED SELL-OUT...COME EARLY!

KING
5 - 1047
STEREO

James Brown
SAY IT LOUD
I'M BLACK AND I'M PROUD

Say It Loud
I'm Black And Proud
Goodbye My Love
Licking Stick
I'll Lose My Mind
AND MANY OTHER HITS

Funk was never ever to sound the same again. Neither was jazz!

James Brown clarified his unassailable position as 'Soul Brother No.1' 'The band is much younger ...it's a new sound...there's a revolution going on and I have to write with these younger guys in mind.'

This he did.

For a time in the early 70s, the level of respect bestowed upon James Brown was also directed towards Sly Stone.

Sadly, ongoing drug-related problems, brushes with the authorities and a lack of self-discipline revealing itself in his failure to show for 26 out of 80 hot ticket dates booked in 1970, would seem to have permanently destroyed Sly's once fertile muse.

But even that can't altogether distract from his wildly influential watershed singles 'Dance To The Music' (1968), 'Everyday People' (1968/No.1), 'I Wanna Take You Higher' (1969) and 'Thank You (Falettin Me Be Mice Elf Agin)' (1970/No.1), 'Family Affair' (1971/No.1) and a triumvirate of big-selling albums 'Stand!' (1969/No.13), 'Greatest Hits' (1970/No.2) and the chart-topping 'There's A Riot Goin' On' (1971).

As far back as 1968, Miles Davis admitted that he wasn't listening to, 'no jazz , but James Brown, Jimi Hendrix & Sly Stone's "Dance To The Music."

That shit he [Sly] was doing was badder than a motherfucker, had all kinds of funky shit up in it. When I first heard Sly, I almost

wore out those first two or three records "Dance To The Music", "Stand" and "Everybody Is A Star".'

Similarly, Brown and Stone were seldom off Hendrix's turntable.

Davis and Hendrix also shared a mutual interest in the Last Poets.

Following the death of Hendrix, shortly before he was to record an album with Gil Evans, and possibly another one involving the trumpet maestro, Davis had become aware that because the guitarist had worked to a white hippy rock audience, few young black kids knew of his existence or the extent of his influence.

Black kids were checking out JB, Sly, Aretha and Motown:

'After playing a lot of these white halls I was starting to wonder why I shouldn't be trying to get to young black kids with my music. They were into funk, music they could dance to.'

June 1972 with JB and Sly foremost in his mind, Davis cut 'On The Corner' with a collective personnel of 15 players (not mentioned on the sleeve) that included Teo Macero, Dave Liebman, Carlos Garnett (saxes), Chick Corea, Herbie Hancock, (keyboards), John McLaughlin (guitar), Colin Walcott (sitar), Jack DeJohnette (drums).

To Davis' eternal chagrin, Columbia promoted 'On the Corner' not as an urban funk release but as a jazz album, and saleswise it suffered badly as a result.

A year later, Herbie Hancock's 'Headhunters' was marketed at young blacks, quickly attaining the lucrative sales figures Miles had anticipated for 'On The Corner'.

Miles Davis: 'Everyone at Columbia said, "Oh. So that's what Miles was talking about!"'

As jazz searched for a new high-profile identity, Herbie Hancock's 'Headhunters' (1973) proved to be as much of a creative signpost as Miles Davis' earlier two-disc 'Bitches Brew' which had come about, in 1970, after the trumpeter had threatened to put together a better rock band than the one that Jimi Hendrix led.

Miles may well have collected the kudos with 'Bitches Brew', 'On The Corner' (1972) and a bunch of other 'live' recordings, but Donald Byrd (then a music educator at Howard University) was as intrigued with Brown and Motown as anything else then available. By turning in a succession of jazz funk albums 'Ethiopian Knights' (1972), 'Black Byrd' (1973), 'Street Lady' (1974), Byrd made the big numbers to reach an even wider listening audience than his fellow hornman.

As the colourfully dressed white rock bands were demonstrating, there was serious money to be earned and the emergent puffball afro-haired brothers wanted a piece of the action and the clothes to go with it. And also, unfortunately, the drugs.

But, whereas rock and roll and jazz were diametrically opposed there were no such demarcation lines in black music – a typical Apollo Theatre bill was just as likely to feature a funk jazz maestro along with a love doctor and a sassy girl group.

Herbie Hancock:

'I listened to James Brown and Sly and said, "Look, I want to find out what this is, and I'm going to go as far as I can." That's why I got some cats who can play funk ...I knew that I had never heard any jazz players really play funk like the funk that I had been listening to.

'Instead of getting jazz cats who knew how to play funk, I got funk cats who knew how to play jazz. So that's what it was.'

Hancock's 'Headhunters' was as much of a financial consideration as it was an artistic endeavour.

'I wanted the audience that read *Cosmopolitan* and *Vogue* as well as the jazz magazine readership. Jazz used to be rebel music, and still is. My own personal brand of rock happened to be R&B, James Brown and Sly Stone stuff, so I worked towards a fusion of standard jazz with that.'

A switch from Blue Note to Warner Brothers resulted in 'Fat Albert Rotunda'; an album based on a Bill Cosby Cartoon Show character which Hancock had originally soundtracked for television.

Conceding that some of the fans were disappointed with this tentative mix of James Brown and bebop, Hancock felt that it should not be compared with his more straight ahead Blue Note canon. 'Fat Albert', he insisted, was his roots album.

'I don't like the idea of having to be stuck within the mainstream of jazz.'

Hancock quit Blue Note, adamant that making 'Fat Albert' on the label would have

been 'almost impossible and a waste.' Blue Note, he was convinced, wanted to pigeon hole him. By his own admission, Hancock discovered there was a lot more to playing funk than he originally anticipated.

'It's a whole different set of criteria, too, based as much on what you don't play as what you do.

'In R&B, solos aren't as important to the overall success as they are in jazz – you can destroy the grooves with extended soloing. those people who want more solos don't know what I know, because I've learned that it doesn't work.

'Oddly enough, the rock listeners can often get to my music easier than the jazz people, who come in expecting something specific and perhaps don't get it.'

Bizarrely, after the release of 'Fat Albert', Hancock was quoted as insisting that 'jazz musicians were being led to the slaughterhouse' and compromised to play rock!

Prior to 'Fat Albert', Hancock had been reduced to existing on his 'Watermelon Man' royalties, having folded his road band. The gold-selling status attained by 'Headhunters' proved a timely rescue.

It's Hancock's opinion that Miles Davis, Weather Report, Donald Byrd together with his own bag of tracks helped to ensure a growing audience for jazz amongst today's youngsters. Indeed, it's allowed him to run parallel careers as both a jazz-funker and a straight ahead doyen. He's even secured cameo roles in movies ['Round Midnight].

Yet, by 1977, Hancock had gathered together all Davis' former acoustic quintet stalwarts Wayne Shorter, Ron Carter and Tony Williams and, with Freddie Hubbard in the role once held by Miles toured and recorded successfully as V.S.O.P.

It wasn't just jazz artists who were busy reinventing themselves. When, in 1971, Stevie Wonder came of age, he presented Motown Records with an ultimatum: the label either allowed him total artistic control over his already spectacularly successful recording career, or he quit. Motown soon renegotiated on Wonder's terms.

Though he was still plastering the world's charts with hit singles, Wonder promptly abandoned Motown's familiar clanking backdrop that serviced the label's entire talent roster, and, against a high-tech electronic battery of ARP synthesizers, clavinet and Moog that owed much to Billy Preston, he celebrated his emancipation with a statement-of-intent, 'Music Of My Mind' (1972). Later, in the same year, he delivered 'Talkin' Book'.

Left: Former Blue Note hard-bopper Donald Byrd, and (above) the group he formed from his college students, The Blackbyrds

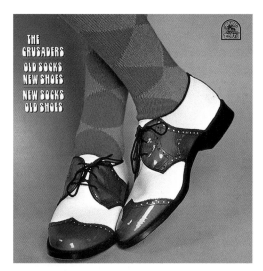

Below: Tenor sax funkster Grover Washington Jr.

Here, amid the sugary 'You Are The Sunshine Of My Life' and other self-absorbed ballads, Wonder drop-kicked his heaviest funk to date in the shape of the relentlessly jagged 'Superstition'.

But, it was on the 1973 follow-up, the Grammy-winning 'Innervisions', that he turned in the cinematic, 'Living For The City', the creative peak of his career. Wonder stepped away from his familiar user-friendly persona to intercut the themes of racial injustice and sprawling urban decay with dramatic *verite* soundbites and a sense of genuine anger he would never again aspire to.

Though not a jazz player, Wonder has paid tribute to Ellington with his No.1 single 'Sir Duke' 1977 and, on two separate occasions, Wes Montgomery, 'Bye Bye World' and 'We All Remember Wes'. Elsewhere, he has phoned-in instantly-recognisable guest-shot harmonica licks on several jazz dates.

Two decades on, 'Innervisions'-era Wonder still maintains a highly negotiable currency, with Acid Jazz acts like Jamiroquai appearing to pick up where Wonder left off.

One of the prime ingredients in the jazz-funk mix was the rhythmic scrubbed 'whucka-chucka, whucka-chucka' wah-wah guitar sound, achieved, in the main, by a Boomerang effects pedal.

The heavyweight practioner at this was Melvin (Wah-Wah) Watson (nee Ragin), who had previously paid dues in a number of soul groups which included Bohannon (where he picked up the 'Wah-Wah' moniker), Motown's Bobby Taylor and The Vancouvers and, along with fellow picker Dennis Coffey, became one of Motown producer Norman Whitfield's much used psychedelic-soul sessioneers – The Funk Brothers – before enlisting with Herbie Hancock.

In the mid-70s, Melvin Wah Wah Watson suggested that jazz virtuosos John McLaughlin and Larry Coryell switched to acoustic guitar as they couldn't handle funk.

'I don't play jazz but I can stir up enough shit and put an element into jazz to make you not think jazz all the time but the jazz shit is still happening, That's very important.

'What is music if it is not a stepping stone? A bridge for the player and the played to Jazz is just one of those bridges. It has no especially divine role, and if players can experiment and find new ways in which they can meet more people, and make them happier, then music will be fulfilling its role much more than if the player is keeping himself restricted.'

Though often dubious storywise, the soundtracks to black exploitation movies *Shaft* (Isaac Hayes), *Superfly* (Curtis Mayfield) and *Trouble Man* (Marvin Gaye) emphasised this new brand of hard funk. The worldwide success of soundtrack albums was also a means of preventing jazz musicians – of the calibre of trombonist J.J.Johnson – from going back to their day job.

There were a few minor drawbacks.

In the quest to attract listeners, numerous album sleeves painfully illustrated, that the sartorial street smarts of those like drummer Alphonse Mouzon were severely called into question as browsers fought hard not to burst into fits of uncontrollable laughter. Even some Isley Brothers covers begged disbelief.

Competition increased with funketeers either sustaining their careers, slipping into obscurity or, worse, unashamedly dashing towards MOR respectability with obscene haste. Yet there was no shortage of seasoned campaigners and fresh-faced conscripts ready to hustle for precious jukebox space.

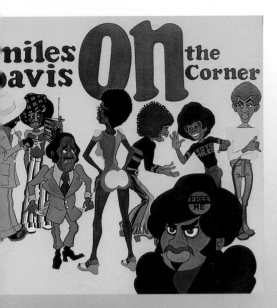

These included Billy Preston ('Outa Space'/1972); Rufus featuring Chaka Khan ('Tell Me Something Good'/1974); The Crusaders ('Southern Comfort'/1974); The Average White Band, ('Pick Up The Pieces'/1974); Lonnie Liston Smith ('Expansions'/1975); The Brecker Brothers ('Sneakin' Up Behind You'/1975); George Benson ('Breezin''/1976), Quincy Jones ('Mellow Madness'/1976); former Pharoah Sanders drummer Norman Connors ('You Are My Starship'/1976); John Handy ('Work Song'/1976); Brothers Johnson ('I'll Be Good To You'/1976); Roy Ayers ('Let's Do It'/1978); Tom Browne ('Funkin' For Jamaica'/1980); Ronnie Laws ('Always There'/1981).

Following the acclaim that greeted George Duke's albums 'Reach For It' (1977) and 'Don't Let Go' (1978), the noisy throwdown jams he cut with bass spanking virtuoso Stanley Clarke as The Clarke/Duke Project (1981) made them jazz festival showstoppers.

It was Earth Wind And Fire that towered above all else commercially. Conceived by former Ramsey Lewis sticksman Maurice White,

a blend of exquisite vocals and hackle-raising horn arrangements, secured EW&F the rare distinction of being heavily programmed on both jazz and soul radio.

Crossover acceptance ensued with albums 'That's The Way Of The World' (1975/No.1), 'Gratitude' (1975/No.1), 'Spirit' (1976/No.2), 'All 'N All' (1977/No.3), 'I Am' (1979/No.3) positioning them as one of the planet's most popular attractions. As visually exciting in person as on record, in the cosmic scheme of things the many-handed EW&F takes its rightful place alongside Ellington and Basie as one of the truly inspired black orchestras.

If Sun Ra insisted he had been beamed down from Saturn, then, in another universe, super showman George Clinton's crazed three-ring Parliafunkadelicment Thang took the funk to its illogical conclusion.

In Clinton's mind, funk was nothing less than a meaning-of-life philosophy. A cosmic cure-all with close on fifty bizarrely-dressed glam-funk party animals gathered together under a 'One Nation Under A Groove' banner.

The Mothership Connection was Groove Central and with James Brown's Bootsy Collins-led rhythm section in the engine room, along with former JB stars Maceo Parker and Fred Wesley, Clinton's self-proclaimed P-Funk (Pure Funk) mutated into mix-and-match units including Parliament, Funkadelic, The Horny Horns, Bootsy's Rubber Band, The Brides Of Funkenstein and others. By the end of the 70s, Clinton took monster funk further out than even the Starship Enterprise had ventured. Sadly, he never quite got back from deep space!

A less hysterical off-shoot of this funky stuff was the esoteric explorations of Ornette Coleman's Prime Time and the marginally popular Defunkt, James Blood Ulmer,

Jamaldeen Tacuma and Ronald Shannon Jackson's Decoding Society.

Jazz-funk came in varying degrees of potency. A popular easy blend created by one-time Verve staff producer Creed Taylor glided from his CTI/Kudu organisation in glossy designer gatefold sleeves. Soon a queue formed headed by George Benson, Freddie Hubbard, Grover Washington, Jr, Airto, Stanley Turrentine, Joe Farrell, Hank Crawford, as Taylor surpassed the bevelled formula he had previously created on Verve with Wes Montgomery and Jimmy Smith.

Taylor's clear recordings, engineered by Rudy Van Gelder, sold in vast quantities with 'Red Clay' (Freddie Hubbard), 'White Rabbit' (George Benson) and 'Mister Magic' (Grover Washington, Jr) being just three releases which, in time honoured tradition, ruffled the purists to where he was branded a heretic.

The battle lines were now drawn.

In a parallel universe, saxophone stylists Grover Washington, Jr, and David Sanborn moved centre-stage to reach a wider audience than most jazz players could ever dream of.

Washington, the smoother of the two, had shown his hand with 'Mister Magic' (1975), Sanborn, at the other extreme, was more exciting in person than his fast-selling albums indicated. Such was the emotional intensity of this former-Butterfield Blues Band altoman, who claimed his style was 'somewhere midway between Louis Jordan's jump jive and Eric Dolphy's cry', that he took jazz funk to a new level, emerging as the most widely imitated sax player since Coltrane.

In company with Cannonball Adderley, Miles Davis, Bill Evans and Wes Montgomery, it could be said that David Sanborn shaped the post-Trane sound of jazz.

The argument continues!

Blaxploitation

Bottom left: Richard Roundtree eyes up the opposition in *Shaft*

Right: Tamara Dobson totes her thing as the avenging angel *Cleopatra Jones*

Stepin Fetchit has a lot to answer for. To the moviegoers of the late 20s and 30s, the gangly, open-mouthed black man epitomised his race. Hollywood black males were perceived as an amiable lot, eye-rolling, singin' n' jivin', ever ready to provide a shoeshine.

WITH THE COMING OF 60s Black Power, Tinsel Town revised its attitude. Suddenly, black movies became Malcolm X-rated and actor Richard Roundtree appeared, not as some hat-tipping descendent of Uncle Remus, but as *Shaft*, a dark avenger, unstoppable, sex-sharp, streetwise and as cool as a Harlem icebox in December. He also came kitted out with his very own soundtrack theme, a funk-filled wah-wah guitar drenched affair crafted by Isaac Hayes, that made everyone aware of his presence. This combination of fights, action, music proved equally unstoppable (and profitable) right through the 70s. Roundtree fought his way through a television series and a couple of further movies, stopping at one point to gain the vocal assistance of The Four Tops as he blasted his way through a gang of unfortunate slave traders (*Shaft In Africa*) who hadn't viewed the original flick and thereby were unaware of the opposition's way with an arms delivery and an attached slice of sock-it-to-'em soul. The final instalment of this big screen trilogy (*Shaft's Big Score*) vibrated to the sound of Freddie Hubbard's 'Symphony For Shafted Souls (The Big Chase)'

This combination of hit movie and attached chart record proved too much for cash-hungry Hollywood to ignore. Before long every ghetto became a set and every soundstage a jukebox. If Roundtree shared annihilation activities with Hayes, then Ron (*Superfly*) O'Neal made mayhem in the company of Curtis Mayfield, Robert (*Trouble Man*) Hooks attempted mass wipeout to the jazz juice of Marvin Gaye and Max (The Mack) Julien attempted all the right sexual and violent movies to the accompaniment of a score fashioned by Motown's Willie Hutch. Not that it was all down to rippling black biceps. Someone, somewhere, figured out that a shapely, karate-dispensing ebony superwoman wouldn't be at all a bad idea.

And so Tamara Dobson became *Cleopatra Jones*, CIA narco queen supreme, as Millie Jackson and Joe Simon warbled soulfully amid thumbs up and J.J.Johnson supplied some atmospheric incidentals. Elsewhere, Pam Grier went into the castration industry as Foxy Brown with Willie Hutch again offering street-sound support.

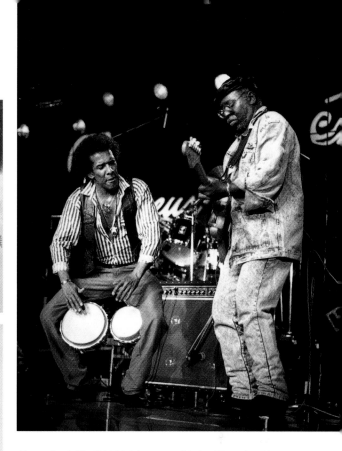

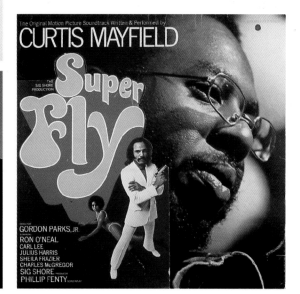

Above: Curtis Mayfield (right), responsible for the music of the worldwide box office blockbuster *Superfly*

RIFFS EQUATED WITH BIFFS right down the line, with Isaac Hayes scoring *Tough Guys* and *Truck Turner,* and also appearing in both.

As the body-count increased, the genre rapidly deteriorated and an inevitable backlash (much of it from black community leaders who saw such movies as stereotyping the black male as murderous and misogynistic) ensued in the wake of such gratuitous violence.

Before such movies all but disappeared from production schedules, there included amongst the fifty or more so blood-bath epics two from James Brown, *Slaughter's Big Rip-Off* and *Black Caesar* (aka *Hell Up In Harlem*), *Across 110th Street* (featuring music by Bobby Womack), *Coffy* (Roy Ayers), *Uptight* (Booker T & The MGs) and *Cool Breeze* (Quincy Jones).

Frequently, the soundtrack on these movies was of much higher quality than both the plot and the script, and while the these last two elements quickly faded from the collective memory, the music – *Shaft* and *Superfly* being two primary examples – was relevant long after as a guiding influence on both urban jazz and future funk.

195

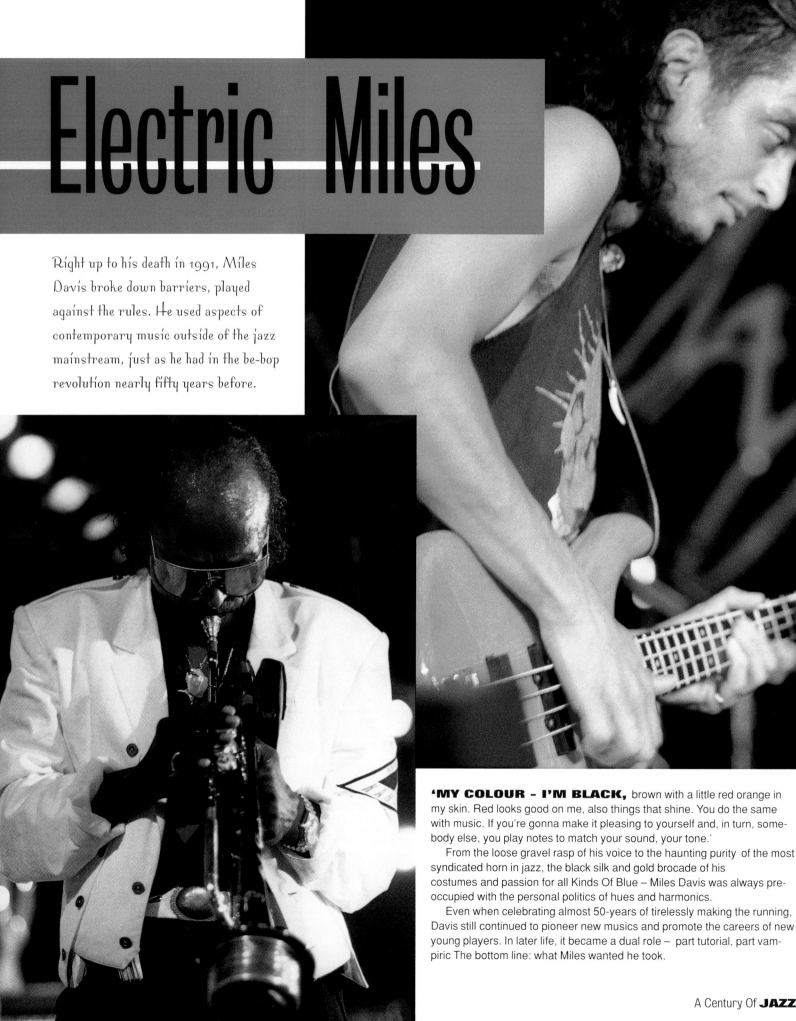

Electric Miles

Right up to his death in 1991, Miles Davis broke down barriers, played against the rules. He used aspects of contemporary music outside of the jazz mainstream, just as he had in the be-bop revolution nearly fifty years before.

'MY COLOUR – I'M BLACK, brown with a little red orange in my skin. Red looks good on me, also things that shine. You do the same with music. If you're gonna make it pleasing to yourself and, in turn, somebody else, you play notes to match your sound, your tone.'

From the loose gravel rasp of his voice to the haunting purity of the most syndicated horn in jazz, the black silk and gold brocade of his costumes and passion for all Kinds Of Blue – Miles Davis was always preoccupied with the personal politics of hues and harmonics.

Even when celebrating almost 50-years of tirelessly making the running, Davis still continued to pioneer new musics and promote the careers of new young players. In later life, it became a dual role – part tutorial, part vampiric The bottom line: what Miles wanted he took.

If jazz was the subject of discussion, Miles persistently placed great emphasis on the distinct characteristics inherent in black and white players. And, you either employ or avoid a faction on the basis of their specific qualities or the lack of them.

Such statements have widely been regarded as either racist or bullshit or both. Others put it down to mere attention-seeking, Miles wilfully going out of his way to be at once provocative and mischievous.

It's no secret that Miles is on record as once mistaking a record by altoist Phil Woods for a black player, Sun Ra as a dodgy Euro-band ('we wouldn't play no shit like that') and insisting that funketeers Earth, Wind & Fire would kick ass had they included a couple of white trumpet players amongst their number.

Then there was the question of three out of the seven members of Miles 'Tutu'-period road band being young, gifted and white. And why did Miles replace John Scofield with yet another white guitarist Robben Ford as opposed to any number of black guitarists?

''Cause most black guys can only play like Jimi Hendrix, and then for not too long', was his dismissive one-liner.

'Robben Ford has the knack of playing the right things in the right style at precisely the the right moment. Another thing he has going for him – he doesn't overplay. Quite an exceptional musician – a rare find.'

When, after six months, Ford left to marry, Miles – unable to find a suitable replacement and having been unable to persuade George Duke to join his band – settled for two electric bass players!

Furthermore, those invited into Miles' Manhattan household or his hotel suite come away talking about how the only albums they ever saw lying around were the latest pop ones. Once, it was Smokey Robinson & The Miracles, Curtis Mayfield, Sly & The Family Stone; later it was Earth Wind & Fire, D-Train, Chaka Khan, Ashford & Simpson and Prince.

Throughout his career, Miles has always had an ear for those pop songs which he felt he could personalise – so his interpretations of 'Time After Time' (Cyndi Lauper), 'Human Nature' (Michael Jackson) and 'Perfect Way' (Scritti Politti) didn't come as a culture shock to those who refused to

If 1986's masterful funk package 'Tutu' honoured the good African Archbishop, then his parting shot for CBS – for whom he'd recorded exclusively for 30-years – denounced the NYPD; 'You're Under Arrest' being a public put down of those cops who frequently flagged down his black Ferrari to harass Miles. The scenario was odious in the extreme: the only reason a black man could be driving such an expensive set of wheels is because it was stolen.

During a career in which he has continually re-invented the most vital areas of contemporary music in his own image, Miles never disguised the fact that he had no love of white American society: what he saw as the hypocrisy, the back-handed Liberalism, the downright lies, and the widespread political corruption.

For many years Miles also avoided, whenever possible, applying the term 'jazz' to his work. If, for the sake of inaugurating a new browser bin marker, Miles' music must be tagged, then tag it 'social dance music' – but don't expect any great explanation. Jazz, Miles felt, is 'white terminology for a black tradition.'

Miles with saxophone superstar David Sanborn

write him off as a lost soul following the release of 'Bitches Brew'.

It's the contemporary pop performers' ability to make their statements within the self-imposed confines of just a few bars that was to continue to intrigue Miles; maybe it reminded him of the days when he and Bird or, for that matter, the 'Birth Of The Cool' band, had the discipline of just one side of a juke-box single to say it all, to give it their best shot.

It's horses for courses and Miles Davis always regarded himself as a quarter horse thorough-bred. Such horses are skilfully trained to give of their best over quarter-of-a-mile.

'I think, it's easier to do what Prince and Quincy (Jones) produce – fill in the cracks.' Though he still enjoyed the luxury of stretching out at will, he admitted that "Bitches Brew" succeeded simply because things were allowed to flow naturally within a set of previously formulated cues.'

His admiration for Prince produced some still-unreleased sessions. 'Prince is also a thorough-bred. He's like an Arabian breed – possesses that extra something. When I hear Prince, I hear James Brown – but it's updated, modified. I also hear Marvin Gaye, Sly Stone – a whole bunch of other good people. That's the part I like.

'Just like when you grab a breast of chicken – or whatever part you prefer and leave the rest. The rest of that stuff I don't like . . . got no use for it, so out it goes.'

What happened was this. Prince sent Miles both a vocal and instrumental version of a song entitled 'Can I Play With You'. Attached to the tape box was a note from Prince that began: 'We think alike. I know how you feel. I know what you're doing.'

Miles stripped down Prince's multi-track tape, adding his own touches and returned it to the composer for some additional vocals. Although he approved of what Miles had done with the 'chicken breast', Prince vetoes the track intended for 'Tutu' feeling that his personal contribution fell short of the album's overall standard. The singer then rang Miles, insisting that the next time they collaborated the two of them should work together in the same studio. They did, and the world still awaits an official release rather than the teasers that have since surfaced on bootleg.

One ambition that Miles Davis never fulfilled was to record with Frank Sinatra. The trumpeter died before Sinatra's all-star 'Duets' project went into production.

'I love the way Sinatra sings – forget every-thing else, if you wanna know the real truth, I learned to phrase from listening to all his early records. So now you know.'

Euro Free

Just as the American Free Jazz movement of the early Sixties broke down the harmonic and rhythmic barriers, as had be-bop before it, so the European avant garde of the Seventies pushed things even further, taking on both the concept of completely free open-ended improvisation, and the introduction of elements from local folk music traditions.

FOR A LONG TIME, it seemed to many that there was only ever one jazz musician to come out of Europe, the Belgian gypsy guitarist Django Reinhardt.

The music had been played in every corner of the Old World since the days of ragtime, but making an international impact was something that eluded most of the musicians working in a local European scene. Even Reinhardt, despite his unique powers as an improviser, was seen as something of a novelty in 'serious' jazz circles, and many Americans refused to take Eurojazz seriously at all.

The truth was, while no major innovations were coming out of Europe in the first decades of the music, the best players brought their own vision to bear on the raw materials of jazz and made something personal and individual out of it – just as the

leading Americans did. During the bop era, for instance, the Swedish clarinetist Stan Hasselgard played with such power in the style that he stood alone as the major bopper on the instrument, even when he went to play in the U.S. So impressed was Benny Goodman with Hasselgard that he invited him to join his group. Only an untimely death in a car accident stopped Hasselgard achieving much wider recognition.

Nevertheless, it wasn't until the early 50s that Europeans created significant extensions of the jazz tradition which didn't rely entirely on American idioms. One of the most important figures was another Swede, Lars Gullin, who played baritone saxophone. Gullin played the new music with as much expertise and passion as anyone, to the point where he was often mentioned in the same breath as Gerry Mulligan and Serge Chaloff.

Furthermore, Gullin brought to jazz a sensibility that was something new; influenced by the folk and classical music of his native country, his writing and playing touched on some of the deepest roots of Swedish music without departing from the jazz vocabulary.

Others followed his example, with elements of their own heritage mixed in with the basic language of jazz. Besides Gullin, Sweden could boast such fine players as Arne Domnerus (alto sax), Putte Wickman (clarinet), and Bengt Hallberg (piano) and trumpeter Rolf Ericson who carved out a successful career Stateside with the likes of Stan Kenton.

Germany had a challenging sax player, Hans Koller, and the superb trombonist Albert Mangelsdorff, whose pioneering work on an unfashionable instrument has taken him from hard bop to free jazz, fusion and beyond. France could be proud of the achievements of pianist-composer-bandleader Martial Solal, whose dazzling virtuosity was enough to earn him a place among any group of masters. Other stellar players included the bassist Pierre Michelot, tenorman Barney Wilen and the pianist-producer Henri Renaud. Italy had keyboard giants of her own in Guido Manusardi and Giorgio Gaslini. And even Spain, an otherwise desolate land as far as jazz is concerned, produced an amazing pianist in the Catalonian Tete Montoliu.

In Britain, the 'traditional' school of the 50s, which at its height had a fanatical following among young fans, ran in parallel with a healthy modern jazz movement. Such performers as Ronnie Scott, Tubby Hayes, Jimmy Deuchar and Don Rendell put their own spin on the hard bop that had filtered through from New York's 52nd Street, and sent back reports of their own, several British albums finding their way into American release schedules. Yet this was still, relatively speaking, a second-hand initiative, just as trad had been with its particular faithful. It wasn't until the 60s that

Above: Norway's tenor giant Jan Garbarek

Opposite: The Swedish baritone sax virtuoso Lars Gullin

Europe began to create a methodology of its own. Ornette Coleman's music inspired many a conversion to jazz free-thinking – Coleman's Croydon concert of 1965 still evokes nostalgia amongst those who were there – and along with the turbulent music of John Coltrane, Eric Dolphy and Albert Ayler, the opening doors of jazz expression were welcomed by many a player outside the U.S.

The whole concept of an avant garde was much more easily digested in Europe, where radical and anarchic art was a comparatively commonplace part of the culture, and the new freedoms in jazz were embraced by a wide variety of players.

In Germany, the music of saxophonist Peter Brotzmann was as challenging and demanding as that of Ayler, and it seems likely that, although there are many parallels between the two players their styles evolved quite independently of each other. Working out of Wuppertal, Brotzmann's earliest recorded work – the still astounding 'For Adolphe Sax' (1967) – boiled all the ingredients of Coltrane's 'Ascension' album down to a trio situation that enraged or delighted bewildered listeners. Brotzmann's tenor sax was used like a flamethrower, and as he roared his way through the music, one felt that jazz itself was being blown apart and reshaped in his sound. Brotzmann went on to create one of the most

powerful sessions of all time in the music of 'Machine Gun', cut for the Free Music Production label in May 1968. Recorded in the basement of an old munitions factory, it featured the leader alongside such kindred tenor playing spirits as Evan Parker and Willem Breuker and drummer Han Bennink on the most unfettered blow-out in the history of the music. Brotzmann may have been among the most extreme of the new European voices, but he wasn't alone. Breuker and Bennink belonged to a radical group of players based in Holland, and along with the pianist Misha Mengelberg they founded an operation called Instant Composers Pool, which began its own independent t- record label, and organised concerts in and around Amsterdam. While Bennink and Mengelberg have remained itinerant spirits to this day, Breuker has formed his own Kollektief, which owes as much to contemporary composition, theatre and the like as to free jazz.

In Germany, the pianist Alex von Schlippenbach formed an orchestra of free players in 1966 to play his composition 'Globe Unity'; and the Globe Unity Orchestra has reconvened, with varying personnel, on and off ever since. Many members of the Orchestra's stellar line-up, including reed player Gerd Dudek, Manfred Schoof (trumpet), Gunter Christmann (trombone), Peter Kowald (bass) Paul Lovens (drums) and others, are major figures in their own right in European free jazz.

Britain had contributed only peripherally to new jazz developments over the years, but for once British players had a major role to play in the

SVEN KLANG'S COMBO
Directed by STELLAN OLSSON   *An Essential release*

SKC-2

Left: Considered by some to be the best jazz movie ever, *Sven Klang's Combo* (Sweden, 1976) was loosely based on the early career of Lars Gullin

furthering of the new avant garde jazz. A handful of performers have become of crucial, international importance in the growth of free music. Derek Bailey, a guitarist from Yorkshire, worked in nightclubs and dance-halls throughout the 50s but became interested in the idea of playing entirely free improvisation when he worked with a trio once a week at a Sheffield jazz club. Thereafter, following a move to London, he became aquainted with a group of players based at Islington's Little Theatre, organised mostly by the late John Stevens, a drummer whose group Spontaneous Music Ensemble (SME) became one of the flagship units of British free jazz.

While Stevens' music was a recognizable evolution from the earliest innovations of Ornette Coleman, Bailey and his associates sought to move ever further from the jazz vocabulary. The guitarist's style – a flux of chords and discords which works to its own illogical logic – seems deliberately removed from that of any other performer on the instrument, and the playing of a saxophonist who worked closely with Bailey for many years, Evan Parker, is equally remote from established patterns. Parker's superhuman solos, often moving in unbroken cycles that his circular breathing can sustain for half an hour, are a mile away from his Coltrane-derived inspirations. Heard live, it can be a shattering experience.

Bailey's enterprise in creating playing situations led him in 1977 to found a freewheeling group called Company. From then until 1994, when he decided to call it a day on the idea, Bailey would organise weeks of concerts where an invited group of players would perform in ad hoc group situations and simply see what kind of music came out of it. In the end, Company created its own dynasty of groups and recordings, heard and

documented around the world. Free jazz in Europe has, indeed, been covered in amazing detail by countless small record labels: besides FMP and Incus, the label run by Bailey himself, there have been Ogun, Matchless, Bvhaast, Horo, Palm and dozens of others. This is in addition to the many European operations dedicated to covering the new kinds of mainstream and hard bop, which have beavered away in every territory: Dragon and Phontastic in Sweden, Splasch and Black Saint in Italy, Jazzhaus in Germany.

Manfred Eicher's ECM operation, based in Munich, has become one of the most eminent jazz labels of its age, building a catalogue of such consistency and quality that it rivals the finest American outfits in the music's history. American musicians have always found a congenial home in Europe as far as live work is concerned; in the 70s and 80s, they found plenty of places to make records, too.

As in America, jazz in Europe has come to mean any number of styles and sounds in the 90s. Little remains of the arguments as to whether this or that method is the true way for the jazz believer, and audiences have settled into following whichever tributary – be it trad, swing, hard bop, fusion or freeform – takes their attention. Yet jazz as a European entity remains undervalued, even by its own audiences, still hung up on the authenticity of American players. A handful of exemplary performers put a good case for thinking otherwise.

The French reed specialist Louis Sclavis, who can play his own highly composed and arranged music one moment and blister through a free-jazz free-for-all the next; his oddball fellow countrymen Urban Sax, a regiment of horn players who stage guerilla-like attacks on stuffy concert

Officium

Jan Garbarek
The Hilliard Ensemble

ECM NEW SERIES

"FINE TOGETHER"
LARS GULLIN

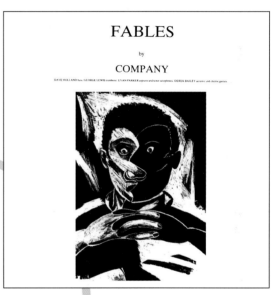

FABLES

by

COMPANY

DAVE HOLLAND bass, GEORGE LEWIS trombone, EVAN PARKER soprano and tenor saxophones, DEREK BAILEY acoustic and electric guitars

platforms with their bizarrely-costumed and choreographed events. British trumpeter Guy Barker, whose extraordinary versatility allows him to run a brilliant hard bop band, be a first-call sessionman for innumerable jazz and non-jazz situations, and even appearing as a guest horn player with Ornette Coleman; Scots tenorman Tommy Smith was one of the first British musicians to record for the Blue Note label, and is a compellingly original voice as a composer; and, from a little further east, the Murmansk-born Russian pianist and general madcap Sergei Kuryokhin, whose uproarious adventures in the fields of jazz, rock and theatre are barrier-busting if anything is.

One musician in particular symbolizes how European jazz has done more than just come of age. Norway is perhaps not the first place one thinks of as a likely spawning ground for one of the most distinctive of jazz voices, but that is where the saxophonist Jan Garbarek hails from. Garbarek was a Coltrane fan when in his teens, gaining early experience working with the American composer George Russell before getting his first wide exposure as a member of the quartet which Keith Jarrett formed with other Scandinavian musicians during the second half of the 70s. Since then his baroque sound and almost mystical delivery have become a major influence on modern saxophone. While Garbarek has explored many settings for his playing, from straight-ahead quartets to fusions with eastern and African players, his music owes much to his interest in the oldest roots of Norwegian music and song, and lends a timbre to his kind of jazz that is steeped in the remote past, just as Ornette Coleman's music reaches back to ancient Texas blues.

In this way, maybe jazz has become the world's music.

LARS GULLIN WITH STRINGS
FEATURING THE ALTO SAXOPHONE OF ROLF BILLBERG

This highly charged occasion symbolized many different things. It not only marked the return of Lars Gullin from his exile abroad but, incredibly enough, it also represented his first genuine concert in Stockholm under his own name. The fact that his comeback, literally on a carpet of strings, was performed hand-in-hand with his twin spirit, Rolf Billberg, undoubtedly added to the auspiciousness of the occasion. Even more significant though was the fact that the event took place at the Museum of Modern Art in Stockholm (on Easter Monday, 1964) and was, as a result, the symbol for a cultural breakthrough by jazz music and an award of social approbation for its practitioners. This was to a large extent the direct outcome of attempts by the jazz musicians themselves. As a result of the awakening of their political consciousness, they made efforts to improve working conditions and extended their energies toward gaining approval for their music and, at the same time, winning their own self respect. These ideals had taken shape about a year earlier, in Emanon, the first association to become founded by Swedish jazz musicians. In the fall of 1963, Emanon began to collaborate with the Museum of Modern Art and with the Swedish Radio broad-

casting corporation. Eight successful concerts were presented during the spring of 1964, which were crowned by the present event and also by the manifestation and appearance of an Emanon Big Band. Until its dissolution in the latter part of the sixties (after which it became succeeded by Modus and F.S.J.), Emanon continued to arrange concerts at the Stockholm Konserthuset and the 'Golden Circle' club, as well as at various other locations and at schools up and down the country, sometimes with support from the Institute for National Concerts (Rikskonserter). Together with City Hall, Emanon were also able to organize the Stockholm Jazzdays in 1964, 1965 and 1966, in additional to promulgating music lessons and arranging a seminar with George Russell who was appointed musical director of the Emanon Big Band in 1965. All in all, the collective endeavours of the members of Emanon led to a good many fruitful activities and some lasting musical memories, of which the concert featuring Lars Gullin and Rolf Billberg represented one of the more memorable ones.

IN CONCERT AT
THE MUSEUM OF MODERN ART
STOCKHOLM

Emanon Vice-chairman 1964, Chairman 1965, 1966. Former manager of the 'Golden Circle' club.

—Åke Abrahamsson

The Young Lions

Jazz in the Eighties also saw a generation of young players steeped in the values of hard bop who, without being retro or revivalist, were the new voice of the mainstream.

O NE HUNDRED OR SO years down the line, it has become increasingly more difficult to add anything genuinely new to the already colourful vocabulary of jazz. But then, the number of true jazz innovators has always been quite small when compared to the plethora of great interpretative masters on every instrument. So, if it is not to become frozen in time like some obsolete museum piece, it has to be the power of individual expression and the manner in which the music is interpreted that remains crucial to its continued survival in a recognizable form.

Right: Guitarist Wes Montgomery, like Bill Evans and Keith Jarret (below), one of the major influences on the new generation of jazz musicians

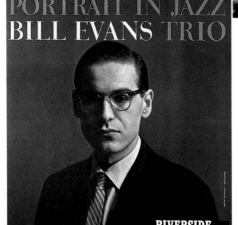

PORTRAIT IN JAZZ
BILL EVANS TRIO

RIVERSIDE

KEITH JARRETT
THE KÖLN CONCERT

ECM

Duke Ellington, Miles Davis and, more recently Joe Henderson, are but three of many high-profile musicians who voiced an opinion that the terminology 'jazz' had out-lived it's purpose to accurately describe a music that has become so diverse. And while, over the years, various unsatisfactory alternatives have been bandied about, the 'jazz' word remains in currency.

The unexpected crossover chart success of 'Mercy, Mercy, Mercy,' in 1967, didn't turn hit-maker Cannonball Adderley's head or cloud his vision. While thoroughly enjoying his moment in the sun, he warned 'The jazz we knew and loved in the 30s, 40s, 50s . . . yes, even the 60s . . .is gone.

'The audience for it is gradually fading away. We enjoy a great deal of success playing what we do, because people don't get enough of a chance to hear it . . . But, there aren't that many playing it.'

Cannonball's doom-laden words may have sounded somewhat melodramatic, but, from his vantage point, there was an element of truth is his pronouncement.

Such was the prominence given to first jazz-rock, and then jazz-funk, that very few new straight ahead artists emerged during the 70s, while most of the musicians who had made their reputations in the previous two decades had to work hard to keep their head above water. Some took the easy route and got a day job. And Blue Note Records, as ever, mirrored those times.

Readers Poll Winners!

downbeat
THE CONTEMPORARY MUSIC MAGAZINE

DECEMBER 1982 $1.75
U.K. £1.30

WYNTON AND BRANFORD MARSALIS

THE CLASH
ORIGINAL ROCK AND ROLL

JAY HOGGARD
CREDIBILITY, MONEY NEXT

WHY ARE THEY SMILING?

Left: Trumpet star Wynton Marsalis and his tenor saxist brother Branford led the new jazz breakthrough Stateside

After 26-years in business, label founder Alfred Lion accepted Liberty Records' generous offer of a buy-out in 1965, but didn't actually retire from the firm until two years later. After his departure, Francis Wolff, his life-long business partner, continued to run the organisation.

By 1971, friends insist, Wolff had worked himself into an early grave as Blue Note's new owners eroded both the label's enviable reputation and unique image by phasing out the trademark sleeve graphics in favour of substandard in-house designs.

It wasn't all bad news, however.

In keeping with the mood of the period, Blue Note's musical policy shifted towards fusion with Donald Byrd's 'Black Byrd' and Bobbi Humphrey, Ronnie Foster, Ronnie Laws, Earl Klugh and Noel Pointer emerging as it's biggest sellers.

A noticeable change in attitude began to occur, when, between 1975 and 1981, Charlie Lourie and Michael Cuscuna started to reissue substantial chunks of the label's pre-fusion back catalogue together with previously unreleased sessions.

Coupled to this, the acquisition by the San Francisco-based Fantasy corporation of the equally-influential Prestige, Riverside and Contemporary labels and the reinstatement of Art Blakey's Jazz Messengers as a College Of Knowledge meant that when, in the 80s, a new generation of young acoustic 'in the tradition' jazz players started to make their presence known, it was easy to pinpoint the contributing elements.

This wasn't a revival in the same sense as when, in the early 40s, a search for the New Orleans Holy Grail brought about Dixieland, 'trad' and the canonization of Bunk Johnson.

Left: Here on soprano sax
on which he doubled with
tenor, Branford Marsalis

Certainly, the seminal influences of jazz history were publicly celebrated, but it didn't concern note-for-note restorations of a bygone time. Nostalgia wasn't on this menu. The music being re-examined hadn't come straight out of cold storage, but was a living, breathing organism.

Similarly, it avoided the bobble hat, food-stained kaftan, orange cords and open-toe sandal fashion statement that had rendered sections of free-jazz so visually unappealing to all but those lookalikes in the audience.

As self-styled keepers-of-the-flame, this fresh generation of young lions dedicated themselves to musical purity and upholding the high moral (as well as technical and artistic) standards that now went with the territory. Drugs and unsocial behaviour were not on the new agenda.

Each era produces natural born leaders. For many, the emergence, in 1980, of 19-year old New Orleans-born trumpet virtuoso Wynton Marsalis with Art Blakey's Jazz Messengers and, soon after, the appearance on the scene of his saxophone playing brother Branford (20), was the much needed impetus.

In the somewhat cynical manner suggested a few years earlier, that if Bruce Springsteen hadn't existed, critics would have invented him, many of these same arguments were directed at the smart-suited Wynton Marsalis, once the initial hysteria had subsided and the first flush of youth had been replaced by musical maturity and manhood.

Unquestionably, it was Marsalis' display of prodigious talent with the Jazz Messengers that thrust Art Blakey back into the limelight, once again affirming his position as a font of all knowledge and constant source of talent.

As for young Wynton, he may have followed in a dynasty that included the likes of Clifford Brown, Kenny Dorham, Donald Byrd, Bill Hardman, Lee Morgan, Freddie Hubbard and Woody Shaw, but there were those who questioned what they perceived as corporate conservatism. Furthermore, the ongoing process, on the part of certain record company executives, of trying to promote Marsalis as the contender to Miles' pre-Electric crown, was both demeaning and unworthy to all concerned.

Right: Courtney Pine, the most prominent British player to break through in the 'new jazz' boom

Below: Courtney Pine and the rest caught the mood across the board, as evidenced in this cover spread in the UK pop music weekly *New Musical Express* in October 1986

ISSN 0028 6362

October 1986   50p   US $1.95 (by air)

NEW MUSICAL NME EXPRESS

Sax maniacs

THE EMPEROR'S NEW CLOTHES?
COURTNEY PINE STRIPPED
BY PAOLO HEWITT

NEW ORDER

WYNTON MARSALIS
NEW BRITISH JAZZ
STYLE COUNCIL
LITTLE RICHARD
NEW BRITISH RAP
JAMES BROWN
PETER CASE

Court in the act by Mike Owen

Other than Louis Armstrong, no one musician has singlehandedly changed the course of jazz, and arguably, undisputed originators of the magnitude of Tatum, Parker, Gillespie and Monk through to Davis, Coltrane, Rollins and Coleman might never again emerge from within a jazz context.

Apart from Pat Metheny – a musician equally at home with Ornette Coleman or David Bowie – there has been a noticeable lack of players, in recent times, possessed with a truly original voice.

Despite the fact that in the past few years, any detectable originality on the guitar, for instance, has all but been restricted to such diverse stalwarts as John McLaughlin, Bill Frisell, John Scofield, Mike Stern and Stanley Jordan – and the before mentioned Pat Metheny – it is still the almost haunting presence of the late Wes Montgomery that continues to loom large over a legion of players ranging from George Benson to Stanley Jordan and beyond.

The same criteria applies in other areas. The majority of trumpet players, however, are so fearful of coming across like Miles Davis

Below: Michel Petrucciani

soundalikes that most sound like nobody in particular. The exception to this has been a pair of outstanding British players Guy Barker and Gerald Presencer.

Young sax players, of which there are many, still take their lead from Coltrane – though some via Michael Brecker. However, as this has proved something of an obstacle, there is now a concerted move – especially among tenor players – to concern themselves with the depth of tonal colour that once so distinguished the greats of the instrument –

DREYFUS JAZZ
MICHEL PETRUCCIANI

AU THÉÂTRE DES CHAMPS-ÉLYSÉES
ENREGISTREMENT PUBLIC INTEGRAL

among them Lester Young, Ben Webster and Coleman Hawkins – from one another.

This leaves the piano players who, from Herbie Hancock, Keith Jarrett and Michael Petrucciani have all looked to Bill Evans as their main point of reference.

So, in an environment where influences can inhibit as much as they inspire, it's in the power of interpretation that a recognisable voice such as Michel Petrucciani or Joshua Redman excels.

At the time of his first solo album release, Redman insisted, 'Success in this country (America) has little to do with artistic worth. Hype is a fleeting thing. I wanted to be sure that other musicians, masters, would want to work with me.'

While attitudes don't quite stretch to strict dress codes, in some areas, jazz has almost become as tribalised as rock, being sectioned off into sub-genres, a number of which only make sense to the faceless marketing executives and radio programmers who created them in the first instance for their own convenience.

This has given rise to various brands of 'near-beer jazz'.

Once, such unobtrusive background sounds would have simply been termed 'cocktail music' and filed under 'Easy

Above: Trumpet virtuoso who led a fiery Blakey-influenced sextet, Roy Hargrove

Left: Hargrove with tenor man Ralph Moore

In another part of the universe, the young and feisty Marsalis boys weren't the only ones seeking true enlightenment, as can be judged from the ability of many post Hard Bop devotees to reach receptive audiences: Terence Blanchard, Wallace Roney, Roy Hargrove, (trumpet); Bobby Watson, Antonio Hart, Vincent Herring, Kenny Garrett, (alto sax); James Carter, Ralph Moore, David Sanchez (tenor sax); Mulgrew Miller, Eric Reed, Danilo Perez, Kenny Kirkland, Geri Allen, (piano); Christine McBride, (bass); Jeff 'Tain Watts', Marvin 'Smitty' Smith (drums).

Not everyone followed the same route.

Tenor player Scott Hamilton and cornetist Warren Vache are but two of a closely-knit coterie of musicians who looked further back than bop for guidance.

Both had worked with Goodman and Herman and were genuinely at ease with a style enjoying popularity long before they were born in 1954 and 1951 respectively.

For Hamilton, it was an extension of the big-toned Coleman Hawkins / Ben Webster / Illinois Jacquet swing tradition. In the case of

Listening'. Nowadays, these casual doodlings have been extricated from their once natural environment of department store elevators and coffee shops, given an expensive make-over and assigned dubious designer-labels ranging from happy-hour 'Lite Jazz' and 'Smooth Jazz' to the more boudoir bound suggestiveness of 'Quiet Storm'.

All style and little content, the concept is to create a carefree after-hours illusion of seductive affluence. It is an opiate so potent that it can make the most mediocre players

often appear reasonably accomplished. The fact that it's often difficult to ascertain whether or not their magazine adverts are promoting music or name-brand shirts says something about how their product is perceived by both seller and buyer.

The undisputed star of this musical nether world of hotel corridors and Club Med wine bars is Kenny G, a soprano saxophone player who has proved himself capable of selling albums literally by the millions and topping the pop charts in the process.

Vache, a remarkable find who had emerged a bit earlier in a climate more receptive to Hard Bop and California Cool, similarities were drawn with Ruby Braff.

Aside from solo careers, Hamilton and Vache have become an integral part of such Festival regulars as the Concord All-Stars and George Wein's Newport All-Stars.

Following a decade when a large section of the British scene had been the territory of jazz rock/funk combos including Ian Carr's Nucleus, Back Door, Barbara Thompson's Paraphernalia and Morrissey-Mullen, an entirely new scene exploded out of two London-based big bands – the all-black Jazz Warriors which had come together in 1985, and the more adventurous Loose Tubes which had formed a year earlier.

The nominal leader of the Jazz Warriors, Courtney Pine, may have claimed that the cover of Rollins' 'Way Out West' – the very same that depicts the Great Man amongst the sagebrush and cacti wearing a ten gallon hat, his sax tucked under his left arm – made him gravitate towards the tenor, but it was to John Coltrane that he, and most every other British saxophone player, first looked to for musical guidance. But most of them didn't come within a sea mile of deciphering the Coltrane codes. Ayler, Sanders and Shepp provide any

alternative muse, if not workable solutions. So it has been to hip hop and such that the attention has shifted.

As the once traditional training ground of big name touring bands, street corner lounges and unsociable-hours clubs has all but vanished, so to have the outlets for musicians to hone their skills in death-or-glory after-hours jam sessions. Far too many now emerge from music colleges and University jazz clinics with awesome techniques but devoid of any personality to distinguish them from the dozens of others like them.

But then, establishing ones credentials and individuality in the jazz world has always been an arduous and thankless task.

Unlike the majority of rock groups, the personnels of which seem to be bound together in lifelong servitude, the jazz life is

most quixotic in its pick 'n' mix approach.

None more so than that of Wynton Marsalis whose vast turnover of work with small, medium and very large combinations constantly makes him a centre of attention, thus enabling him to reach a public as broad as the Carnegie Hall regulars or the rock crowds at the annual British rock event at Glastonbury.

For some, it's what Marsalis represents rather than what he actually plays that is of the greater importance. But there are few occasions when Marsalis (or any other young blood for that matter) has performed with such passion than he did on his set around midnight on the last day of the 1995 Glastonbury Rock Festival.

At a time when the crowd was expected to either head for home or the comfort of their tents, most remained transfixed as the crystal clear sound of Wynton's 'In This House, On This Morning' band wafted on the still warm night air across the heavily populated valley and into the nearby hills.

Like that most legendary of fellow New Orleans trumpet players, Buddy Bolden, perhaps his horn could be heard as far as 14 miles away?

As Duke Ellington once said 'Music must move forward. It can't stand still or go back, It's like language – always changing.'

CD CHECKLIST

WYNTON MARSALIS
Standard Time (Columbia)
ROY HARGROVE
The Vibe (Novus)
JOE LOVANO
Tenor Legacy (Blue Note)
CHARLIE HADEN
Quartet West (Verve)
ART BLAKEY
Keystone Three (Concord)
JOE HENDERSON
The State Of The Tenor (Blue Note)
VARIOUS
The Young Lions (Elektra)

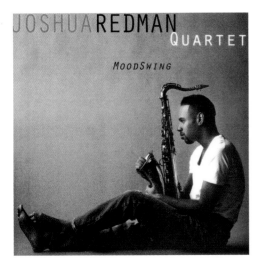

JOSHUAREDMAN QUARTET

MoodSwing

THE BIG GUNDOWN
John Zorn plays the music of Ennio Morricone

JOE LOVANO TENOR LEGACY

JOSHUA REDMAN
MULGREW MILLER
CHRISTIAN McBRIDE
LEWIS NASH
DON ALIAS

TOCJ-5884

KEYSTONE 3

ART BLAKEY
AND THE JAZZ MESSENGERS
DONALD BROWN
CHARLES FAMBROUGH
BRANFORD MARSALIS
WYNTON MARSALIS
BILL PIERCE

New Moon Daughter

CASSANDRA wilson

ROY HARGROVE QUINTET
WITH THE TENORS
OF OUR TIME

SCOTT HAMILTON

Race Point

GERRY WIGGINS
ANDY SIMPKINS
JEFF HAMILTON
HOWARD ALDEN

CCD-4492

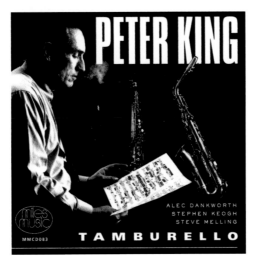

PETER KING

ALEC DANKWORTH
STEPHEN KEOGH
STEVE MELLING

MMCD083

TAMBURELLO

Twylight

Socially rooted in the club-based dance culture of the Nineties, with promoters and disc jockeys often the main driving force, the Acid Jazz movement nevertheless has a thoroughbred musical pedigree that has involved some of the finest new young jazz players active on either side of the Atlantic.

Future funk— Acid

Above: Guru and Roy Ayers
Left: Guru
Overleaf: Pioneer DJ Gilles Peterson

CID JAZZ was a misnomer from the start – it had no real musical links with the Acid House boom from which it deliberately borrowed its name, nor was it jazz in the sense that the more conventional of music critics would have recognised over the preceding decades.

And yet this new genre, which to many started out as nothing more than a controversial tag, has helped revitalise the mainstream genre as well as introducing this, and future, generations to the idea of jazz as an organic, living, growing force. A force in which they – in the case of young musicians, disc jockeys and promoters – might just have a stake.

The roots of all this lie in the Jazz Dance scene of the early 8Os, where hip hop – funk and electro influenced rap played on a bass-heavy tip – updated Donald Byrd's 70s blend of jazz and funk, returning jazz to its pre-war status of good-time DANCE music.

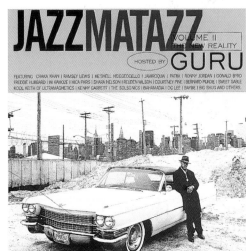

Jazz

But Acid Jazz was, and to a remarkable degree still is, much more than that. A blend of beatnik innocence, punky edginess and post-60s soul – a beat for the feet; James Brown on acid, the astringent alto saxes of Lou Donaldson and the JB's Maceo Parker merging at someone else's rap party, the perfect blend of urban hip hop rhythms and classically based jazz melodies.

The ultimate musical antidote to the cultural problems of the confused and confusing 1990s – comforting with its frequent use of samples and standard formulas yet vital and challenging in its sheer exultant energy and diversity.

By late 1983, hip young promoter Paul Murphy had made his jazz nights at the Electric Ballroom, Camden Town the talk of London's more aware youngsters. Every week they were pulling in the best jazz dancers in Europe with attractions such as The Tommy Chase Quartet, Working Week and DJs armed with floor-filling jazz tracks.

Guitarist Simon Booth of Working Week later said 'I started Working Week to give the Ballroom's dancers something jazzy that was new, something new that they could do their stuff to.' But even as Booth spoke, most of the British recording artists then starting out in the young jazz field – Working Week, Paul Weller's post-Jam group The Style Council, female crooners Sade, Carmel and Tracey Thorn – were being gently ushered, via the vacuous style-obsessed glossies, into a dead-end.

Most young people aspired to a fake sophistication that somehow seemed apt to those who had just been through the ridiculously youthful extremes of mid-70s Punk and New Romanticism. It was, essentially, the cocktail circuit all over again, one big blue rondo a la turkey, endlessly recycling bleached 60s Bossa Nova-type sounds while the audience posed, well-heeled feet tapping an outdated and kitsch cha-cha-cha.

Everyone, including most of the above, simply *had* to be in Julien Temple's two hour pop promo of a movie *Absolute Beginners*, which began filming in 1984. The latter was a cinematic turkey as sterile as the formal British society that Colin MacInnes' original book had hoped was dying. Everyone sipped cappuccino at the Soho Brasserie and dreamt about filling their Filofaxes with brochures from Docklands and Porsche. Flash zoot suits and Yuppie values were in. Jamming and improvisation were out. To sound smooth, detached even, was everything.

By the time *Absolute Beginners* was finally released, in 1986, the newish music it featured – despite being technically competent and, at times, entertaining – represented a dead scene. It was not raw enough to reflect the cultural upheaval of a society in flux. Nor did its polished tones mirror the frenetic energy of the jazz dancers (at another Camden nighterie, Dingwall's) with their ever-changing steps and fashions.

Elsewhere, the scene was quietly growing. On the south coast, the Brighton Bops, for instance, were rapidly taking on legendary status as American artists from Terry Callier to Big John Patton were hauled out of semi-obscurity to star, and yet there was still obviously something missing. But half a dozen minor events occurred just after the mid point of the 80s that changed everything.

Britain's premier music magazine, the weekly *New Musical Express*, issued three jazz cassettes of classic jazz grooves. 'Stompin' At The Savoy' was a 40s and early-50s compilation that juxtaposed doo-wop with bebop, while 'Straight No Chaser' and 'Night People' joyfully plundered the Blue Note, Prestige and Riverside vaults to cover everything from Wes Montgomery and Cannonball Adderley to Miles, Monk and the Messengers.

These three titles racked up unprecedented mail order sales in excess of 50,000 (a massive figure for the UK) and, since only one of the three, 'Stompin' At The Savoy', was on vinyl, this led to various club DJs besieging an indifferent BMG Records in an attempt to get a key Wes Montgomery track re-released.

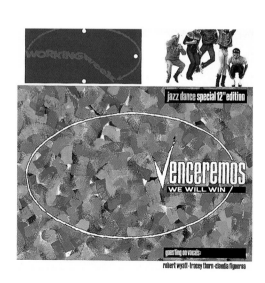

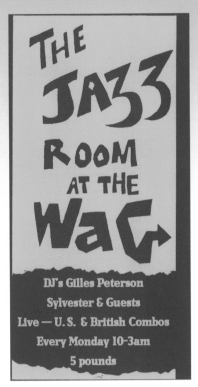

These *NME* tapes also introduced a generation to the idea of jazz as something lively and vital, and paved the way for further releases featuring Billie Holiday, Charlie Parker, Latin Jazz and the cream of contemporary Brit-bop (including Courtney Pine, Steve Williamson, Andy Sheppard, Working Week and Tommy Chase).

Then the laconically hip masters of live, controlled hysteria, the young veteran Herbie Hancock, the revolutionary Gil Scott Heron, the ever-popular and ever-funky Roy Ayers and the more mainstream jazz giants Art Blakey and the still-respected Miles Davis ('Tutu' made the UK Top 40 album chart) began, once again, to make regular forays to the UK and, this time, with hundreds and then thousands of people under 25 in the audience.

Some of London's top Rap DJs – Norman Jay, Jay Strongman and Animal Nightlife's Mac – began programming some jazz influenced soul gems from the 1966-73 Golden Age. A few from the Blue Note stable, most from the post-Motown world of psychedelic soul.

Since most of the B-sides and bootlegs they played – Tommy Stewart's 'Bump'n'Hustle Music', The Honeydripper's 'Impeach The

President', The Jackson Sisters 'I Believe In Miracles' – were rarer than hen's teeth, this sub-genre was initially labelled Rare Groove.

And, most importantly of all, DJs like Baz Fe Jazz and the young Gilles Peterson began to do their own club nights. Baz Fe Jazz helped establish a Monday night at the Wag Club in Soho that ran for half a decade (this is the equivalent of decades in club terms) and reclaimed the Wag from an audience previously inclined towards 'dinner jazz'. Gilles Peterson's night was called, bombastically enough, 'Talking Loud And Saying Something' and, after various false starts in 1987, it became a regular event at Dingwall's, Camden Lock, in spring 1988.

At Talking Loud's Sunday afternoon sessions there were none of the, often racist, door restrictions of the West End; no banning of trainers or jeans and the place was soon rammed with young black and white music fans. With a funk underlay, Peterson concocted a mix of Rare Groove, hard bop, Brazilian, Afro-Cuban, modal and avant garde jazz. As the man himself said: 'The original essence of Talking Loud was taking influences of the best before and now so that the original Dingwall's playlist included everything from A Tribe Called Quest to Sun Ra.'

Visits to Talking Loud inspired Jonathan Rudnick to launch New York's Groove Academy, made Gang Starr's Guru start his Jazzamatazz revue, motivated fellow rappers the Dream Warriors to record with Slim Gaillard, led first Ace Records in London and later, San Francisco's Luv 'n' Haight label to successfully trawl the Fantasy/Prestige/Riverside archives and also, of course, brought the likes of tenor legend Pharoah Sanders to the attention of a fresh young audience and made some British musicians think twice.

People with the undoubted musical potential of saxman Courtney Pine and guitarist Ronny Jordan no longer assumed that they would be forced to play their lives away in the sub-Karaoke vein inhabited by mainstream plastic soul and reggae bands – jazz was fast becoming a young man's game once again.

In the Summer of 1988, as the 120 beats-per-minute thudding of Chicago's Acid House first swept the dance-floors of Britain – providing the soundtrack to much 'E'-taking and subsequent newspaper headlines – the DJ Gilles Peterson linked up with a Northern Soul fan and hustlin' young mod-about-town Eddie Piller, to form a record company that would reflect this new funky eclecticism.

Peterson and Piller had met through Nicky Holloway's soulboy nights – events known as The Special Branch, which had occurred all over England, coastal Spain and Ibiza. As a joke, initially, Peterson and Piller hit on the name Acid Jazz records. Piller had played the DJ himself,

in various Northern Soul venues, and he thought that a label with just the right inflammatory name – 'just the right buzz term' – would infuriate the old guard at the same time as it attracted the younger element, the teens and twenty-somethings, bringing together the hitherto separate tribes of jazzers, the soulboys, mods and the hip hop funkees.

The term 'Acid Jazz' defined the latest and greatest noises of the underground – laid-back pieces of silky strut like the Stetsasonic cut 'Talkin' All That Jazz' – and it defined them at the same time as it gave them a certain outlaw glamour. What could be more infamous than being linked with the House dance'n'drugs underground that the media was then busy exposing and condemning? What started as a near-prank, a vehicle for re-releasing jazz-funk rarities so 'we could make some beer money', was taken so seriously by music biz insiders that it rapidly escalated into an authentic forum for new sounds. Most jazz magazine editors had very little time for the new tag-stroke-genre, but – to those of a certain, young, age – this only confirmed the burgeoning street credibility of Acid Jazz.

Acid Jazz became undeniably successful at sharpening the soul tip of jazz, at getting some deserved media attention for a hitherto neglected scene. And it helped continue, by all means necessary, the happening vibe that Northern Soul had once epitomised, keeping alive the original spirit of jazz as a genuinely 'popular' music form. It was a label that could, and did, record and release material by some seasoned campaigners like Hammond organist James Taylor, Simon Booth and The Jazz Renegades (with former Tommy Chase alto-star Alan Barnes), as well as by a host of complete newcomers.

The breezily defiant 'Frederick Lies Still', by Peterson's old pal Rob Gallagher and his group Galliano, was the first release and an instant cult hit. Others quickly followed as new blood flowed in – Urban Species with their protest raps and dub touches, poppy jazz-soul chartsters US3 with their skilful blend of commercial rap and authorised Blue Note label sampling, the precociously talented pin-up Jay Kay of Jamiroquai, the Brand New Heavies with their Rare Groove grounding and amazing live shows, the militant funk of The Young Disciples. And new magazines (*Soul Underground*, *Straight No Chaser*), new clubs (Club Sandino, Confusion De Londra, La Monde, Low Rider), new venues (The Jazz Cafe, The Blue Note) and new record companies sprang up to cater for them.

The Acid Jazz label, which went on to own and run the Blue Note club in London's East End, has sold millions across the US, Japan, Germany, Greece, Holland and Italy, out-gunning some labels with far bigger budgets. 'I like to see the major record labels screw up', Piller has said, 'I like the integrity of being the little guy on the street telling the big conglomerate which way to jump. The majors don't have a bloody clue what's going on at street level, they need people like me to blow a bit of fresh air up their arses!'

Acid Jazz records has now been joined by dozens of boutique labels, while Gilles Peterson in 1990 elected to form his own Talkin' Loud label distributed worldwide by mighty Phonogram. Between 1991 and 1994 the Brand New Heavies' self-titled Acid Jazz album went gold, likewise, the Dream Warriors' 'My Definition Of A Boombastic Style', while the unstoppable Jamiroquai stole the show at the annual Glastonbury Festival as The Young Disciples, Incognito, Marxman and JTQ (the renamed James Taylor Quartet) joined them in the charts with hits of increasingly diverse sounds.

As the 1990s winds to a close we have also seen acts like US3 break into America's Top Ten to give Blue Note it's biggest-selling album ever, while Galliano wows 'em live in the Big Apple as the Acid Jazz roster continues to grow. And, this is surely an amazing

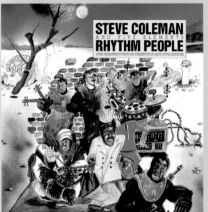

Left: New York's crossover specialist Steve Coleman fusing hip hop, funk and be bop

M Base

If any new trend is to succeed it is invariably as a result of openly rejecting existing ones.

A RESPONSE to what young musicians in Brooklyn and Bedford-Stuyvesant viewed as the conservatism of Wynton Marsalis' elevation to jazz icon, the M-Base collective was the shared vision of Steve Coleman (alto) and Graham Haynes (cornet), M-Base standing for Macro-Basic Array Of Structured Extemporization.

Though it first took shape in 1981, it wasn't until the mid-80s that Coleman (by then thirty years old) and his band Five Elements (a name purloined from a martial arts movie) began attracting media attention.

With a core personnel including fellow altoist Greg Osby, singer Cassandra Wilson plus David Gilmore (guitar), Geri Allen (piano), Reggie

Washington (bass), Marvin 'Smitty' Smith (drums) plus occasional fellow-travellers Craig Handy, Ravi Coltrane, Roy Hargrove and Kevin Eubanks, M-Base took to the streets for the latest hip-hop break beats and funk rhythms upon which to construct original horn lines.

Coleman originally took his cue from Bird, then subsequently both he and Greg Osby proved to be more parts Maceo Parker than Charlie. And, like his Prime Time namesake Ornette, exhibited an irregular angular slant to the M-Base beat.

While the 1995's 'Def Trance Beat' revealed Coleman's ability to deconstruct Jerry Goldsmith's theme to 'Flint' and Dizzy Gillespie's 'Salt Peanuts', the previous year's 'Steve Coleman And Metrics/A Tale Of 3 Cities' saw the exchange between horn players and street rappers being mutually beneficial.

Originally on JMT, the key players branched out with Steve Coleman's prolific output on BMG's Novus imprint, Graham Haynes with Verve and both Greg Osby and Cassandra Wilson pacting with Blue Note.

Osby turned heads with '3-D Lifestyles' and 'Black Book' while Wilson's 'Blue Light Til Dawn' and 'New Moon Daughter' – a brace of albums flavoured with poles-apart material by Robert Johnson, Hank Williams and The Monkees! – sold in pop-like quantities, finally establishing her as a major league attraction.

Meanwhile, the M-Base beat goes on.

Above: Incognito

Left: The Young Disciples, August 1991

Overleaf, right: Jamiroquai

sight -- the ultimate British invasion, the old UK selling jazz, the musical phenomenon of the age, back to the continent that spawned it – and re-sold not as a po-faced Opera style museum piece, existing purely to be analyzed and dissected by broadsheet intellectuals, but instead as a vibrant, living form of music, a way of life to be felt, experienced and danced to. Although sometimes it will over-promote the under-ripe, the Acid Jazz scene has helped create a music that undeniably communicates across the genres and the generations. This was how things were, and indeed continue to be, a young broad church perpetuating a brand new beat (which also embraces the fast emerging drum 'n' bass culture) that will take us from this dying century and on, into the next.

Acid Jazz? Long may it continue Talkin' Loud.

Bandleader, composer, arranger, pianist, trumpet player, producer, record executive; his roles are as varied as his career, which has ranged from big band be-bop to hip-hop.

Quincy Jones

TWO CELEBRITY studded albums 'Back on The Block' and 'Q's Jook Joint' depict Quincy Jones looking backwards over his shoulder as he looks forward towards the future. Both albums feature hip hop tracks.

'Ice T, Kool Moe Dee and the others were very happy that I was getting involved in hip hop . . . they all said that it gives them credibility in the business and I was glad that this would happen.

Hip Hop is the new Bebop . . . no question about it.

No matter what anybody says, it is, 'cause I was there the first time around and I see the many similarities.

It's very close to scat singers like Babs Gonzales and Eddie Jefferson and all of that, but they don't know that because they don't know what their musical roots are.

L.L Cool J once asked me, "what do the musicians and singers think about us?" And,

220

years ago and are now really finding out what people were about . . .Bird and Dizzy, Miles and Coltrane, James Brown, Sly & The Family Stone.

So what's happening now is the most natural combination in the world . . . this fusion with bebop, it's the only place to go.

Much of it is improvised and some of those guys are so cleaver, so creative, very fast and spontaneous. This is the new jazz but when I used to tell people that, they'd just laugh.'

The title track to Quincy's 1989 album 'Back On The Block', features rappers Ice T, Melle Mel, Big Daddy Kane and Kool Moe Dee. Also included is a version of Joe Zawinul's 'Birdland' which is prefaced by 'Jazz Corner Of The World' and a motor-mouth introducing by Kool Moe Dee and Daddy Kane. Both tracks feature contributions from Miles Davis, Dizzy Gillespie, George Benson, James Moody, Sarah Vaughan and Ella Fitzgerald.

'When I asked Daddy Kane to introduce all these artists he didn't have a clue who these artists were. I had a rhythm track which was the same tempo as "Birdland" and so I said, write me an introduction for Ella Fitzgerald – eight bars. Do the same for Miles Davis, and he'd ask "Who's Miles Davis?"

I'd throw him a few words like "Birth of the Cool" and tell him a little bit about it. I didn't want him to do more than one at a time because I didn't want him to think about it . . . just get the feeling.

With Ella . . .I'll never forget that one. "Who's Ella?" I told him Ella was the First Lady of Song

and that she was more like a musician than a singer. Then it hit me, Ella along with Louis Armstrong, they invented what they did . . . and these hip hops are also inventing what they do.

I went out in the hallway where we were recording and there's Big Daddy Kane standing there in the corner trying to look all cool and mean and he beckoned me over: "Hey Q, let me hear you use the world sterile in a sentence" and right away I knew what he was going for, but he didn't know how to use the word, though.

I understand that some people regard certain rappers as bad role models, I'm not saying that I always approve of the stance some artists take, but for many it's a last desperate attempt to find some self-esteem . . . a desperate attempt to have some pride. And the girls are saying, great we like young brothers like that because they're strong instead of succumbing to that system and shuffling around like that.

All this goes way back. Starting with slavery, they've been conditioned in a country to where their self worth is being diminished.

The original programme was to take the family apart, to take all their validation and their roots and self-esteem away.

It was purposely done so that hopefully they would be made into non-thinking objects there for labour. If they had to deal with a slave that could do mathematical equations and knew all about literature, then he could be dangerous to a slave system.

The same thing still happens. They don't teach them at schools. And, because the every-day scuffle is so hard to survive means that they don't go back too far . . . haven't the time.

In 1944 the United States government published a book called *Discovering Music,* and it said something to the effect that jazz is not the right music to study for appreciation because it came from a feebled stock race that was incapable of anything other than repetition.

If you keep telling people they're nothing . . . that because of their skin colour they have no capacity to learn or sell, they'll start believing it . . . If I'm nothing . . . why bother to go to school if I'm not going to university?

If that's the case, then I just might as well sell crack . . . earn 1,500 dollars a day pushing dope . . . get me a gun.

The result is that a lot of young kids are killing each other.

What people don't realise is . . . that it takes a very intelligent mind to run a dope gang.

Organisation, leadership, economics, everything . . . and it's illegal.

Think what could be achieved if such minds were put to good use.'

that was the first time I ever thought about them not considering themselves as musicians and perhaps that's why they sold, because they dont know anything about music

A lot of these guys were so poor when they started out, couldn't afford instruments or music lessons, most only thing they had was a record turntable, a few records and a microphone and from just that they created something entirely new. I don't believe anyone has ever started out and created so much from so very little. And, it's entirely their music. It's not a product of some big corporate machine.

I feel more at home with hip hop than I do with rock'n'rollers, no question about it. They have a sensibility that utilises the opposite descriptions of everyday emotions, which to those who don't understand might sound like negative connotations.

What they're saying, reminds me of when I was in New York and somebody would ask "How was Bird last night?" And we'd say, "terrible, Man!" – but we meant the opposite.

If you ask hip hoppers "How was the concert?' they'll reply, "Dope or it was Hype . . . Phat." But that's a slang that goes back to slavery – using the reverse word to what you really mean, instead of saying it was wonderful or marvellous. And, that's a sensibility that I understand, because it's exactly the same sensibility that Bird, Miles and myself had back then.'

Despite reservations from certain sectors of the music industry, Quincy Jones approves of sampling, not only of artists such as Jams Brown, Sly Stone and George Clinton, but of his own recordings.

'For some strange reason good things are happening. Kids are going back into their musical history much more than they did 20

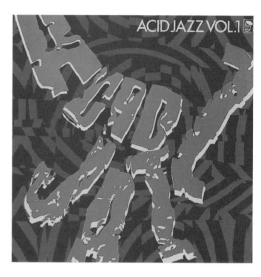

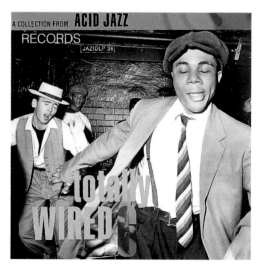

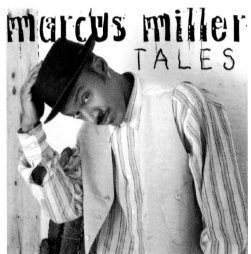

Still Blue After All These Years

From outdoor festivals to beer commercials, blues musicians, having survived the lean years, have enjoyed a revival in fortune during the Nineties.

THROUGHOUT THE 70s and 80s, blues musicians both black and white struggled for recognition.

B.B. King was lucky enough to be drawn into the mainstream of American pop culture, under Johnny Winter's aegis (a guitarist once toted as the great albino blues hope and Hendrix successor) Muddy Waters' record-making career enjoyed a late resurgence with albums such as 'Hard Again' (1977), 'I'm Ready' (1978) and 'Live' (1979) before his death in 1983, and Albert King's remarkable collaboration with the Stax house band on 'Born Under A Bad Sign' (1968) was one of the few truly creative innovations from the period. But other prominent players like Albert Collins, Buddy Guy and Otis Rush, toiled on but failed to catch the eye of

Below: The Blues Brothers
Opposite: Stevie Ray Vaughan (left) and Johnny Copeland

a fickle, albeit international, audience. But there was one significant new artist to emerge from this period, hailed as the new voice of the blues, Robert Cray. Beginning with 'Bad Influence' (1983), his Hightone albums achieved an increasing recognition and sales, helped in no small way in 1986 by his label's affiliation with Mercury for 'Strong Persuader'. Subsequent releases have not fared quite as well, although he remains a popular live performer.

His only serious competition, Joe Louis Walker, also made his debut album, 'Cold Is The Night' (1986) for the Hightone label. Walker's output stayed closer to the mainstream of the blues than did that of Cray, and his move to Verve for the 1993 album 'Blues Survivor' and those that followed ensured that he too achieved a higher profile.

The emergence of what came to be a second, more significant Blues Boom, was signalled by the success of John Lee Hooker's multi-million selling album, 'The Healer' (1989) and the follow-up albums 'Mr Lucky' (1991), 'Boom Boom' (1992) and 'Chill Out' (1995). Garlanded with every conceivable award, the homburg-hatted Hooker also became the

acceptable face for advertisers of everything from jeans (Lee) to brandy (Hennessey) and heart treatments (ICI), while Lonnie Brooks (falling through the stereotypical front porch) also demonstrated the efficacy of Heineken lager drinking.

There was more of this commercial-break cashflow to come; blues songs such as Muddy Waters' 'Mannish Boy' and Howlin' Wolf's 'Smokestack Lightning' were chosen as suitably masculine soundtracks for Levi jeans and Budweiser beer.

Not to be left out, female blues veteran Etta James made the charts in 1996 when her version of 'I Just Want To Make Love To You' was used as the background music to a Pepsi television commercial.

White blues bands such as Roomful Of Blues and The Fabulous Thunderbirds had spent the 80s working regularly but getting very little critical notice or overt commercial success, as also did the now-expatriot John

Opposite: Robben Ford (left) and BB King
Top Right: Eric Clapton with Muddy Waters
Centre Right: A poster for the Clapton concert that proved to be Stevie Ray Vaughan's final appearance

Mayall, John Hammond and Stevie Ray Vaughan – the latter making his eventual breakthrough into big name status after a show-stopping appearance at the 1982 Montreux Jazz Festival.

Vaughan's untimely death in 1990, in a helicopter crash, prevented his accession to the throne of white blues king. That vacancy is still being contested by the likes of Tinsley Ellis, Walter Trout and Bob Margolin.

Eric Clapton's annual season of concerts at London's Royal Albert Hall became more and more devoted to the blues end of his varied repertoire. The success of his most successful album ever, 'Unplugged' (1992) – rumoured to have sold more than 12-million copies worldwide – enabled Clapton to make the move back to blues playing full-time, which resulted in his 1994 collection of oldies 'From The Cradle' (featuring songs he had been influenced by as a young player) and the world tour that promoted it.

Unlike the previous boom, this latest one has ensured that black artists have also reaped the benefits. Buddy Guy, Otis Rush and, until his death in 1993, Albert Collins have all enjoyed a higher profile and made albums that received critical and financial laurels. Other performers like Larry Garner, Sherman Robertson, Tutu Jones and Jay Owens have also emerged, proving that the blues has not been entirely rejected by the community that spawned it in the first place.

Meanwhile, in a remarkable volte face, the blues has been embraced by the unlikliest of institutions, the US Post Office, by way of a series of 29-cents stamps depicting Robert Johnson, Muddy Waters, Howlin' Wolf, Jimmy Rushing, Bessie Smith, Ma Rainey and such as part of their Legends Of American Music series, while both the African state of Tanzania and the former Soviet Republic of Kyragystan have commemorate John Lee Hooker's 75th birthday with a stamp.

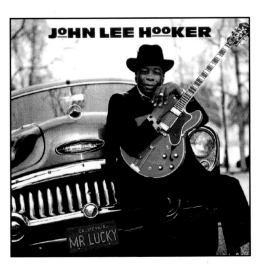

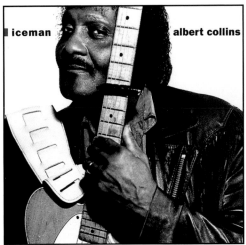

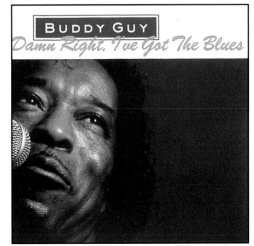

Jazz Festivals

THE SIX DAY LONG International Jazz Congress, staged in Chicago in 1926, could probably have staked a claim as the first ever jazz festival, but the festival which acted as the yardstick for the now familiar modern day event was the Grande Parade du Jazz which took place in 1948, in Nice in the South of France where Louis Armstrong starred.

The French were clearly pioneers in the field – a year later the Festival International du Jazz staged in Paris enticed the Charlie Parker Quintet, the Miles Davis-Tadd Dameron Band and Sidney Bechet to perform.

Founded in 1954, by Louis & Elaine Lorillard, but organised by Boston (Storyville) nightclub owner-cum-pianoman George Wein, the Newport Jazz Festival promptly became the Main Event of the year, with a West Coast equal – Monterey – up and running by 1958.

From there, a worldwide circuit steadily evolved to the point where European venues such as Montreux, Perugia, Umbria, Marciac and the North Sea have become among the most coveted of dates in the jazz yearbook.

Often seen as a modern cultural statement in conjunction with public Arts Festivals, there are now more international jazz festivals staged throughout the world each year than equivalent rock music events.

Left and Right: Freddie Hubbard (trumpet) and Joe Henderson (tenor) live at the Montreux Festival

And in the same way that George Wein became synonymous with Newport, so too did the individual styles of Jimmy Lyons (Monterey), Claude Nobs (Montreux) and Paul Acket (North Sea) become identified with the outstanding events that they created.

People who might rarely feel the desire to spend their evenings hanging out in smoky jazz clubs frequently make up a large section of the summertime festival-going audience. And, with so many alternative forms of entertainment vying for public attention and disposable incomes, the audience for jazz – both live and recorded – demands value.

Furthermore, the opportunity to catch a parade of major artists all in the space of a few days has special appeal, especially if it's staged in some idyllic location like Antibes, Montreux, Jamaica, St. Lucia or at the foot of Japan's Mount Fuji where Blue Note's past-and-present alumni often turn out in force.

THE 12TH ANNUAL Floating Jazz Festival
ABOARD THE S/S NORWAY
22–29 OCTOBER 1994

NCL AND HOSS PRESENT

LEGENDS

The ULTIMATE CARIBBEAN JAZZ SPECTACULAR
A Tribute to OSCAR PETERSON
MAJESTY OF THE SEAS
28 May – 4 June 1995

Left: Van Morrison / Bottom right: Pat Metheny / Below: Gerry Mulligan and Anita O'Day backstage at Newport in *Jazz On A Summer's Day* / Bottom centre: Dizzy Gillespie at Montreux
Bottom left: Dexter Gordon (he was with the group from *'Round Midnight*) at Montreux / Centre left: The riots at Newport, 1960

Not to pretend there haven't been problems.

They may have been rioting at Newport as early as 1960, but come 1971, a combination of 'progressive' rock and campus beer monsters finally terminated the world's most famous open air jazz jamboree.

After a much-needed clean up, the event relocated from its (once tranquil) Rhode Island base to the 24-hour bustle of Manhattan, and venues ranging from Radio City Music Hall to The Yankee Stadium.

En route, it also changed its name and its corporate sponsors several times, but, even in exile, it's still regarded as the Newport bash.

(In fact, the role of sponsor and product placement has becomes paramount to the success of large multi-concert events as both the annual JVC-branded [New York] and Capital [London] roll-outs attest).

Newport works on many levels and, over the years, has been responsible for instantly revitalising the sagging careers of artists of the calibre of Miles Davis and Duke Ellington. The surprise hit of a 1955 all star jam also involving Gerry Mulligan, Zoot Sims, Thelonious Monk, Percy Heath and Connie Kay, a puzzled Davis was heard to enquire backstage 'What's all the fuss? I've always played this way'.

It was at Newport, the following year, that Duke Ellington also experienced a reversal of his fortunes. During a rendition of 'Diminuendo And Crescendo In Blue', Paul Gonsalves suddenly cut loose on his tenor sax to roar his way through a 27-chorus marathon. The crowd was on its feet, wildly cheering him along and, by the end of the set, The Duke and his band was again a hot commercial property, with the souvenir album-of-the-event an instant best-seller.

The ability to rise to the occasion has not only halted many an artist's box office decline, but launched big time careers of relative newcomers: Charles Lloyd at Monterey, and both Cuban pianist Gonzalo Rubalcaba and Texas bluesman Stevie Ray Vaughan at Montreux being perfect examples.

Though it didn't stretch as far as actually turning its camera on the event, by 1956 even Hollywood saw the merits of using the Newport Jazz Festival as a back-drop for *High Society* and including Louis Armstrong & His All Stars amongst a blue chip cast headed by Bing Crosby, Frank Sinatra and Grace Kelly. A single of Bing and Satchmo duetting on 'Now You Has Jazz' even made the Hot 100 chart.

Two years on, it was to be Bert Stern's 1958 award-winning documentary *Jazz On A Summer's Day* that vividly immortalised the Newport shindig. Few can forget the movie's evocative opening sequence with shots of spectators intercut with close-ups of Jimmy Giuffre, Bob Brookmeyer and Jim Hall chuggin' through their rustic hop 'The Train And The River'.

Some years later, Clint Eastwood (a self-confessed jazz fanatic) featured footage of Cannonball Adderley on stage at the Monterey Festival in his 1971 box office smash *Play Misty For Me*.

Long gone are the times when a festival was simply a parade of pick-up bands running familiar changes.

NEWPORT IN NEW YORK '72
Roberta Flack, B. B. King, Curtis Mayfield
Herbie Mann, Les McCann, Billy Eckstine

JOHN HANDY
RECORDED LIVE AT THE MONTEREY JAZZ FESTIVAL

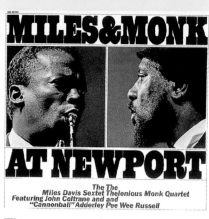

MILES & MONK
AT NEWPORT
The The
Miles Davis Sextet Thelonious Monk Quartet
Featuring John Coltrane and and
"Cannonball" Adderley Pee Wee Russell

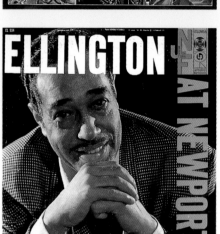

ELLINGTON AT NEWPORT

Fujitsu-Concord
jazz festival in japan '87
THE CONCORD ALL STARS

VOLUME III "TAKE 8"

DAN BARRETT   RED HOLLOWAY
ED BICKERT   DAVE McKENNA
SCOTT HAMILTON   JIMMIE SMITH
                   WARREN VACHÉ
                   STEVE WALLACE

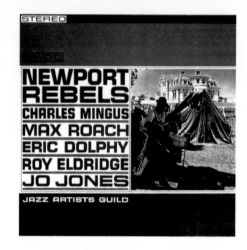

STEREO

NEWPORT REBELS
CHARLES MINGUS
MAX ROACH
ERIC DOLPHY
ROY ELDRIDGE
JO JONES
JAZZ ARTISTS GUILD

The Johnny Otis Show
Live At Monterey!
The Historic Rhythm & Blues Extravaganza
That Rocked The 1970 Monterey Jazz Festival

PABLO LIVE
PABLO LIVE
CD 2620-115
OSCAR PETERSON
LIVE AT THE NORTHSEA JAZZ FESTIVAL
THE HAGUE, HOLLAND, 1980
JOE PASS   TOOTS THIELEMANS
NEILS HENNING ØRSTED PEDERSEN

Left: Quincy Jones with
Montreux Festival organiser
Claude Nobs

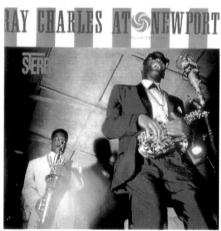

RAY CHARLES AT NEWPORT
STEREO

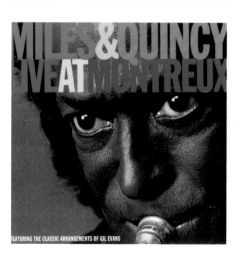

MILES & QUINCY
LIVE AT MONTREUX
FEATURING THE CLASSIC ARRANGEMENTS OF GIL EVANS

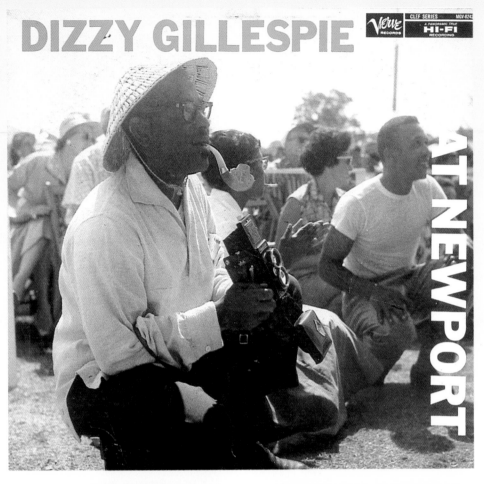

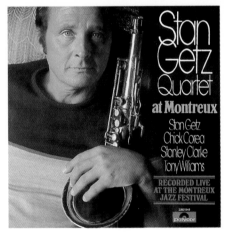

PABLO LIVE
MONTREUX '77
The Pablo All Stars Jam
Oscar Peterson, Milt Jackson, Clark Terry, Ronnie Scott, Joe Pass, Niels Pedersen, Bobby Durham

Some festivals are devoted to a single theme, such as Bix Beiderbecke (Davenport, Indiana) or, as in the case of the increasing popular jazz cruises, take to the high seas with top dollar talents like Oscar Peterson as main attraction.

More likely they are multi-themed, cross-over spectaculars like Montreux and New York where individual nights showcase the best of blues, Brazil, acid jazz, fusion, singers, post-hard bop, avant garde and R&B.

On the subject of rhythm'n'blues, it was no stranger to outdoor British beanos, as early as 1963 The Rolling Stones appearing bottom of the bill on the 3rd National Jazz Festival.

The following year was a different story when the Stones became the stars of the Friday night R&B show, while, over the next two days, Manfred Mann, The Yardbirds, Graham Bond and Georgie Fame mixed it up with, amongst others, Tubby Hayes' Big Band, Memphis Slim, Chris Barber, Ronnie Scott, Mose Allison and blues singer Jimmy Witherspoon.

The National Jazz Festival had sprung into being after ugly confrontations between modern and traditional jazz fans finally grounded the Beaulieu Festival which, between 1955 and 1961, had been held in the vast grounds of Lord Montagu's stately home.

And as British beat groups were successfully invading America, the UK National Jazz Federation gradually changed its emphasis. Come 1967, the NJF not only switched it's three-day gathering from Richmond to Windsor but also its booking policy. Renamed the 'National Jazz, Pop, Ballads & Blues Festival' it was acts such as Cream, Jeff Beck, Donovan, the Small Faces, John Mayall's Bluesbreakers and the debut of Peter Green's Fleetwood Mac that took top billing, with the once large jazz contingent being reduced to the Chris Barber Jazz Band, the Zoot Sims-Al Cohn Quintet and Yusef Lateef.

Nowadays, most festivals pride themselves on their eclecticism, effortlessly accommodating acts as diverse as Van Morrison, Simply Red and Eric Clapton or B.B. King, Ray Charles and Chaka Khan with the same enthusiasm as it will announce the presence of Tito Puente, Caetano Veloso and Youssou N'Dour or Wynton Marsalis, Phil Woods and Joshua Redman.

As Pharoah Sanders once observed 'It's not that easy to find good places to play in the States. For that reason, so many musicians tour Europe and the Far East. The festival circuit is lucrative for the majors and offers good exposure for emergent talent. The audiences are more appreciative as are working conditions – they're much more advanced and more willing to listen to the more creative side of the music.'

Record company executives are the first to admit that the best exposure for any jazz artist is out there on the road giving a good account of themselves on as many high-profile festival bills that they can clamber on.

Nowadays, festivals can make or break talent. Unlike in pop, where artists are required to tour almost immediately their new album hits the check-out, and then milk it for as many singles as humanly possible, a jazz artist might wait up to six months for an album to break before packing their bags and heading for the airport.

On the other hand, reunions are always good crowd-pullers. Chico Hamilton reformed his original Quintet, Flip Phillips guested with his former JATP tenor adversary Illinois Jacquet, the

Above: At Montreux, (l to r) Robin Kenyatta, Clark Terry, Chuck Mangione and George Benson (and insert) Opposite: Bobby McFerrin with impromptu choir

Brecker Brothers polished up their funk shoes, while Miles and Quincy teamed up for a replay of Gil Evans' orchestrations in Montreux when both the tapes and cameras were rolling. But the passing of so many great jazz stars means that a search for veterans of a proven lineage could result in a number of original-era players finally making it big time on the circuit and, in doing so, attain the level of success their talents deserve.

Situations frequently occur at festivals that would never happen elsewhere – be it Havana or Manhattan – with some memorable impromptu jams entering the realms of legend.

In 1972 an 11-piece band sporting a sax team comprising Zoot Sims, Dexter Gordon, Rashaan Roland Kirk, James Moody and Flip Philips stopped a New York audience in its tracks.

Similarly, at a Jazz Messengers get-together in 1989 organised in Leverkusen, Germany, the former Blakey conscripts Terence Blanchard, Freddie Hubbard, Curtis Fuller, Jackie McLean, Wayne Shorter, Benny Golson, Walter Davis Jr,

Buster Williams plus Roy Haynes got to grips with the gig at hand with no tantrums over billing!

Fortunately, few such moments pass unrecorded, festivals being a continuous source of strong-selling albums.

Between them, Montreux and Newport have spawned well over a couple of hundred alone. Memorable moments from Montreux include the million-plus selling 'Swiss Movement' by Les McCann and Eddie Harris, plus sets by Bill Evans, Stan Getz and the now legendary Miles & Quincy partnership

Newport notables are many, and a cross-section comprises big band blow-ups by Maynard Ferguson, Dizzy Gillespie, Quincy Jones, Count Basie and Duke Ellington, combo sets featuring Thelonious Monk, Miles Davis, John Coltrane, Dave Brubeck, Ella Fitzgerald, Billie Holiday, Cecil Taylor and Ray Charles.

Never one to miss an opportunity, Herbie Mann enjoyed three bites of the cherry – 'Live

At Newport', 'Standing Ovation At Newport' and 'New Mann At Newport'.

The Antibes festival kept collectors happy with recordings by Ella & Duke, plus a sensational 1961 onslaught from the Charles Mingus band with Eric Dolphy.

Sessions from Monterey again embraced Mingus, while contributions by Woody Herman, John Handy, Charles Lloyd, Don Ellis and the Johnny Otis Show are still talked about. As is a set by the ever-resourceful Cannonball Adderley when he delivered the goods during a torrential rainstorm in Comblain-La-Tour.

Quite the opposite from hole-in-wall joints where musicians once learnt their trade. In the absence of those neighbourhood jazz bars and the kind of clubs usually only written about in hard-boiled crime novels, the festival circuit can be seen as being the music's modern-day salvation, and a means of steady income in an otherwise insecure profession. The truth is, were it not for the festival circuit, there are many musicians who might still be scratching a living in the relatively few remaining club venues. Or worse still, sorting mail for the Post Office.

The roots of jazz may well be in Africa, but as far back as the Fifties, observers noted that the importation of American popular music was eroding the identity of its own indigenous jazz scene. Moreover, the politics of South Africa meant that jazz actually became a music in exile.

BIG JAZZ NIGHT
★ HEAR THIS GROUP ★
says JOHN MARLEY, Jazz Critic, Brighton & Hove Herald

For One Appearance only
- SOUTH AFRICA'S TOP MODERN JAZZ GROUP -
CHRIS McGREGOR'S BLUE NOTES
at
Brighton's Luxurious Late-Night Jazz Spot
CLUB 65
Crystal Room, Hare and Hounds, Preston Circus
THURSDAY, DECEMBER 16th
8 p.m. - Midnight
Fully Licensed until Midnight

THE BLUE NOTES: Chris McGregor, Piano; Johnny Dyani, Bass; Louis Mohola, Drums; Dudu Pukwana, Alto; Mongezi Feza, Trumpet

Sensational stars from Cape Town who appeared in 1964 Antibes Jazz Festival. SMASH SUCCESSES at Africana Club, ZURICH, Blue Note Club, GENEVA, and Ronnie Scott Club, LONDON

CLUB 65 presents modern jazz stars every Thursday night : Licensed bar: Reduced rates for students

For news of the club and who's coming when, read John Marley's "Jazz Talk" column each Friday in the Brighton and Hove Herald . . . the leading local jazz column, the leading local newspaper.

Above: Chris McGregor's Blue Notes with (l-r) Johnny Dyani, Chris McGregor, Mongezi Feza, Louis Moholo and Dudu Pakwana.

Out of Africa

Left: The 'Soul Makossa' man, Cameroons tenor sax star Manu Dibango

THE INTRODUCTION OF Apartheid in South Africa in 1948, and the Group Areas Act of 1950, created a racist dictatorship which left South African musicians of the calibre of trumpet player Hugh Masekela and pianists Dollar Brand (Abdullah Ibrahim) and Chris McGregor – a white man fronting an all-black combo – with no alternative but to go into exile.

Masekela was the first to leave Johannesburg. Arriving Stateside in 1960, with his then wife Miriam Makeba, the 21-year old musical refugee received a stony welcome. But come 1968, Masekela enjoyed cult status when his album 'The Promise Of The Future' spawned a summer hit, the four-million selling fusion fingerpopper 'Grazing In The Grass'.

A Capetown resident, Abdullah Ibrahim (and his fiancee, singer Sathima Bea Benjamin) turned up in Europe in 1963, from where the album 'Duke Ellington Presents The Dollar Brand Trio' (Reprise) launched him internationally.

Contrary to the name, Chris McGregor & The Blue Notes quickly switched from hard bop to an organic mix of free jazz and township jive (kwela). With a personnel comprising the best South Africa had to offer – Dudu Pakwana (alto), Mongezi Feza (trumpet), Johnny Dyani (bass) and Louis Moholo (drums), McGregor later expanded the Blue Notes as the aptly named Brotherhood Of Breath (1970).

More recently two unique tenormen, the political activist Fela Anikulapo Kuti (Nigeria) and 'Soul Makossa' hitmaker Manu DiBango (Cameroons) plus Franco et TPOK Jazz (Zaire) have proved central to the World Beat phenomenon. But, to most, the music of modern day (South) Africa is associated with the distinctive textured sounds that the fleet-fingered guitarist Ray Phiri brought to Paul Simon's 'Graceland' project, plus the overlapping fusion of African funk, rock and jazz found in the artistry of Salif Keita (Mali) and Senegalese stars Youssou N'Dour and Baba Maal.

Jazz Licks

Who would have thought that the 'peoples' music born in the honky tonks of New Orleans would be celebrated, along with poets and presidents, on postage stamps.

In 1956 Riverside Records used facsmile stamps to promote the album 'The Unique Thelonious Monk'

LEGENDS OF AMERICAN MUSIC SERIES

JAZZ SINGERS/BLUES SINGERS

Though individual commemorative stamps for Duke, W.C. Handy, Scott Joplin and Satchmo have previously been struck by the U.S. Postal Service, more recently they have gone one better with a multi-stamp series that has embraced seminal rock & roll and R&B legends (Elvis Presley, Buddy Holly, Otis Redding, Dinah Washington etc), jazz & blues singers (above, including Bessie Smith, Billie Holiday and Robert Johnson), Country Music pioneers (Bob Wills, Hank Williams), popular singers (Bing Crosby, Ethel Waters, Nat 'King' Cole) a selection of no less than ten jazz greats (right) Armstrong, Blake, Coltrane, Garner, Hawkins, Johnson, Mingus, Monk, Morton and Parker, plus perforated tributes to Big Band leaders (below) including Basie, Goodman, Miller and the Dorsey Brothers.

LEGENDS OF AMERICAN MUSIC SERIES
Big Band Leaders

Below left:
The Carribean island of Grenada saw fit to honour Charlie Parker and Miles Davis with a 'Grammy Award' stamp

GRENADA GRENADINES $3 Charlie Parker — GRENADA GRENADINES $3 Miles Davis — Grammy Awards

Perhaps the oddest jazz stamp issued to date comes courtesy of the British Post Office. No portraits of deceased local heroes Tubby Hayes or Joe Harriott were utilised for a jazz image which was included as part of a multi-stamp greetings set. Instead, the sole jazz stamp (right) had a picture of West Coast bass player Curtis Counce and the New York bebop trumpeter Kenny Dorham in action.

Above: It's not always on postage stamps that such acknowledgements have been paid; the memory of the great Ella Fitzgerald was honoured with this tribute on a French telephone card

Ad fab

Things have come a long way since Louis Armstrong extolled the power of a Scandinavian laxative or hard-swigging Eddie Condon endorsed not the demon drink, but daily roughage-rich Kelloggs.

DIZZY GILLESPIE may have lent his name to Chicago clothier Harold C. Fox's hand-finished berets, jackets and bop shades while Billy Eckstine turned a fast buck with his Mister B Flex-Roll Collar shirts and Chet Baker picked up some extra cash and a few samples promoting neckties, but jazz has usually endorsed hi-fi, cigarettes, booze and hair care products. It comes with the territory.

John Lee Hooker has bolted his name and image to such diverse marques as Couvoisier brandy, Lee Jeans and ICI pacemakers, leaving Lonnie Brooks and Harmonica Fats to star in arguably one of the most memorable of recent commercials promoting Heiniken.

When not promoting airlines, B.B.King was featured in an M&Ms campaign, while Bo Diddley was the focus of a Nike campaign. Elsewhere, Miles Davis has been pictured next to a Honda motorcycle ('I'd have preferred a Ferrari') and a bottle of Japanese firewater called Van (though not at the same time), while the Young Lions Roy Hargrove (trumpet) and Joshua Redman (tenor sax) can hardly contain their delight after being kitted out respectively by Levi and DKNY.

And you don't have to be alive to act as a star salesman: Louis' image has been used for Building Society services, while the likenesses of Cannonball Adderley, Art Blakey, Clifford Brown and Bobby Hackett have accompanied adverts for cigarettes and hi-fi.

Meanwhile, Thelonious Monk (Ford), Nina Simone (Chanel), Louis Armstrong (Guinness), Muddy Waters (Levi), and Howling Wolf (Budweiser) are just some who soundtrack radio and television commercials.

But perhaps one of the greatest of all ironies involves doomed trumpeter Bunny Berigan, who drank himself into an early grave, recently being resurrected to promote whisky!

From the top, clockwise: Miles Davis in the Japanese ad for a bottle of Van, John Lee Hooker with Martell, Roy Hargrove looking cool in his Levi 501s and the ghost of Bunny Berigan serenading a bottle of bourbon

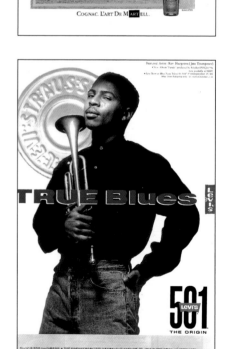

For over fifty years he was the embodiment of jazz in the minds of both musicians and public alike, and the changes his contribution wrought in the development of the music were to impact directly on the evolution of all popular music, of which he was one of the century's leading figures.

Satchmo

THERE WAS A TIME WHEN Louis Armstrong – aka 'Satchmo' and 'Pops' – was in danger of forever being considered the Clown Prince of Jazz. The facial muggin' with the ever-present brow-wiping handkerchief, the repertoire riddled with non-worthy pop songs, and final growled 'Oh yeahhhh' became the trademarks that kept an array of second-rate impressionists off the breadline. Pure stupidity.

For years it was believed that Louis was (conveniently) born on 4 July 1900, but it is now established that he was born just over a year later on 4 August 1901, and if he had never accomplished more than the series of unbelievable trumpet and cornet choruses on such early recordings as 'Potato Head Blues', 'West End Blues' and 'Sweethearts On Parade', it would have been enough to ensure his premier position in the Jazz Hall of Fame. Throughout his career his many small band recordings, from the Hot Five and Hot Seven (1925-28) right through to the sessions with the All-Stars between 1947 and the end of the 50s, have remained the yardstick for New Orleans jazz.

But Louis was no mere musician, he moved on to become the complete entertainer. A singer whose voice defined jazz vocals and scat singing, whose appeal would register with generation after generation, and whose hits would span from 1926 ('Muskrat Ramble') to 1994 ('We Have All The Time In The World'). Such was his universal appeal that even at the height of Beatlemania, Louis was able to elbow the Fab Four's 'Can't Buy Me Love' from the very top of the U.S. singles chart, in May 1964, with 'Hello, Dolly!'

As a screen actor Louis won hearts rather than Oscars in vehicles as diverse as *High Society* and *Paris Blues*. He was always Louis. Nobody expected anything else, and nobody wanted anything more. His personality was everything. Louis was wide-screen before wide-screen had been invented, adding warmth, humour and love to just about any script thrust his way.

But it was as a musician that the one-time kid from a New Orleans' waifs home really proved influential. Even today, many confess to being unashamed believers in all things Louis.

Lew Soloff regards him as 'The Master', Dizzy Gillespie insisted 'Louis not only influenced trumpet players, he changed the modus operandi of music by inventing the solo.' Wynton Marsalis rarely does an interview without providing an Armstrong namecheck, and veteran Benny Carter confesses 'No matter what we play, there's a lot of Louis in us all.'

Louis Armstrong was arguably the true realisation of the Great American Dream. Unlike Bird, Lady Day, Dean, Monroe, Elvis or a dozen other troubled icons, his life story didn't evolve into a tragedy of Jacobian proportions. Armstrong achieved just about everything he aspired to and, despite the physical frailty of his last years, his success never soured or his spirit self-destruct.

A goodwill ambassador, who toured the world, greeting royalty as only a jazz royal ought, the much travelled Louis explained shortly before his death: 'Musicians don't quit, they just stop when there ain't no more gigs.' The gigs finally ran out for Louis on 6th July, 1971. But the tributes never ceased.

Boxing Clever

The CD has meant that whole sections of a musicians' work – sometimes the complete recordings – can be housed in one box.

BACK IN THE

early days of the vinyl long playing album, Blue Note was one of a number of enterprising labels adept at rushing out two-disc souvenirs of live dates by Art Blakey (Birdland), The Jazz Messengers (Cafe Bohemia), Sonny Rollins (Village Vanguard) and Stanley Turrentine (Minton's) while out on the West Coast Contemporary had found takers for both pianoman Hampton Hawes' inexhaustible three disc 'All Night Session' and four successive albums that captured the adrenalin rush of Shelly Manne & His Men in action at San Francisco's famed niterie, The Blackhawk.

When not indulging in huge recording sessions with Oscar Peterson and Art Tatum, Verve Records boss Norman Granz wasn't adverse to boxing up a few discs by Ella Fitzgerald, Stan Getz or his money-making JATP troupe.

But it was Savoy Records who were the first to demonstrate that there was even a large receptive market for multiple false starts, incomplete performances and alternate takes with the breakthrough release of a five disc extravaganza devoted to every single note that Charlie Parker had blown for the Newark-based label.

Next, Bird's extensive output for Ross Russell's Dial operation was given a similar high-profile treatment, paving the way for EMI-Japan to grab a piece of the same action when successfully putting together a three album box devoted to assorted broadcasts.

Other labels toyed with a few collections, but it was to take the inauguration of the Mosaic mail order operation in 1983, with the 49-track/four disc 'The Complete Blue Note Recordings Of Thelonious Monk' to firmly establish future guidelines.

Run by former United Artists/Blue Note marketing executive Charlie Lourie and the ubiquitous producer/writer Michael Cuscuna, Mosaic's aim was true. The premise was to put back into circulation long out of print classics and unissued material in a form commensurate with their importance.

The Monk project was the realisation of their mission statement. For some time prior to Mosaic, Cuscuna had become recognised as Blue Note's Keeper Of The Flame – both he

and Lourie having been responsible for resurrecting its fortunes in 1975 – and while researching the label's cache of Monk master tapes uncovered 'thirty-minutes of worth-while unreleased alternate takes and hitherto unknown tracks.'

As with so many previous ad hoc re-issues, Blue Note's two volume 'Thelonious Monk: Genius Of Modern Music' had been victim of 'scrambled eggs' programming – tracks being scattered over both discs without thought given to chronological order.

Mosaic's box re-compiled all 49 of Monk's tracks (originally recorded between 1947 and 1952) in chronological order, including the 14 previously unissued tracks that Cuscuna had discovered of which the two takes of the never-before-heard Monk original 'Sixteen' and the only known version of 'I'll Follow You' were alone worth the price of admission.

The records were handsomely packaged with a large-format booklet that contained a detailed commentary, session notes and

Miles in the studio with Gil Evans (far left)

period photographs. Hand numbered and released in a limited edition of just 7,500 vinyl sets worldwide, the Thelonious Monk 'box' collected a Grammy Nomination in 1983 before going on to be voted Reissue Of The Year in *Down Beat* magazine's prestigious 1984 International Critics Poll.

A standard had been set.

Soon after, Mosaic followed through with releases featuring The Gerry Mulligan Quartet, Albert Ammons / Meade Lux Lewis, Clifford Brown, Art Pepper and Chet Baker. And true to the spirit of the enterprise, the Mosaic programme didn't just concern itself with artists of a recognised pedigree. With the releases of boxes by tenor sax player Tina Brooks and pianist Herbie Nichols, these previously undervalued talents were accorded the kudos they had both been denied during their short lifetimes.

Miles Davis & Gil Evans

THE COLLABORATION between trumpet supremo Miles Davis and master arranger Gil Evans crated some of the greatest orchestral music of the 20th century. Seven years had elapsed since they had first made music together on the 'Birth Of The Cool' sessions for which Evans had supplied 'Boplicity' and 'Moon Dreams'.

Whereas for the 'Cool' collection, Davis had used the Claude Thornhill Band as a template: 'We wanted that sound, but the difference was that we wanted it as small as possible,' for the first of a trilogy of albums it was panoramic vista all the way.

Recorded between 1957 and 1960, Gil Evans created a whole new aural paintbox utilising tone colours even more vibrant than those he'd previously employed when arranging for Thornhill. 'I loved working with Gil because he was so meticulous and creative . . . I trusted his musical arrangements completely. We had always been a great musical team and I realized it when we did "Miles Ahead" that Gil and I were something special together musically.' This was plainly evident in the opening track 'Springsville'. According to Miles, Gil would phone him in the early hours of the morning insisting: 'If you ever get depressed, just listen to "Springsville".' For the second instalment, a much darker, at times brooding reworking of George Gershwin's music for 'Porgy & Bess' (1958) gave way to the heavily atmospheric 'Sketches Of Spain' (1959) with it's extended version of Joaquin Rodrigo's 'Concierto De Aranjuez (Adagio)' as the centrepiece.

Here, Miles' haunting Moorish-sounding horn was called upon to interpret the music in an altogether different style than usual. 'Saeta' – a Holy Week religious song of Andalusian origin – cast the trumpeter in the role of a woman singer who stands on an iron railing balcony singing with passion to the parade passing beneath her.

'That was the hardest thing for me to do on "Sketches Of Spain"; to play the parts on the trumpet where somebody was singing, especially when it was ad-libbed, like most of the time.' However, Rodrigo was nonplussed with what Miles and Gil had achieved: 'His composition was the reason I did "Sketches Of Spain" in the first place,' growled Miles. 'Let's see if he likes it after he starts getting those big royalty cheques.'

All this together with other tracks, some of which would remain unheard until1996, are majestically restorted on the historic 5-CD set 'Miles Davis & Gil Evans: The Complete Columbia Studio Records' (Columbia/Legacy).

One final project, 'Tosca' may have been on the agenda for years, but never got beyond wishful thinking, though Miles insisted: 'All Gil has to do is phone and I'll be there.'

Left: Chet Baker
(right) with (l-r)
Jimmy Rowles,
Carson Smith and
Shelly Manne

Right: A Blue Note
publicity shot of
Jimmy Smith

Far right: From a
1951 movie *The
Strip*, Jack
Teagarden and
Louis Armstrong,
with Mickey
Rooney playing a
jazz drummer

Below: Baker,
Smith and Satch
all collected on
the Mosaic label

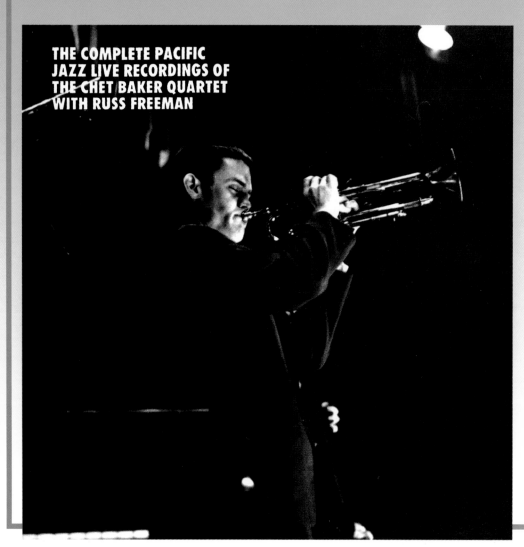

THE COMPLETE PACIFIC
JAZZ LIVE RECORDINGS OF
THE CHET BAKER QUARTET
WITH RUSS FREEMAN

THE COMPLETE FEBRUARY 1957
JIMMY SMITH BLUE NOTE SESSI

THE COMPLETE DECCA STUDIO RECORDINGS OF LOUIS ARMSTRONG AND THE ALL STARS

Western Swing

As far as the jazz purists are concerned, Western Swing simply never happened. Yet the fiddle-led front lines of country jazz were as potent a part of the swing era as their more celebrated big city cousins.

BOB WILLS, a fiddle-player who is to Western Swing what W.C. Handy is to blues, plus singer Milton Brown, started out with a band known as the Light Crust Doughboys. Following a dispute with their sponsor (from whom came the name) the hard-drinking Wills quit in 1933 and formed his Texas Playboys, salesman Brown also moving on to create his rival Musical Brownies. Both leaders opted for a swing band approach with country overtones, western waltzes slotting in alongside the blues and stomps, with fiddle teams substituting for sax sections.

It was Wills who really set the pace. By the mid-30s he was leading a 13-piece outfit, which grew to be 18-strong by the 40s. His early recording sessions were nothing if not eclectic, tracks such as Wills' own 'Osage Stomp', plus 'St Louis Blues', 'Trouble In Mind', 'Basin Street Blues' and the Original Dixieland Jazz Band's 'Bluin' The Blues' figuring on early sessions alongside 'Mexicali Rose' and more cornball items. Bob logged several hits on the US pop charts before being paralysed by a stroke, but he carried on with various dates, albeit in a wheelchair. He cut records up to 1973, before being victim to another, fatal, stroke in 1975.

Milton Brown, whose band featured jazz guitarist Bob Dunn – the first musician in country music to electrify his instrument – also followed Wills' swingin' way of things, but his life was terminated in a car crash in 1936.

Oklahoma's Spade Cooley, another fiddle-player, went as far as to dub himself 'The King Of Western Swing'. Settling on the West Coast, his band, which sometimes numbered two dozen musicians, won recording, radio, TV and film contracts. Jailed for murdering his wife, Cooley suffered a heart attack in 1969, while on release to play a sheriff's benefit concert.

But Western Swing survived the loss of all such legendary figures. Wills sidemen like guitarists Eldon Shamblin and Tiny Moore, along with fiddler Johnny Gimble, continued to inspire future generations of country stars and young rock-

Opposite: Movie and recording 'cowboy' star Gene Autrey with Duke Ellington

Left: The real king of Western Swing, Bob Wills

era country bands such as Commander Cody's Lost Planet Airmen, Asleep At The Wheel and Alvin Crow's Pleasant Valley Boys, while jazz vibes virtuoso Gary Burton and bassist Steve Swallow (following in the path of Stan Kenton, who recorded with Tex Ritter, and Charlie Parker, who had jammed with Ray Price's Cherokee Cowboys) headed into RCA's Nashville studios during 1966 to cut 'Tennessee Firebird', a fusion album that found them swapping eights with such Nashville stalwarts as Buddy Spicher (fiddle), Ken Buttrey (drums), Charlie McCoy (bass/harmonica), Chet Atkins (guitar) and Buddy Emmons, who had recorded the first-ever pedal steel jazz album some three years earlier.

But it's not always been a one-way traffic; guitarist Hank Garland and drummer Joe Morello, for instance, were with Paul Howard's Arkansas Cotton Pickers in their early days. And despite the 'official' line in jazz history books, there have been numerous examples of similar country cross-overs since – Gimble and The Nashville Pickers delivering Benny Golson's 'Killer Joe', Vassar Clements cutting two albums of 'Hillbilly Jazz', guitar-picker Roy Clark forming a bootin' big band – the list is endless.

Jazz Movies

The cinema's treatment of jazz has matured over the years, but it's been a long haul, romanticised biopics or shocking 'exposés' being the silver screen's stock in trade for decades.

'I DON'T KNOW what the hell that boy thinks a trumpet will do. That note he was going for, that thing he was trying for — there isn't any such thing. Not on a horn'. *Young Man With A Horn* (Dorothy Baker 1938)

A lifelong jazz buff, actor Clint Eastwood (and the director of *Bird*) concedes that jazz and the movies might well be considered America's greatest artistic contribution to the 20th Century, but the two seldom have yet to team up with any real compatibility. And Oscars? Forget it.

Only singer Peggy Lee and tenor saxist Dexter Gordon have so far received nominations for their noteworthy acting roles in two of the best efforts, *Pete Kelly's Blues* and *'Round Midnight*.

The jam session has been a favourite cliché of jazz movie-makers; Paul Newman (left) teamed up with Louis Armstrong in *Paris Blues* (1961) while (above) a more factual cutting contest featured in Robert Altman's *Kansas City* in 1996

A recurring problem is the destructive downside of jazz life, rather than the humorous aspects, being given priority with unsociable behaviour big on the menu. Yet few things are funnier than musicians swapping yarns.

Maybe a jazz comedy is the option? Had the musical content of *Some Like It Hot* (1959) not been so throwaway, it might have been reshaped into a possible contender. Perhaps Woody Allen should take it on.

Having said that, films of the quality of *Pete Kelly's Blues* (1955), *The Sweet Smell Of Success* (1957), *Sven Klang's Quintet* (1976), *New York, New York* (1977), *'Round Midnight* (1986) and *Kansas City* (1996) can be viewed as relatively successful in their efforts to reflect the jazz life or the environment in which it exists.

The Sweet Smell Of Success and *Sven Klang's Quintet* are about as good as they come, while the Dale Turner character (a composite of Bud Powell and Lester Young) – as portrayed by Dexter Gordon in Bernard Tavernier's *'Round Midnight* – was a serious attempt to develop a real, believable persona rather than parcel up a bunch of tired clichés.

In the Swing era, name band leaders were often weaved into predictable Tinsel Town plots. High amongst those enlisted were Artie Shaw (*Second Chorus*,1940), Glenn Miller (*Orchestra Wives*,1942), Benny Goodman and Count Basie (*Stage Door Canteen*,1943)and Harry James (*Kitten On The Keys*,1946), while Armstrong, Barnet, Dorsey, Goodman and Hampton all appeared in the 1948 Danny Kaye comedy *A Song Is Born*.

Black audiences were similarly catered for, being served a bizarre diet of cheaply-made Westerns starring Ellington heart-throb Herb Jeffries in titles such as *Harlem Rides The Range* (1939), or knockout comedies built around Slim Gaillard (*Ovoutie O'Rooney*,1946) and Louis Jordan (*Reet, Petite And Gone*,1947).

An outcome of all this was the forerunner of MTV-style pop videos. Between 1941 and 1947, over 2,000 three-minute 'Soundies' were made for visual jukeboxes, while more enterprising studios such as Warners (*Melody Master Bands*), RKO (*Jamboree*), Paramount and Universal made low-budget series of musical shorts, nine to fifteen minutes in duration.

Jack Webb (right), of *Dragnet* fame, made a convincing portrayal of the title role in *Pete Kelly's Blues* (1955), one of the better jazz films of the 50s, which he also directed

Left: Tony Curtis mimes to Buddy Collette's flute in 1957's *The Sweet Smell of Success*, with the Chico Hamilton Quintet (l-r) Chico Hamilton (drums), Carson Smith (bass), actor Martin Milner, Paul Horn (clarinet) and Fred Katz on cello

Left: Danny Kaye in a 1948 adaptation of *Snow White* (!), *A Song Is Born*, with a line-up including Benny Goodman, Tommy Dorsey, Charlie Barnet and Louis Armstrong Below left: Kaye as Red Nichols, who is looking on in this shot, in *The Five Pennies* (1959)

Above left: Goldie Hawn (centre) and Kurt Russell in 1984's *Swing Shift*, in which Russell plays a war-time jazz trumpeter

Centre: Kirk Douglas miming to the trumpet of Harry James (with Hoagy Carmichael on piano) in *Young Man With A Horn*, from the novel by Dorothy Baker inspired by – but not based on – the life of Bix Beiderbecke (1950)

Right: Dave Brubeck and the British trumpeter Bert Courtley in the UK-made 'jazz thriller' from 1961 (which was based on *Othello*) *All Night Long*

Above: Gerry Mulligan in the 1960 screen version of Jack Kerouac's beat generation novel *The Subterraneans*

Left: Cab Calloway in *Stormy Weather* (1943)

Right: Robert Wagner with singer Pearl Bailey in *All The Fine Young Cannibals (1960)*, based loosely on the life of trumpeter Chet Baker

Sensing an even faster buck, the majors then pumped out formula rags-to-riches biopix of varying authenticity. Top of the pile were *The Fabulous Dorseys* (1947), *The Glenn Miller Story* (1953), *The Benny Goodman Story* (1955), *The Gene Krupa Story* [aka *Drum Crazy*] (1959), *The Five Pennies* [Red Nichols] (1959) and, later, *Lady Sings The Blues* [Billie Holiday] (1972). Most were nothing more than re-vamped Hollywood showbiz musicals, the remainder, cliched melodramas.

It fell to Clint Eastwood to bring Charlie Parker to the screen, in 1988, with *Bird,* and a script which concerned itself more so with his relationship with Chan Richardson rather than why he was one of the most influential jazz musicians of all time.

While biopix on Miles Davis, Louis Armstrong, Jimi Hendrix and Robert Johnson are in development, the most intriguing is a treatment, in Eastwood's possession, concerning the wild exploits of Bird's one-time sidekick and doper, the trumpeter Red Rodney.

Following stints playing for Elvis Presley in Las Vegas, and working as a San Francisco gumshoe, Red spent the late 50s masquerading as US military disbursement officer General Arnold T MacIntyre – heisting large amounts of the military's cash in the process. His downfall came when, grabbing ten grand from the Atomic Energy Commission in Nevada, Red accidentally hoovered up some top secret documents which almost resulted him being charged with espionage.

Where jazz invariably comes into its own, is when underscoring on-screen action. When filmed in stringent black and white, the sound of yearning saxes and skyscraper brass matched those powerful atmospheric night-time images of long shadows and neon-reflected wet-pavements.

Those tense, fast moving themes Leith Stevens composed and Shorty Rogers arranged for *The Wild One* (1953) and *Private Hell 36* (1954), followed by Rogers' collaboration with Elmer Bernstein on *The Man With The Golden Arm* (1955) and Bernstein's own scores for *Johnny Staccato* (1959/60) – a television series starring John Cassavetes as a piano-playing private eye – created their own genre.

Above: Robert De Nero and Liza Minnelli in Martin Scorsese's evocative impression of the jazz life *New York, New York* (1977)
Below: Samuel E. Wright and Forest Whitaker as Diz and Bird in Clint Eastwood's 1988 Charlie Parker biopic *Bird*
Below right: Frank Sinatra, Buddy Collette and Tony Curtis in the jazz-tinged Army drama from 1958 *Kings Go Forth*

But, contrary to belief, it was not all blaring brass and flying cymbals. A fixture of the Modern Jazz Quartet's repertoire, 'The Golden Striker' came from the score John Lewis had composed for *Sait En Jamais?* [*No Sun In Venice*] (1957), while The Chico Hamilton Quintet established a suitably moribund mood for one of the most acclaimed films of 1957, *The Sweet Smell Of Success*. Equally haunting were the Johnny Mandel / Gerry Mulligan charts unique to *I Want To Live* (1958).

The French were quick to react as Miles Davis recorded live-on-the-studio-floor improvisation for *Ascenseur Pour L'Echafaud* [*Lift To The Scaffold*] in 1957, and The Jazz Messengers greatly enhanced *Des Femmes Disparaissent* [*Girls Disappear*] (1959) and *Les Liaisons Dangereuses* [*Dangerous Relationships*] in1959.

Duke Ellington's music for *Anatomy Of A Murder*, (1959), Sonny Rollins' written-overnight *Alfie* (1966) and Henry Mancini's jazz-flavoured contribution to *Touch Of Evil* (1957) also proved perfect foils. Mancini would again hit paydirt scoring the hip private eye TV series *Peter Gunn* (1958-61).

Add to this the extensive work of the likes of Lalo Schifrin, Herbie Hancock, Quincy Jones and Mark Isham, and it becomes apparent that if the studio bosses possessed just a fraction of the imagination as demonstrated by soundtrack suppliers then the jazz film might well become a credible genre after all.

But up to now, in terms of credibility, it has to be documentaries that have usually presented jazz in the most sympathetic and accurate light.

In this respect Gjon Mili's highly stylised Oscar-nominated ten-minute short *Jammin' The Blues* (1944) featuring Lester Young, Illinois Jacquet and Harry 'Sweets' Edison, and Bert Stern's record of the 1958 Newport Festival *Jazz On A Summer's Day*, have to be the classic yardsticks.

Meanwhile, the Jazz Movie, as a main feature, remains a genre that continues to intrigue and exasperate film makers.

One day, somewhere, somebody will get it right? Maybe!

Above: (l to r) Herbie Hancock, Dexter Gordon, Pierre Michelot and John McLaughlin in a scene from *'Round Midnight*
Below left: Bille Holiday and Louis Armstrong in the 1947 movie *New Orleans*
Below: Diana Ross as Billie Holiday in *Lady Sings The Blues*

WHO DID WHAT!

Lloyd Bradley Caribbean Cool

Brian Case The Harder They Come

Richard Cook The Windy City & The Big Apple, The New Thing, Euro Free

Fred Dellar Cornet Kings, Boogie Woogie, Stride, Call Me Mr Big, Crooners, Up Jumped The Blues, Progressive Big Bands, We'll Always Have Paris, Blaxploitation, Satchmo, Western Swing

John Fenton Charles Mingus

Neil Slaven Way Down Yonder In New Orleans, Woke Up This Morning, The Blues Brothers, Jazz Plugs In, Still Blue After All These Years

Phil Strongman Future Funk – Acid Jazz

Roy Carr V-Discs, The Be Bop Revolution, Jazz At The Phil, The Dixieland Revival, Cool On The Coast, Shorty Rogers, Chet Baker, John Coltrane, So Far Soho, Good Rockin' Every Night, Soul To Soul, The Organ, That Latin Tinge, Jazz On The Juke Box, The Charts, Jazz Funks Out, Electric Miles, The Young Lions, M-Base, Quincy Jones, Jazz Festivals, Out Of Africa, Jazz Licks, Ad Fab, Boxing Clever, Jazz At The Movies

PICTURE ACKNOWLEDGEMENTS:

Ace / Fantasy, Adrian Korsner, Arista Records, Atlantic Records, Barry Plummer, BBC / Jazz 625, Blue Note Records, Bob Flemming / NJF, British Film Institute, Capitol Records, Chess Records, Columbia Records, Crescendo / PRT, David Redfern / RCC, Decca Records, EMI Records, Epic Records, Franco Milano, Good Time Jazz / Fantasy / Ace, Granada TV, Gretsch Drums, Herbie Mann, Herman Leonard, Howard Rumsey, Hulton Getty Picture Collection, Jak Kilby / MM, Jazz at the Philharmonic, John Fenton Collection, Lesley Howling, Malpaso, MCA / Universal, MCA Records, Melody Maker Archive (MM), Mercury Records, Metronome Records, Motown, Mr R & B, National Jazz Federation (NJF), Pacific / PRT, Polydor, Polygram, Precision Records & Tapes (PRT), Prestige / Fantasy Records, RCA Records, Redferns / Bob Willoughby, Reuters, Roulette Records, Roy Carr, Savoy Records, Spotlite Records, Talkin' Loud Records, The Collection of Roy Carr, The Collection of Val Wilmer, Val Wilmer, Verve Records, Warner Bros., WEA. The postage stamps illustrated in this book are the copyright of the United States Post Office & United States Postal Service.

We would also like to acknowledge the following film distributors:
20th Century Fox; Orchestra Wives-1942, Stormy Weather-1943 / Carlton Films; All Night Long-1960 (Rank) / Columbia; Don't Knock The Rock-1956, Make Believe Ballroom-1949 / Contemporary Films; Jazz on a Summers Day-1959 / Electric Pictures; Kansas City-1976 / Paramount; A Song is Born-1948, King Creole-1958, Lady Sings The Blues-1972, The Five Pennies-1959 / United International Pictures; Cool and Groovy-1957, Swing Parade of 1946 / Warner Brothers; All The Fine Young Cannibals-1960 (MGM), Ballad in Blue-1964, Bird-1988, The Blues Brothers1980, Cleopatra Jones-1973, The Fabulous Dorseys-1947, Get Yourself a College Girl-1964, I Want to Live!-1958, Kings Go Forth-1958, New Orleans-1947, New York, New York-1977, Paris Blues-1961 (UA), Pete Kelly's Blues-1955, 'Round Midnight-1986, Shaft-1971, Sweet Smell of Success-1957, Swing Shift-1984, The Girl He Left Behind-1956, The Subterraneans-1960 (MGM), Young Man with a Horn-1950.

ACKNOWLEDGEMENTS

In appreciation of their special talents and eternal friendship, I dip the shades and doff the proverbial beret to:
Paul Aarons, Lloyd Bradley, Brian Case, Richard Cook, Fred Dellar, John Fenton, Neil Slaven, Phil Strongman,
and Mike Evans and Kay

and the following individuals and organisations without whose generous assistance – and seemingly inexhaustible knowledge and patience – this tome would have never come about :
Roger Armstrong (Ace), John Beecher (Rollercoaster/Bear Family), Bleecker Bob, Paul Bradshaw (Straight No Chaser), Glyn Callingham, Edna & Tony Carr, Ted Carroll (Ace Records), Ted Cummins (MCA-Universal), Michael Cuscuna (Mosaic), Mike Doyle, George Duke, Bob Fisher (Westside), Wendy Furness (Blue Note/EMI), Andrea Gibbs (Warner Bros/ESP), Jo Hagger (Warner Bros/ESP),Tony Hall, Barry Hatcher (Castle/Concord), Mark Haywood (Vinyl Experience/UFO), John Jack (Cadillac Distribution), Allan Jones (Melody Maker/Uncut), Quincy Jones David Kassner (President), Danny Keene (MCI), Chunky La Plage, Herman Leonard, George McManus (Polydor), Kerstan Mackness (New Note), Big Cliff Malani, Gavin Martin, Gaylene Martin (Coalition), John Martin, Hazel Miller (Cadillac Distribution), Jonathan Morrish (Sony), Rob Partridge (Coalition), John Pearson (MCA-Universal), Harold Pendleton (NJF), Karen Pitchford, Natasha Porter (Mercury), Rachel Rayfield (Verve), David Redfern, Samantha Richards (Charly), Alan Robinson (Demon), Vinnie Romano, David Sanborn, Steven Sanderson (New Note), Adam Sieff (Sony/Columbia), Iain Snodgrass (MCA-Universal), Neil Spencer, Becky Stevenson (Verve), Jay Vickers, Joop Visser, Tony Wadsworth (Parlophone/EMI), Cliff White, Bob Willoughby, Val Wilmer, Trevor Wyatt
plus
Ron and Mitch at Acorn Studios
Tony Williams at Quicksilver

Pete King & the staff of Ronnie Scott's Club (London)
Claude Nobs & the staff of the Montreux Jazz Festival (Switzerland)
Fraser Kennedy & Les 'Ted' Clifford
The Hyatt, Eden Du Lac and Palace Hotels (Montreux)

The ever-helpful press and promotions departments of numerous record and motion picture companies for assistance in tracing original material:
Ace, Acid Jazz, Atlantic, Blue Note, BMG, Cadillac, Charly, Columbia, Demon, Direct Distrubution, East-West, Electric Pictures, EMI, GRP, Island, Malpaso, MCA-Universal, MCI, Milan, MGM, Mosaic, New Note, Ogun, Paramount, Polydor, PolyGram, Sony, Talkin' Loud, UIP, United Artists, Verve, Warner Brothers.

The British Film Institute
The John Fenton Archive
The Franco Milano Archive

The following publications: Down Beat Magazine, Jazziz, Jazz Times, Melody Maker, New Musical Express, Straight No Chaser, Swing Journal

Bleecker Bob's Golden Oldies Stores (Greenwich Village and Los Angeles),
Ray, Glyn Bob, Alex, Ski & Mike at Ray's Jazz Shop (London), Pete at Mole Jazz (London),
Rock On (London)

22 and 625 Entertainments

Gone, but not forgotten: Miles Davis, Slim Gaillard, Shorty Rogers and Ronnie Scott

For Leon and the next century

at the JAZZ CORNER of the World

BIRDLAND

proudly presents a few of the great

JAZZ artists who will appear

in *1955*

CHET BAKER

COUNT BASIE

ERROLL GARNER

STAN GETZ

DIZZY GILLESPIE

STAN KENTON

MODERN JAZZ QUARTET

GEORGE SHEARING

SARAH VAUGHAN

DINAH WASHINGTON

BIRDLAND
52nd St. & B'way
New York, N.Y.
JUdson 6-1368